Memorable Moments Begin With Unforgettable Fare

HOLIDAYS and celebrations throughout the year are special moments to gather with family and friends. Home-cooked foods make the occasions more endearing — and the memories more enduring.

Taste of Home Holiday & Celebrations Cookbook 2008 showcases 256 recipes to make Christmas, Thanksgiving, Easter and any celebration throughout the year even more memorable for you and your family. Plus, we make entertaining easy on the hostess because we do the menu planning for you!

'Tis the Season. From formal sit-down dinners and cocktail parties to casual movie nights and lunches, the Christmas season is abuzz with events. This chapter presents a merry array of 110 recipes, including Turkey Scaloppine with Marsala Sauce, Crab 'n' Cheese Spirals, Roasted Red Pepper Bisque and White Chocolate Cream Torte. For festive finales, sweets from around the world, fast-to-fix desserts and classic cookies and candies are always welcome. We even offer innovative ideas for homemade gifts from the kitchen.

Giving Thanks. Are you hosting a crowd-pleasing, casual buffet? Maybe a sit-down dinner for four is more your style. Either way, we've got you covered with fabulous fall fare, such as Always-Tender Roasted Turkey, Duo Mashed Potatoes and Apple Butternut Squash. For a twist on pumpkin pie, try any of the chapter's 11 featured pleasing pies and tarts, including Layered Caramel-Pear Tart, Pecan Meringue Pie, Chocolate Hazelnut Tart and Butternut Squash Pie.

Easter Gatherings. Tired taste buds will rise and shine with a beautiful brunch of Wine 'n' Cheese Strata, Champagne Punch and Raspberry-Rhubarb Coffee Cake. Are you cooking an Easter dinner? You'll love lively selections like Marinated Grilled Lamb, Roasted Asparagus with Leeks and Mashed Parsnips 'n' Potatoes. Round out any springtime supper with seasonal sides and sweet or savory muffins and scones.

Special Celebrations. You'll find 73 family-favorite recipes for other occasions throughout the year, including the Indy 500, Father's Day, neighborhood block parties, Oktoberfest, wedding anniversary celebrations and Halloween.

Can-Do Decorating Ideas. There are dozens of ideas for timeless table toppers (see the Giving Thanks Gourds on page 117), festive decor (such as the Lighted Wine Bottles on page 37) and fun party favors (turn to page 23 for Christmas Poppers).

With unforgettable fare, perfect party menus and easy decorating ideas, *Taste of Home Holiday & Celebrations Cookbook 2008* will help you make magical memories with family and friends all year long!

WOULD YOU like to see one of your family-favorite recipes featured in a future edition of this timeless treasury? See page 256 for details!

Taste of Home
HOLIDAY & Celebrations
COOKBOOK
2008

Project Editor: Julie Schnittka
Art Director: Gretchen Trautman
Associate Editor: Sara Lancaster
Craft Editor: Jane Craig
Content Production Supervisor: Julie Wagner
Proofreaders: Linne Bruskewitz, Victoria Soukup Jensen
Editorial Assistant: Barb Czysz
Editorial Intern: Heather Miller

Taste of Home Test Kitchen
Food Director: Diane Werner
Test Kitchen Manager: Karen Scales
Recipe Editors: Mary King, Christine Rukavena
Contributing Copy Editor: Kristine Krueger
Associate Food Editor: Annie Rundle
Contributing Home Economists: Anne Addesso,
Jackie Josetti, Lorri Reinhardt

Taste of Home Photo Studio
Senior Food Photographer: Rob Hagen
Food Photographers: Lori Foy, Dan Roberts, Jim Wieland
Set Stylists: Jennifer Bradley Vent (Senior),
Stephanie Marchese (Senior), Dee Dee Jacq, Melissa Haberman
Food Stylists: Sarah Thompson (Senior), Kaitlyn Besasie,
Tamara Kaufman
Photo Studio Coordinator: Kathy Swaney

Vice President, Executive Editor/Books: Heidi Reuter Lloyd
Senior Editor/Books: Mark Hagen
Creative Director/Creative Marketing: James Palmen
Creative Director: Ardyth Cope
Chief Marketing Officer: Lisa Karpinski
Senior Vice President, Editor in Chief: Catherine Cassidy
President, Food & Entertaining: Suzanne M. Grimes
President and Chief Executive Officer: Mary G. Berner

Taste of Home Books
©2008 Reiman Media Group, Inc.
5400 S. 60th Street, Greendale WI 53129
International Standard Book Number (10): 0-89821-625-7
International Standard Book Number (13): 978-0-89821-625-7
International Standard Serial Number: 1535-2781

Cover photo of Glazed Racks of Lamb (p. 46) by Dan Roberts.
Food styled by Jennifer Janz. Set styled by Stephanie Marchese.

'TIS THE *Season*

GIVING *Thanks*

EASTER *Gatherings*

SPECIAL *Celebrations*

'TIS THE
Season

If you're hosting a formal Yuletide event,
you'll reel in raves with a special seafood Christmas dinner
or a classy cocktail party featuring hors d'oeuvres.
We also present casual menus for a family holiday movie night
and a Christmas friendship luncheon. Desperate for desserts?
Check out our sweets from around the world,
in-a-dash desserts and classic cookies and candies.
You'll also find festive entrees and gifts from the kitchen.

Delightful Christmas Dinner

IF IT'S up to you to host Christmas dinner every year, you may be looking for a way to liven up your holiday menu.

Instead of reaching for the typical beef, poultry or pork recipe, why not try this festive, from-the-sea fare? It's sure to catch on with guests gathered around your dinner table!

You won't have to angle for compliments when you present friends and family with Honey-Mustard Glazed Salmon. Served upon a bed of colorful Creamed Spinach, the enticing entree will reel in raves.

Everyone will be hooked on the deliciously different Shrimp Scampi Topped Potatoes. This hearty side dish features garlic-infused shrimp and creamy twice-baked potatoes. (All recipes shown at right.)

SPECIAL SEAFOOD SUPPER

(Pictured above)

Honey-Mustard Glazed Salmon (p. 12)

Creamed Spinach (p. 14)

Shrimp Scampi Topped Potatoes (p. 12)

COUNTDOWN TO CHRISTMAS DINNER

A Few Weeks Before:

- Prepare two grocery lists—one for non-perishable items to purchase now and one for perishable items to purchase a few days before Christmas Day.
- If desired, make the Merry Mosaic Trees on page 15.

Two to Three Days Before:

- Buy remaining grocery items.
- Thaw the frozen bread dough for Caramelized Onion Breadsticks as directed on package.

Christmas Eve:

- Set the table.
- Prepare Banana Nog; refrigerate.
- Make the caramelized onions for the breadsticks. Store in an airtight container and chill.
- Chop onions for Creamed Spinach; refrigerate in an airtight container.
- Make Italian Cream Cheese Cake; refrigerate.
- For Pepper-Crusted Tenderloin Crostini, make caramelized onions, prepare the horseradish spread and roast the tenderloin. Let cool and refrigerate in separate containers.
- Make the twice-baked potatoes for Shrimp Scampi Topped Potatoes if desired; cover and chill. Peel and devein the shrimp; refrigerate in an airtight container.

Christmas Day:

- In the morning, bake Caramelized Onion Breadsticks.
- Assemble Pepper-Crusted Tenderloin Crostini but don't top with the onions; cover and chill.
- Just before guests arrive, reheat the caramelized onions for the crostini; place on top of the beef.
- Serve the crostini and Banana Nog.
- Bake Honey-Mustard Glazed Salmon.
- Prepare Creamed Spinach.
- Reheat the twice-baked potatoes in the microwave. Saute the shrimp and place on top of hot potatoes; drizzle with pan drippings.
- Set out the breadsticks.
- For dessert, serve Italian Cream Cheese Cake.

Pepper-Crusted Tenderloin Crostini

(Pictured at right)

Caramelized onions add a touch of sweetness to this elegant appetizer from our Test Kitchen. Use the higher range of pepper if you like a little more zip.

2 large onions, chopped
6 tablespoons butter, softened, *divided*
2 teaspoons sugar
1 tablespoon olive oil
1 beef tenderloin (1-1/2 pounds)
2 to 3 teaspoons coarsely ground pepper
2 garlic cloves, minced
3/4 teaspoon salt
2 teaspoons prepared horseradish
1 French bread baguette (10-1/2 ounces), cut into 30 slices

In a large skillet over medium-low heat, cook onions in 3 tablespoons butter for 5 minutes or until tender. Add sugar; cook over low heat for 30-40 minutes longer or until onions are golden brown, stirring frequently.

Meanwhile, rub oil over tenderloin.

Combine the pepper, garlic and salt; rub over beef. In a large skillet, brown beef on all sides. Transfer to a baking sheet. Bake at 425° for 20-25 minutes or until meat reaches desired doneness (for medium-rare, a meat thermometer should read 145°; medium, 160°; well-done, 170°). Let stand for 10 minutes.

In a small mixing bowl, beat horseradish and remaining butter until blended. Spread over bread slices. Place on a baking sheet. Broil 3-4 in. from heat for 2-3 minutes or until lightly golden brown. Thinly slice the beef; place on toasted bread. Top with caramelized onions. **Yield:** 2-1/2 dozen.

Editor's Note: You can roast the tenderloin the day before; cover and refrigerate. The next day, slice the beef and assemble Pepper-Crusted Tenderloin Crostini as directed.

Banana Nog

(Pictured at far right)

During my family's annual cookie exchange, we ran out of our beloved eggnog...much to everyone's horror! So into the kitchen I went to create this cool, creamy concoction. It was a hit.
—Jennae LeFebvre, Aurora, Illinois

3 cups milk, *divided*
3 cups half-and-half cream, *divided*
3 egg yolks
3/4 cup sugar
3 large ripe bananas
1/2 cup light rum
1/3 cup creme de cacao
1-1/2 teaspoons vanilla extract
Whipped cream and baking cocoa, optional

In a large heavy saucepan, combine 1-1/2 cups milk, 1-1/2 cups cream, egg yolks and sugar. Cook and stir over medium-low heat until mixture reaches 160° and is thick enough to coat the back of a metal spoon.

Place bananas in a food processor; cover and process until blended. Pour milk mixture into a pitcher; stir in the banana puree, rum, creme de cacao, vanilla, and remaining milk and cream. Cover and refrigerate for at least 3 hours before serving.

Pour into chilled glasses. If desired, garnish with whipped cream and sprinkle with cocoa. **Yield:** 11 servings (about 2 quarts).

Swiss-Bacon Spinach Tartlets

I developed this recipe as a way to entice my husband to eat spinach.
When I first made the tarts for Christmas, they disappeared within minutes.
—Kimberly Carr, Akron, Ohio

1/2 pound sliced bacon, diced
2/3 cup chopped sweet onion
1 garlic clove, minced
1 package (10 ounces) frozen chopped spinach, thawed and squeezed dry
2 tablespoons sugar
1 teaspoon Worcestershire sauce
1/2 teaspoon salt
1/2 teaspoon pepper
1/2 teaspoon Liquid Smoke, optional
1 package (2.1 ounces) frozen miniature phyllo tart shells
2/3 cup shredded Swiss cheese

In large skillet over medium heat, cook bacon until crisp. Remove to paper towels; drain, reserving 1 tablespoon drippings. Saute onion and garlic in drippings until tender.

Reduce heat to medium. Stir in the spinach, sugar, Worcestershire sauce, salt, pepper and Liquid Smoke if desired; heat through. Stir in the bacon.

In each phyllo tart shell, layer 1 teaspoon of Swiss cheese, 1 tablespoon of spinach mixture and another teaspoon of cheese. Place on an ungreased baking sheet.

Bake at 350° for 12-15 minutes or until cheese is melted. Serve warm. Refrigerate leftovers. **Yield:** 15 appetizers.

Italian Cream Cheese Cake

(Pictured at right)

Buttermilk makes every bite of this awesome dessert moist and flavorful. I rely on this recipe year-round.
—Joyce Lutz, Centerview, Missouri

1/2 cup butter, softened
1/2 cup shortening
2 cups sugar
5 eggs, *separated*
1 teaspoon vanilla extract
2 cups all-purpose flour
1 teaspoon baking soda
1 cup buttermilk
1-1/2 cups flaked coconut
1 cup chopped pecans
CREAM CHEESE FROSTING:
2 packages (one 8 ounces, one 3 ounces) cream cheese, softened
3/4 cup butter, softened
6 cups confectioners' sugar
1-1/2 teaspoons vanilla extract
3/4 cup chopped pecans

In a large mixing bowl, cream the butter, shortening and sugar until light and fluffy. Add egg yolks and vanilla; beat until combined. Combine flour and baking soda; add to creamed mixture alternately with buttermilk. Beat just until combined. Stir in coconut and pecans.

In a small mixing bowl, beat egg whites until stiff peaks form. Fold a fourth of the egg whites into batter, then fold in remaining whites. Pour into three greased and floured 9-in. round baking pans.

Bake at 350° for 20-25 minutes or until a toothpick inserted near the center comes out clean. Cool for 10 minutes before removing from pans to wire racks to cool completely.

In a large mixing bowl, beat cream cheese and butter until smooth. Beat in confectioners' sugar and vanilla until fluffy. Stir in pecans. Spread frosting between layers and over top and sides of cake. Store in the refrigerator. **Yield:** 12 servings.

Honey-Mustard Glazed Salmon

(Pictured on page 7)

You won't need to fish for compliments from your dinner guests
when you serve our home economists' spectacular salmon!

10 salmon fillets (5 ounces *each*)
2/3 cup packed brown sugar
2 tablespoons Dijon mustard
2 tablespoons honey
1/2 teaspoon salt

Place fillets, skin side down, on a greased baking sheet. In a small bowl, combine the brown sugar, mustard, honey and salt; spoon over salmon.

Broil 3-4 in. from the heat for 8-12 minutes or until fish flakes easily with a fork. **Yield:** 10 servings.

Shrimp Scampi Topped Potatoes

(Pictured on page 7)

Our Test Kitchen's impressive twice-baked potatoes feature
garlic-infused cooked shrimp. These "spuds" could be a meal by themselves!

10 medium potatoes
3 tablespoons olive oil
1-1/2 teaspoons salt
FILLING:
1/2 cup sour cream
1/4 cup heavy whipping cream
4 garlic cloves, minced
1 tablespoon minced fresh parsley
1 tablespoon prepared horseradish
1/2 teaspoon salt
TOPPING:
3 garlic cloves, minced
2 tablespoons olive oil
10 uncooked jumbo shrimp, peeled and deveined
2 tablespoons minced fresh parsley
2 tablespoons lemon juice
2 tablespoons white wine *or* chicken broth
1/8 teaspoon salt

Scrub and pierce potatoes; rub with oil and salt. Place on a baking sheet. Bake at 400° for 1 hour or until tender. Cool slightly; cut a thin slice off the top of each potato and discard. Scoop out pulp, leaving a thin shell.

In a large mixing bowl, mash pulp with the sour cream, whipping cream, garlic, parsley, horseradish and salt until blended. Spoon into potato shells; keep warm.

In a large skillet, saute garlic in oil until tender. Add shrimp; cook for 1 minute on each side. Add the parsley, lemon juice, wine or broth and salt; cook 2-3 minutes longer or until shrimp turn pink. Top each potato with a shrimp; drizzle with pan drippings. **Yield:** 10 servings.

Editor's Note: The twice-baked potatoes can be prepared the day before. Cover and refrigerate. Reheat in the microwave before topping with the sauteed shrimp and pan drippings.

Caramelized Onion Breadsticks

(Pictured at right)

*I'm a sixth grade special education
teacher with little time on my hands.
These easy-to-make breadsticks
go well with my vegetable beef soup.*
—*Jennifer Bermingham
Shillington, Pennsylvania*

1 large sweet onion, halved and
   thinly sliced
6 tablespoons butter, *divided*
1 teaspoon sugar
1 loaf (1 pound) frozen bread
   dough, thawed

In a large skillet over medium-low
heat, cook onion in 4 tablespoons butter for 5 minutes or until tender. Add
sugar; cook over low heat for 30-40
minutes longer or until onion is gold-
en brown, stirring frequently.

On a lightly floured surface, roll
bread dough into an 18-in. x 12-in. rectangle. Spoon onion mixture lengthwise over half of the dough; fold plain
half of dough over onion mixture. Cut
into eighteen 1-in. strips. Twist each strip twice; pinch
ends to seal.

Place 2 in. apart on greased baking sheets. Melt the remaining butter; brush over breadsticks. Cover and let rise
in a warm place until doubled, about 40 minutes.

Bake at 350° for 12-15 minutes or until lightly browned.
Serve warm. **Yield:** 1-1/2 dozen.

Spiced Pear Risotto

We love risotto and are always in search of fun and different ways to prepare it.
I like to serve this fruity version with pork tenderloin.
—*Kim Berto, Port Orchard, Washington*

6 cups chicken broth
1/2 cup finely chopped sweet onion
1/2 cup finely chopped sweet red pepper
1 garlic clove, minced
3 tablespoons butter
3 cups uncooked arborio rice
1/2 teaspoon Chinese five-spice powder
Dash cayenne pepper
1/4 cup apple cider *or* juice
1 large pear, peeled and chopped
1/2 cup grated Parmesan cheese, *divided*
1/2 teaspoon coarsely ground pepper

In a large saucepan, heat broth and keep warm. In a Dutch oven, saute the onion, red pepper and garlic in butter until tender, about 3 minutes.

Add the rice, five-spice powder and cayenne; cook and stir for 2-3 minutes. Reduce heat to medium; add cider. Cook and stir until all of the liquid is absorbed.

Add warm broth, 1/2 cup at a time, stirring constantly. Allow the liquid to absorb between additions. Cook just until risotto is creamy and rice is almost tender. (Cooking time is about 25 minutes.)

Add the pear, 1/4 cup Parmesan cheese and pepper; cook and stir until heated through. Sprinkle with remaining Parmesan cheese. Serve immediately. **Yield:** 10 servings.

Creamed Spinach

(Pictured on page 7)

Cooked spinach makes a perfect accompaniment to many entrees, especially salmon.
This simple version of creamed spinach comes from our Test Kitchen.

4 packages (9 ounces *each*) fresh spinach, torn
2 medium onions, finely chopped
1 tablespoon butter
2 teaspoons all-purpose flour
1/8 teaspoon salt
1/8 teaspoon white pepper
1/3 cup milk
1 tablespoon heavy whipping cream
3 tablespoons grated Parmesan cheese

In four batches, place spinach in a steamer basket; place in a large saucepan over 1 in. of water. Bring to a boil; cover and steam for 3-4 minutes or until wilted. Transfer to a large bowl; keep warm.

In a large skillet, saute the onions in butter until tender. Stir in the flour, salt and pepper until blended. Gradually add the milk and cream. Bring to a boil; cook and stir for 2 minutes or until thickened. Stir in the Parmesan cheese. Drain the spinach; add the sauce and toss to coat. Serve immediately. **Yield:** 9 servings.

Merry Mosaic Trees

(Pictured at right)

Instead of topping your table with evergreens, add a little more color by making these mosaic trees! You can select tiles that work with your color scheme.

Mirror tiles (1/2-in. x 1/2-in. and 1- x 1/4-in.) in silver and different shades of blue
Double-sided tape (1/2-in. wide)
3 Styrofoam tree shapes (9-, 12- and 15-in. tall)
Small silver ball ornaments for tree toppers

Wash mirror tiles in warm water and dishwashing detergent; dry thoroughly.

Place a strip of double-sided tape around the bottom of one tree. Adhere 1/2-in. x 1/2-in. mirror tiles onto the tape in any pattern you desire. Place another strip of tape around the tree close to the top of the tiles you just attached. Adhere tiles onto the tape. Repeat until all but about 1/2 in. at the top of the tree is covered with tiles. Add tape. Adhere 1-in. x 1/4-in. tiles vertically around the top of the tree. Glue a silver ball ornament on top. Repeat the process with the other two Styrofoam trees.

Editor's Note: The number of tiles needed depends on the size of the trees used. To cover one 9-in., one 12-in. and one 15-in. tree, we used about 800 silver 1/2-in. tiles, 200 blue 1/2-in. tiles and 33 silver 1- x 1/4-in. tiles.

'TIS THE *Season*

A Merry Movie Night

THE hustle and bustle of the Christmas season can have you reeling. Why not slow down and gather with friends and family for a casual, fun-filled movie night?

After rounding up a selection of holiday movie favorites, focus on the food!

Welcome guests in from the cold with such oven-fresh snacks as Crab 'n' Cheese Spirals and Hot Antipasto Sandwiches.

Restless kids won't act up when you set out a tray of Pizza Egg Rolls. (All recipes shown at right.)

These hot and hearty appetizers are just a sneak peek of the fabulous, family-friendly foods you'll find on the following pages!

PICTURE-SHOW SNACKS
(Clockwise from top left)

Crab 'n' Cheese Spirals (p. 18)

Pizza Egg Rolls (p. 18)

Hot Antipasto Sandwiches (p. 22)

Crab 'n' Cheese Spirals

(Pictured on page 16)

These pretty pinwheels are loaded with cheese, imitation crabmeat and black olives.
Using refrigerated crescent rolls is so convenient.
—Lisa Harke, Old Monroe, Missouri

2 packages (8 ounces *each*)
   cream cheese, softened
2 cups chopped imitation
   crabmeat
1 can (4-1/4 ounces) chopped
   ripe olives
1/4 cup minced chives
3 tubes (8 ounces *each*)
   refrigerated crescent rolls
3/4 cup shredded part-skim
   mozzarella cheese
3/4 cup shredded Parmesan
   cheese

In a small bowl, beat the cream cheese, crab, olives and chives. Unroll one tube of crescent dough into one long rectangle; seal seams and perforations.

Spread with 1 cup cream cheese mixture; sprinkle with 1/4 cup of each cheese. Roll up jelly-roll style, starting with a long side; pinch seam to seal.

Using a serrated knife, cut into 10 slices; place cut side down on a greased baking sheet. Repeat with remaining crescent dough, cream cheese mixture and cheeses.

Bake at 375° for 14-16 minutes or until golden brown. Serve warm. **Yield:** 2-1/2 dozen.

Pizza Egg Rolls

(Pictured on page 17)

Our home economists give traditional pizza a twist by rolling up
the usual toppings in egg roll wrappers, then deep-frying them. Yum!

1 package (3-1/2 ounces) sliced
   pepperoni, chopped
1 cup chopped fresh
   mushrooms
1 medium green pepper,
   chopped
1/2 cup grated Parmesan cheese
1/2 teaspoon pizza seasoning *or*
   Italian seasoning
14 egg roll wrappers
14 pieces string cheese
Oil for deep-fat frying
1 can (15 ounces) pizza sauce,
   warmed

In a small bowl, combine the pepperoni, mushrooms, green pepper, Parmesan cheese and pizza seasoning. Place an egg roll wrapper on a work surface with a point facing you; place a piece of string cheese near the bottom corner. Top with about 2 tablespoons pepperoni mixture.

Fold bottom corner over filling. Fold sides toward center over filling. Using a pastry brush, wet the top corner with water; roll up tightly to seal. Repeat with remaining wrappers, cheese and filling.

In an electric skillet or deep-fat fryer, heat oil to 375°. Fry egg rolls, a few at a time, for 1-2 minutes on each side or until golden brown. Drain on paper towels. Serve with pizza sauce. **Yield:** 14 egg rolls.

Grinch Punch

(Pictured at right)

My family expects to see this frothy beverage on my buffet each Christmas. It always satisfies a crowd.
—Janice Hodge, Custer, South Dakota

1/3 cup sugar
  6 tablespoons plus
    1-1/2 teaspoons water
1/3 cup evaporated milk
1/2 teaspoon almond extract
 12 drops neon green food
    coloring
  1 bottle (2 liters) lemon-lime
    soda, chilled
  2 pints vanilla ice cream

In a large saucepan, combine sugar and water. Cook and stir over medium heat until sugar is dissolved; remove from the heat. Stir in milk and extract. Transfer to a bowl; cool to room temperature. Cover and refrigerate until chilled.

Just before serving, transfer milk mixture to a punch bowl. Stir in the food coloring and soda. Top with scoops of ice cream. **Yield:** 4 quarts.

Chocolate Peanut Clusters

(Pictured at far right, bottom)

I turn to my slow cooker to prepare these convenient nutty chocolate treats. Making candies couldn't be any easier!
— *Pam Posey, Waterloo, South Carolina*

1 jar (16 ounces) salted dry roasted peanuts
1 jar (16 ounces) unsalted dry roasted peanuts
1 package (11-1/2 ounces) milk chocolate chips
1 package (10 ounces) peanut butter chips
3 packages (10 to 12 ounces *each*) vanilla *or* white chips

2 packages (11-1/2 ounces *each*) 60% cacao bittersweet chocolate baking chips

In a 5-qt. slow cooker, combine the peanuts. Layer with the remaining ingredients in order given (do not stir). Cover and cook on low for 2 to 2-1/2 hours or until chips are melted.

Stir to combine. Drop by tablespoonfuls onto waxed paper. Let stand until set. Store in an airtight container at room temperature. **Yield:** 4 pounds.

Garlic Parmesan Popcorn

I came up with this recipe one night when I was craving a salty snack.
It's a great change from ordinary salted popcorn.
— *Rita Scarborough, Barrington, New Jersey*

12 cups popped popcorn
6 tablespoons butter, cubed
2 garlic cloves, peeled and chopped
1/2 cup grated Parmesan cheese
1/2 teaspoon salt
1/2 teaspoon dried basil

Place popcorn in a large bowl; set aside. In a small skillet, melt butter over medium heat. Add garlic; cook and stir for 1-2 minutes. Strain butter, discarding garlic.

Drizzle butter over popcorn. Sprinkle with Parmesan cheese, salt and basil; toss to coat. **Yield:** 3 quarts.

AVOIDING "OLD MAIDS"

POPCORN kernels that don't pop are called "old maids" and are the result of insufficient water content in the kernel.

According to the Popcorn Board, you can rejuvenate kernels when they no longer pop into fluffy popcorn. Here's how: Fill a one-quart jar three-fourths full of kernels. Add 1 tablespoon of water. Cover and shake every five to 10 minutes or until all the water is absorbed. Let sit 2 to 4 days before using.

Vanilla Caramel Corn

(Pictured at right, top)

This recipe gives a sweet and tasty twist to microwave popcorn. When I first tried it at a party, I couldn't stop eating it!
—Janel Andrews, Jerome, Idaho

   3 packages (3.3 ounces *each*) butter-flavored microwave popcorn
1-1/3 cups packed brown sugar
   1/2 cup light corn syrup
   2/3 cup sweetened condensed milk
   1/2 cup butter, cubed
     1 teaspoon vanilla extract

Pop popcorn according to manufacturer's directions. Transfer to two very large bowls; discard any unpopped kernels.

In a large heavy saucepan, combine brown sugar and corn syrup. Bring to a boil over medium heat; cook and stir for 3 minutes. Carefully stir in milk and butter; return to a boil. Remove from the heat; stir in vanilla. Pour over popcorn and toss to coat. Spread in a single layer on greased 15-in. x 10-in. x 1-in. baking pans.

Bake at 250° for 40 minutes, stirring once. Remove from pans and place on waxed paper to cool. Break into clusters. Store popcorn in airtight containers or plastic bags. **Yield:** 7 quarts.

Hot Antipasto Sandwiches

(Pictured on page 17)

I usually make this stromboli as an appetizer for holiday get-togethers.
But I also like to serve it with salad as a satisfying meal.
—Lisa Berry, Fayetteville, West Virginia

2 tubes (8 ounces *each*) refrigerated crescent rolls
1/4 pound thinly sliced hard salami
1/4 pound thinly sliced deli ham
1/4 pound sliced pepperoni
1/4 pound sliced provolone cheese
2 eggs
Dash pepper
1 jar (7 ounces) roasted sweet red peppers, drained and patted dry
2 tablespoons grated Parmesan cheese
1 egg yolk, beaten

Unroll crescent roll dough into two rectangles; seal seams and perforations. Press one rectangle onto the bottom and 3/4 in. up the sides of a greased 13-in. x 9-in. x 2-in. baking dish. Layer with salami, ham, pepperoni and provolone.

Whisk eggs and pepper; pour over cheese. Top with roasted peppers and Parmesan cheese. Place remaining crescent dough rectangle over the top; pinch edges to seal. Brush with egg yolk.

Cover and bake at 350° for 30 minutes. Uncover; bake 15-20 minutes longer or until golden brown. Cut into eight triangles; serve warm. **Yield:** 8 servings.

REINDEER FOOD PARTY FAVOR

WHEN setting out a plate of cookies for Santa on Christmas Eve, don't forget about his flying friends! Make a big batch of magic Reindeer Food for kids to sprinkle on the lawn on Christmas Eve night. To make the "food," simply combine equal parts of oats and colored sugar. Pour into cellophane bags; seal. Attach the following poem to each bag:

Sprinkle on the lawn at night.
The moon will make it sparkle bright.
As Santa's reindeer fly and roam,
This will guide them to your home.

Hand out the filled bags as pint-size guests leave your fun-filled holiday party.

Cute Christmas Poppers

(Pictured above)

KIDS OF ALL AGES will agree that a party just isn't the same without fun favors to take home! So before hosting your Merry Movie Night, enlist little ones to help you make these festive poppers.

Weeks before your party, start collecting cardboard tubes from rolls of paper towels and toilet paper. Then gather colorful tissue paper and ribbon as well as trinkets (wrapped candy, small toys, pencils, stickers, etc.) to hide inside the poppers.

Cut a piece of tissue paper that is about 4 inches wider than the length of the tube and long enough to cover the tube. Cut another color of tissue paper that is about 1 inch wider than the first color. Layer the tissue paper with the wider piece on top. Wrap the cardboard tube with the paper and tape to secure it.

Tie curling ribbon around one end of the tube. Put trinkets into the tube through the open end. Tie curling ribbon around the open end of the tube. If desired, curl the ribbon on both ends.

'TIS THE Season

Holiday Cocktail Party

ALTHOUGH cocktail parties had their heyday in the 1950s, they truly never went out of style!

An upscale cocktail party featuring elegant appetizers and beverages can be a fun-filled way to gather with friends over the holiday season.

One sip of an Orange Razzletini will chase away the winter doldrums.

As you mingle with guests, present a platter of bite-sized Prosciutto Bundles. A chive "ribbon" on each adds a festive flair.

There's no need to prepare a formal meal when you offer hot and hearty appetizers like Coconut Shrimp, Roasted Rosemary Beet Skewers and Goat Cheese-Pesto Crostini. (All recipes are shown at right.)

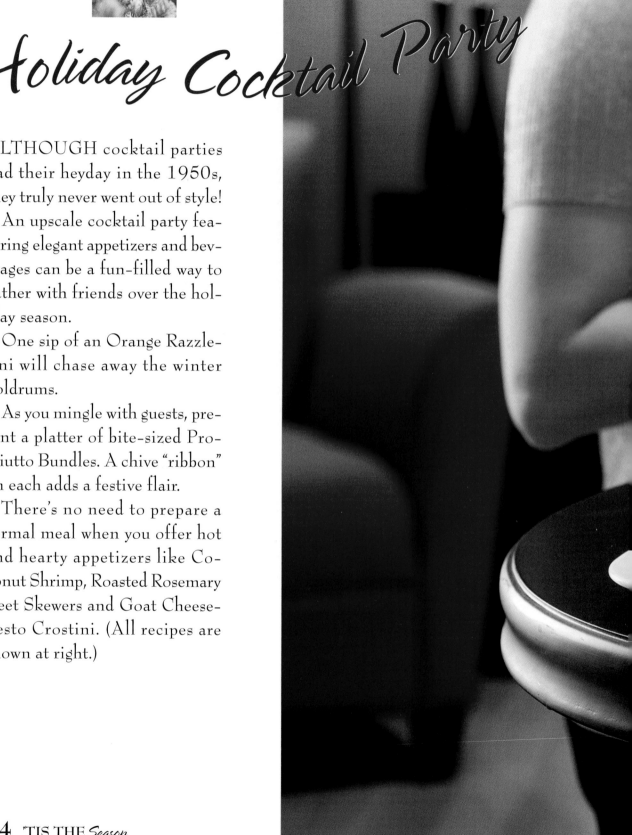

Elegant Hors d'Oeuvres
(Pictured above)

Roasted Rosemary Beet Skewers (p. 26)

Coconut Shrimp (p. 30)

Goat Cheese-Pesto Crostini (p. 28)

Prosciutto Bundles (p. 28)

Orange Razzletini (p. 30)

Roasted Rosemary Beet Skewers

(Pictured on page 25)

*Guests will never guess that beets are the featured ingredient in this
deliciously different appetizer. But they will agree the flavor is fabulous!*
—*Cheryl Perry, Elizabeth City, North Carolina*

  3 medium fresh beets (about
     1 pound)
 24 fresh rosemary sprigs
     (3 inches)
1/4 cup olive oil
  1 tablespoon grated orange peel
  2 teaspoons minced fresh
     gingerroot
  1 teaspoon pepper
1/2 teaspoon salt
POMEGRANATE SAUCE:
  1 cup pomegranate juice
2/3 cup sugar
1-1/2 teaspoons lemon juice
  1 tablespoon brown sugar
  1 tablespoon water

Scrub beets; cut each into 16 wedges. Poke a hole through each wedge with a wooden skewer. Thread two wedges onto each rosemary sprig. Place in a greased shallow baking pan.

In a small bowl, combine the oil, orange peel, ginger, pepper and salt. Drizzle over the beets; gently toss to coat. Bake at 350° for 20-30 minutes or until the beets are tender, turning once.

Meanwhile, in a small saucepan, combine the pomegranate juice, sugar and lemon juice. Bring to a boil. Reduce heat; simmer, uncovered, until mixture is syrupy and reduced by half. Stir in brown sugar and water. Serve with beets. **Yield:** 4 dozen (2/3 cup sauce).

HINTS FOR HOSTING A COCKTAIL PARTY

- **Pick a date and time.** To avoid having to serve a meal, start the festivities after the dinner hour. Send out invitations or invite people by phone a few weeks in advance.
- **Make the menu.** Plan on offering both hot and cold hearty appetizers. Also purchase nuts and snack mixes for guests to nibble on. A few desserts and coffee serve as a nice finishing touch.
- **Plan your beverages.** Plan on having beer and wine as well as ingredients for other cocktails. Don't forget the ice!

- **Arrange the room.** Remove or rearrange large furniture to allow for open spaces and easy mingling. Set up chairs and smaller tables for more intimate conversations.
- **Create stations.** Set out two linen-covered tables: one for beverages and another for food. To reduce traffic, place the tables away from each other, even in different rooms.
- **Plan the atmosphere.** Have the room dimly lit with plenty of candles. Set the mood with '50s-inspired cocktail lounge music like Frank Sinatra and Dean Martin.

Chilled Raspberry Soup

(Pictured at right)

*To make this lovely soup a little lighter,
I often use sugar substitute
and reduced-fat sour cream.
—Amy Wenger, Severance, Colorado*

1/3 cup cranberry juice
1/3 cup sugar
**5-1/3 cups plus 12 fresh
    raspberries, *divided***
**1-1/3 cups plus 2 tablespoons sour
    cream, *divided***

In a blender, combine the cranberry juice, sugar and 5-1/3 cups raspberries; cover and process until blended. Strain and discard seeds. Stir in 1-1/3 cups sour cream. Cover and refrigerate for at least 2 hours.

To serve, pour 1/4 cup of soup into 12 cordial glasses. Top each with a raspberry and 1/2 teaspoon sour cream. **Yield:** 12 servings.

Bubbly Cranberry Mixer

*Our home economists like to bring out a little bubbly on special occasions.
Here champagne mixes with cranberry juice for a refreshing beverage.*

**1 bottle (48 ounces) cranberry
    juice, chilled**
3/4 cup limeade concentrate
**2 bottles (750 milliliters *each*)
    champagne, chilled**

In a large pitcher, combine cranberry juice and limeade. Refrigerate until serving.

For each serving, pour 1/4 cup cranberry mixture into a champagne glass; add 1/4 cup champagne. **Yield:** 24 servings.

Prosciutto Bundles

(Pictured on page 25)

Slices of salty prosciutto pair well with a lightly seasoned cream cheese filling in these bite-size snacks.
—*Gina Quartermaine, Alexandria, Virginia*

1 package (8 ounces) cream
   cheese, softened
1/2 cup minced fresh parsley
1 can (4-1/4 ounces) chopped
   ripe olives, drained
2 green onions, chopped
2 tablespoons finely chopped
   red onion
2 garlic cloves, minced
1/4 teaspoon pepper
16 thin slices prosciutto (about
   10 inches x 3-1/2 inches)
32 whole chives

In a small mixing bowl, beat the cream cheese, parsley, olives, onions, garlic and pepper until combined.

Cut each prosciutto slice in half widthwise; place about 2 teaspoons of filling on the center of each piece. Bring up corners of prosciutto and tie with a chive, forming a bundle. Refrigerate until serving. **Yield:** 32 appetizers.

PREPARE BUNDLES AHEAD

NOT ONLY are Prosciutto Bundles a lovely addition to an appetizer party, they can also be made in advance. Prepare the bundles as directed. Place in an airtight container and refrigerate for up to 8 hours.

Goat Cheese-Pesto Crostini

(Pictured on page 25)

Guests will think you fussed over these elegant appetizers. But the recipe conveniently calls for jarred pesto.
—*Cindie Haras, Boca Raton, Florida*

6 tablespoons olive oil
6 tablespoons prepared pesto
3 tablespoons grated Parmesan
   cheese
1 French bread baguette
   (10-1/2 ounces), cut into
   24 slices
8 bacon strips, diced
1 package (4 ounces) herbed
   goat cheese
1/2 cup fresh arugula *or* baby
   spinach, finely chopped
3 tablespoons pine nuts,
   toasted

In a small bowl, combine the oil, pesto and Parmesan cheese. Place bread slices on an ungreased baking sheet; brush with pesto mixture. Broil 3-4 in. from the heat for 3-4 minutes or until edges are lightly browned.

Meanwhile, in a large skillet, cook bacon over medium heat until crisp. Remove to paper towels to drain.

Combine goat cheese and arugula; spread over bread. Sprinkle with bacon and pine nuts. Serve immediately. **Yield:** 2 dozen.

Pork 'n' Pear Lettuce Wraps

(Pictured at right)

When the weather's mild, I like to prepare the pork and pears on the grill. No matter how you make it, this Asian-inspired dish is delicious!
—Cheryl Perry
Elizabeth City, North Carolina

2 cups pear nectar
3 tablespoons minced fresh
    gingerroot
2 tablespoons butter
1/2 teaspoon coriander seeds,
    crushed
1/2 teaspoon ground cumin
1 tablespoon brown sugar
1/2 teaspoon cayenne pepper
2 Asian pears, peeled, halved
    and cored
4 garlic cloves, minced
1 teaspoon salt
1 pork tenderloin (3/4 pound)
10 green onions, cut into
    1-inch pieces
10 Bibb *or* Boston lettuce leaves

In a small saucepan, combine the first five ingredients. Bring to a boil; reduce heat. Simmer until the sauce is reduced to 1-1/4 cups; keep warm.

Combine brown sugar and cayenne; sprinkle over pears. Place on a greased broiler pan. Rub garlic and salt over tenderloin. Place on broiler pan with pears.

Broil 4-6 in. from the heat for 9 minutes. Turn; broil 7-9 minutes longer or until a meat thermometer reads 160° and pears are lightly browned. Let stand for 5 minutes.

Cut each pear half into five slices. Cut pork into 10 slices. Place two slices of pear, a slice of pork and onions on each lettuce leaf. Top with sauce; wrap lettuce around filling. Serve immediately. **Yield:** 10 wraps (1-1/4 cups sauce).

Orange Razzletini

(Pictured on page 25)

*Our home economists combined orange juice and raspberry rum
to create this fruity martini. The sunny, bright color is appealing.*

Ice cubes
  1/2 cup orange juice
    2 ounces raspberry-flavored
      rum
  1/2 ounce Triple Sec
Orange slices and fresh raspberries,
  optional

Fill a mixing glass or tumbler three-fourths full with ice. Add the orange juice, rum and Triple Sec; stir until condensation forms on outside of glass.

Strain into two chilled cocktail glasses. Garnish with orange slices and raspberries if desired. Serve immediately. **Yield:** 2 servings.

Coconut Shrimp

(Pictured on page 25)

Tender shrimp are nicely coated with crumbs and coconut in this elegant hors d'oeuvre.
—Elaine Bonica, Bethel, Maine

1 egg
1 tablespoon water
1 cup panko (Japanese) bread
  crumbs
1 cup flaked coconut
1 pound uncooked large
  shrimp, peeled and deveined
Oil for deep-fat frying
  1 jar (12 ounces) orange
    marmalade
  1/4 cup rum

In a shallow bowl, whisk egg and water. In another shallow bowl, combine bread crumbs and coconut. Dip shrimp into egg mixture, then roll in crumb mixture.

In an electric skillet, heat 1/4 in. of oil to 375°. Fry shrimp, a few at a time, for 1-2 minutes on each side or until golden brown. Drain on paper towels.

Meanwhile, in a small saucepan, bring orange marmalade and rum to a boil. Reduce heat; simmer, uncovered, for 5 minutes. Serve with shrimp. **Yield:** 2 dozen (1-1/3 cups sauce).

PANKO POINTER

PANKO bread crumbs (also called Japanese bread crumbs) have a coarser texture than ordinary bread crumbs and produce a lighter, crunchier coating. Look for panko bread crumbs in the Asian foods section of larger grocery stores. Regular bread crumbs can be substituted but the texture of the coating will not be as crisp.

Tuscan Kabobs

(Pictured at right)

With chicken, bacon, tomatoes and bread cubes, this is a hearty appetizer that all guests will clamor for. The sauce provides the fantastic finishing touch.
—Elaine Sweet, Dallas, Texas

16 bacon strips, cut in half
    widthwise
1-1/2 pounds boneless skinless
    chicken breasts
  1 loaf (1/2 pound) French bread
32 fresh basil leaves
32 cherry tomatoes
1/2 cup lemon juice
  5 tablespoons olive oil
  1 teaspoon salt
  1 teaspoon pepper
RED PEPPER AIOLI:
  1 cup mayonnaise
1/2 cup roasted sweet red peppers
  4 garlic cloves, peeled and
    halved
1/2 teaspoon crushed red pepper
    flakes

In a large skillet, cook bacon over medium heat until partially cooked but not crisp. Remove bacon to paper towels to drain.

Cut chicken breasts into 32 cubes, about 1 in. each. Wrap a bacon piece around each cube. Cut bread in half lengthwise, then cut into 32 slices.

On 32 metal or soaked wooden appetizer skewers, thread a wrapped chicken cube, basil leaf, bread slice and cherry tomato. Place on baking sheets. In a small bowl, combine the lemon juice, oil, salt and pepper; brush over kabobs. Let stand for 10 minutes.

Broil kabobs 3-4 in. from the heat for 6-8 minutes or until chicken juices run clear, turning frequently. Meanwhile, place the aioli ingredients in a food processor; cover and process until blended. Serve aioli with kabobs. **Yield:** 32 kabobs (1-1/4 cups sauce).

Honey-Tangerine Chicken Skewers

I developed this recipe one day when I was trying to think of something new
to do with chicken. My family gobbles them up.
—Lillian Julow, Gainesville, Florida

2 pounds boneless skinless
   chicken breasts, cut into
   1-inch cubes
1/4 teaspoon salt
1/4 teaspoon pepper
1/2 cup tangerine juice
1/4 cup butter, melted
1/4 cup honey
4 teaspoons dried oregano
4 teaspoons ground cumin
2 to 4 teaspoons hot pepper
   sauce
2 tablespoons vegetable oil

Sprinkle chicken with salt and pepper. In a large bowl, combine the tangerine juice, butter, honey, oregano, cumin and hot pepper sauce. Add chicken and toss to coat.

Thread chicken onto 16 metal or soaked wooden appetizer skewers. In a large skillet, cook skewers in oil in batches over medium-high heat for 4-5 minutes or until chicken is no longer pink. **Yield:** 16 servings.

Hazelnut Hot Chocolate

Vanilla beans and Frangelico liqueur lend to the sophisticated flavor
of this hot chocolate. With such rich taste, it could be served as a dessert.
—Michael Compean, West Los Angeles, California

3 vanilla beans
9 cups milk
2-3/4 cups heavy whipping cream,
   divided
15 squares (1 ounce *each*)
   bittersweet chocolate, chopped
1/2 cup chocolate hazelnut spread
2 tablespoons dark brown sugar
1 tablespoon sugar
1/4 teaspoon salt
3/4 cup hazelnut liqueur
1 square (1 ounce) semisweet
   chocolate, shaved
1/4 cup chopped hazelnuts,
   toasted
Cinnamon sticks, optional

Split vanilla beans in half lengthwise. With a sharp knife, scrape the beans to remove the seeds. Set seeds aside; discard the beans.

In a large saucepan, heat milk and 3/4 cup cream over medium heat just until mixture comes to a simmer. In a large heat-proof bowl, combine the bittersweet chocolate, hazelnut spread, sugars, salt and vanilla seeds. Pour warm milk mixture over chocolate mixture. Let stand for 1 minute.

Meanwhile, whip the remaining cream. Whisk chocolate mixture until smooth; stir in the liqueur.

Fill mugs or cups three-fourths full. Top with whipped cream, shaved chocolate and chopped hazelnuts. Garnish hot chocolate with a cinnamon stick if desired. **Yield:** 22 servings (1/2 cup each).

Cherry Brandy Old-Fashioned

(Pictured at right)

This recipe from our home economists features brandy instead of whiskey. The addition of maraschino cherry juice makes it a little sweeter.

1 maraschino cherry
1 teaspoon bitters
1/2 teaspoon chopped candied *or* crystallized ginger
1/3 cup ice cubes
1/3 cup ginger ale, chilled
1-1/2 ounces brandy
1/2 to 1 ounce maraschino cherry juice
Maraschino cherry with a stem, optional

In a rocks glass, muddle the cherry, bitters and ginger. Add ice. Pour in the ginger ale, brandy and cherry juice. Garnish with a cherry if desired. **Yield:** 1 serving.

Chocolate Cheesecake Phyllo Tartlets

A crisp phyllo shell holds a mousse-like filling in this festive treat. The bite-size portion is perfect for parties.
—Giovanna Kranenberg, Cambridge, Minnesota

1 package (8 ounces) cream cheese, softened
1/4 cup sugar
1/4 cup semisweet chocolate chips, melted
1/2 teaspoon vanilla extract
2 packages (2.1 ounces *each*) frozen miniature phyllo tart shells
Chocolate curls, optional

In a small mixing bowl, beat the cream cheese, sugar, melted chocolate and vanilla until smooth.

Cut a small hole in the corner of a pastry or plastic bag; insert #32 star pastry tip. Fill the bag with cream cheese mixture; pipe into tart shells. Garnish with chocolate curls if desired. Refrigerate until serving. **Yield:** 2-1/2 dozen.

Caramel Vanilla Martinis

(Pictured at far right)

*Our Test Kitchen came up with this rich and delicious
after-dinner drink. The chocolate swirl inside the glass adds a festive touch.*

Ice cubes
   3 ounces Amaretto
   2 ounces caramel-flavored Irish
     cream liqueur
1-1/2 teaspoons vanilla vodka
Chocolate syrup, optional

Fill a mixing glass or tumbler three-fourths full with ice. Add the Amaretto, Irish cream liqueur and vodka; stir until condensation forms on outside of glass.

Drizzle chocolate syrup on the inside of two chilled cocktail glasses if desired. Strain Amaretto mixture into glasses. Serve immediately. **Yield:** 2 servings.

Curried Scallop Wonton Cups

*Cumin and curry add fabulous flavor to these seafood cups.
In place of the scallops, I've also used shrimp, crab, chicken and turkey.*
— Pam Norby, Amery, Wisconsin

 36 wonton wrappers
3/4 pound bay scallops
1/2 cup mayonnaise
1/4 cup minced fresh cilantro
  2 tablespoons lime juice
  1 tablespoon mango chutney
  1 teaspoon minced fresh
    gingerroot
1/4 to 1/2 teaspoon curry powder
1/4 to 1/2 teaspoon ground cumin
1/8 teaspoon cayenne pepper

Press wonton wrappers into greased miniature muffin cups, forming a cup. Bake at 350° for 8-9 minutes or until edges are golden.

Meanwhile, wrap scallops in microwave-safe paper towels. Microwave on high for 2-1/2 to 3 minutes or until firm and opaque.

In a small bowl, combine the remaining ingredients; stir in scallops. Spoon into wonton cups. Serve immediately. **Yield:** 3 dozen.

Editor's Note: This recipe was tested in a 1,100-watt microwave.

Miniature Napoleons

(Pictured at right)

It can be a challenge to enjoy an elegant dessert while mingling at a cocktail party. These impressive, bite-size sweets from our Test Kitchen are easy to eat.

6 tablespoons sugar
2 tablespoons cornstarch
1/4 teaspoon salt
1 cup milk
1 egg yolk, beaten
2 tablespoons butter, *divided*
1/2 teaspoon vanilla extract
1 sheet frozen puff pastry, thawed
1/2 cup heavy whipping cream
2 squares (1 ounce *each*) semisweet chocolate, chopped

In a small saucepan, combine the sugar, cornstarch and salt. Add milk; stir until smooth. Cook and stir over medium heat until mixture comes to a boil. Stir a small amount into egg yolk; return all to the pan. Bring to a gentle boil, stirring constantly; cook 2 minutes longer.

Remove milk mixture from heat; stir in 1 tablespoon butter and vanilla. Pour into a small bowl; cool to room temperature. Cover surface of custard with waxed paper. Refrigerate, without stirring, for 2-3 hours or until chilled.

Unfold puff pastry; place on an ungreased baking sheet. Prick dough thoroughly with a fork. Bake according to package directions. Remove to a wire rack to cool.

In a small mixing bowl, beat cream until stiff peaks form. Fold into custard. Use a fork to split pastry in half horizontally. Spread filling over the bottom half; replace top. Cover and freeze for 4 hours or until firm.

Cut into 1-1/2-in. x 1-in. rectangles. In a microwave-safe bowl, melt chocolate and remaining butter; stir until smooth. Drizzle over pastries. Freeze until serving. **Yield:** 4-1/2 dozen.

Wonton Ravioli

I created this recipe as a quick yet elegant meal. But it also works well as an appetizer.
You can experiment with the filling ingredients to suit your taste.
—Jenny Johnson, White Bear Lake, Minnesota

1	pound ground beef
1/3	cup chopped onion
1/2	teaspoon minced garlic
1/2	teaspoon dried oregano
1/2	teaspoon dried basil
88	wonton wrappers
2-3/4	cups shredded part-skim mozzarella cheese
2	tablespoons butter, melted

Grated Parmesan cheese, optional
Spaghetti sauce, warmed

In a large skillet, cook the beef, onion and garlic over medium heat until meat is no longer pink; drain. Stir in oregano and basil.

Place eight wonton wrappers on a greased baking sheet; top each with 1 tablespoon meat mixture and 1 tablespoon mozzarella cheese. Moisten edges with water; top with another wonton wrapper. Pinch edges with a fork to seal. Repeat with remaining wrappers, meat mixture and cheese.

Brush the wontons with butter. Sprinkle with the Parmesan cheese if desired. Bake at 350° for 10-12 minutes or until golden brown. Serve ravioli with the spaghetti sauce. **Yield:** 44 appetizers.

Marinated Shrimp and Olives

This is my favorite appetizer to serve party guests. The flavors in this colorful dish
blend beautifully, and the shrimp are tender and tasty.
—Carol Gawronski, Lake Wales, Florida

1-1/2	pounds cooked medium shrimp, peeled and deveined
1	can (6 ounces) pitted ripe olives, drained
1	jar (5-3/4 ounces) pimiento-stuffed olives, drained
2	tablespoons olive oil
1-1/2	teaspoons curry powder
1/2	teaspoon ground ginger
1/4	teaspoon salt
1/4	teaspoon pepper
2	tablespoons lemon juice
1	tablespoon minced fresh parsley *or* 1 teaspoon dried parsley flakes

Combine shrimp and olives in a 2-qt. dish; set aside. In a small saucepan, heat oil over medium heat. Combine the curry, ginger, salt and pepper; whisk into hot oil. Cook and stir for 1 minute. Remove from the heat; stir in lemon juice and parsley. Immediately drizzle over shrimp mixture; toss gently to coat.

Cover and refrigerate for up to 6 hours, stirring occasionally. Serve with toothpicks. **Yield:** 15-20 servings.

Lighted Wine Bottles

(Pictured at right)

DECORATING a basement bar or rec room can cost a fortune. But Bill Lehman from Muskego, Wisconsin shares this fun idea for turning wine bottles into inexpensive art!

First gather several empty wine bottles and corks. Wash the bottles inside and out with hot, soapy water. Any glue reside from the label can be removed with a penetrating oil spray like WD-40®.

Make a simple wooden V-shaped fixture to hold the bottle while drilling.

Wearing eye protection and work gloves, slowly and carefully drill a hole 1 to 2 inches up from the bottom of each bottle using a 1/2-in. drill bit designed for glass.

Rinse bottle to remove any glass particles.

If desired, use a clear sealant to cover any rough edges of glass.

For each bottle, you need a single-plug strand of 20-25 lights. Feed the non-plug end into the drilled hole, leaving a length of cord extending from the opening.

To make it easier to put the cork back into the bottle, drill an 1/8-in. hole lengthwise into each cork. Insert a cork into each bottle top.

Editor's Note: If the glass has any defects, it may crack during drilling. So plan on having a few extra empty bottles on hand.

'Tis The Season

Feast on Festive Entrees

SPECIAL occasions call for extraordinary entrees. Whether you're gathering with friends for a casual holiday supper or are hosting a formal family Christmas dinner, this chapter offers a merry array of main courses for every event.

By adorning your table with the eye-catching Glazed Pork Roast (shown at right), your holidays are sure to be happy!

Other elegant entrees on the following pages include Tomato-Cream Stuffed Chicken, Angel Hair Pasta with Lobster and Champagne Baked Ham.

For classy yet casual Christmas fare, Meatball Rigatoni Alfredo and Paella are sure to please.

Regal Roast
(Pictured above)

Glazed Pork Roast (p. 40)

Glazed Pork Roast

(Pictured on page 38)

You don't need many ingredients to prepare this oh-so-good entree.
It's a hit with old and young alike at my holiday table.
—*Gloria Carrara, West Warwick, Rhode Island*

1 bone-in pork loin roast
 (4 to 5 pounds)
1 can (16 ounces) jellied
 cranberry sauce
1/2 cup water
1/3 cup packed brown sugar
1/3 cup molasses
1/4 cup cider vinegar
1/4 teaspoon ground cloves
1/4 teaspoon ground cinnamon

Place roast fat side up on a rack in a shallow roasting pan. In a small saucepan, combine the remaining ingredients. Bring to a boil. Reduce heat; simmer, uncovered, for 14-16 minutes or until smooth and slightly thickened. Pour over pork.

Bake, uncovered, at 325° for 2 to 2-1/2 hours or until a meat thermometer reads 160°, basting with pan juices every 30 minutes. Let stand for 10 minutes before slicing. **Yield:** 10 servings.

Angel Hair Pasta with Lobster

A light, lemon-garlic wine sauce enhances the flavor of
tender lobster in this extra-special dish. Arugula adds a bit of color.
—*Carole Resnick, Cleveland, Ohio*

2 fresh *or* frozen lobster tails (8
 ounces *each*), thawed
2 garlic cloves, minced
3 tablespoons olive oil
1/2 cup white wine *or* chicken
 broth
2 tablespoons tomato puree
1/2 teaspoon salt
1/4 teaspoon pepper
8 ounces uncooked angel hair
 pasta
1 cup fresh arugula *or* baby
 spinach, coarsely chopped
2 tablespoons lemon juice
1 tablespoon grated lemon peel
Shredded Romano *or* Parmesan
 cheese, optional

Carefully remove lobster meat from shells; cut into 1-in. pieces and set aside.

In a large skillet over medium heat, saute garlic in oil until tender. Add the wine or broth, tomato puree, salt and pepper. Bring to a boil over medium heat. Reduce heat. Stir in lobster; simmer, uncovered, for 5-6 minutes or until the lobster is firm and opaque.

Meanwhile, cook pasta according to package directions. Drain pasta; add to lobster mixture and toss to coat. Stir in the arugula, lemon juice and peel; cook for 1-2 minutes or until arugula is wilted. Garnish with cheese if desired. **Yield:** 4 servings.

Tomato-Cream Stuffed Chicken

(Pictured at right)

For a pretty presentation at your next gathering, reach for this impressive recipe. The sun-dried tomato sauce is great alongside chicken and with grilled veggies.
—Jaqui Humphrey
Kirkland, Washington

1/2 cup cream cheese, softened
1/2 cup shredded part-skim
    mozzarella cheese
1/2 cup chopped fresh spinach
1/2 cup oil-packed sun-dried
    tomatoes, chopped
  2 garlic cloves, minced
  4 bone-in chicken breast halves
    (8 ounces *each*)
1/4 teaspoon salt
1/4 teaspoon pepper
  3 tablespoons butter
  1 tablespoon olive oil
SAUCE:
  3/4 cup white wine *or* chicken
    broth
1/4 cup oil-packed sun-dried
    tomatoes, chopped
  3 teaspoons chopped shallot
  3 garlic cloves, minced
  6 fresh basil leaves, thinly
    sliced
  3/4 cup heavy whipping cream
1/4 cup butter, cubed

In a small bowl, combine the first five ingredients. Carefully loosen the skin on one side of each chicken breast to form a pocket; spread cheese mixture under the skin. Sprinkle with salt and pepper.

In a large skillet, brown chicken on both sides in butter and oil. Transfer to an ungreased 13-in. x 9-in. x 2-in. baking dish. Bake, uncovered, at 400° for 20-25 minutes or until juices run clear.

Meanwhile, in a small saucepan, combine the wine or broth, tomatoes, shallot, garlic and basil. Bring to a boil over medium-high heat; cook until reduced by half. Add cream and butter. Bring to a boil. Reduce heat; simmer, uncovered, until thickened, stirring occasionally. Serve with chicken. **Yield:** 4 servings.

Turkey Scaloppine with Marsala Sauce

My family requests this entree at least once a month.
The slightly sweet marsala sauce is yummy over the turkey slices and hot noodles.
—Briana Knight, Ferndale, Washington

1 cup all-purpose flour
1 teaspoon salt
1 teaspoon pepper
1 package (17.6 ounces) turkey breast slices
2 tablespoons olive oil
1-1/2 cups marsala wine
3 tablespoons butter
Hot cooked linguine, optional
3 tablespoons shredded Parmesan cheese
Thinly sliced green onions, optional

In a large resealable plastic bag, combine the flour, salt and pepper. Add turkey slices and shake to coat.

In a large skillet over medium heat, cook turkey in oil for 3-4 minutes on each side or until juices run clear. Remove and keep warm. Add wine to the skillet; cook over medium heat for 8-10 minutes or until liquid is reduced by a third. Stir in butter until melted. Return turkey to the pan; heat through. Serve with linguine if desired. Garnish with Parmesan cheese. **Yield:** 4 servings.

Roasted Pork and Vegetables

Cooking the vegetables and pork roast together lets you concentrate on
other parts of the meal. Rosemary and garlic nicely flavor the meat.
—Lillian Julow, Gainesville, Florida

1 boneless lean pork roast (3 to 4 pounds)
1/4 teaspoon salt, *divided*
1/4 teaspoon pepper, *divided*
2 garlic cloves, sliced
3 fresh rosemary sprigs
3 tablespoons olive oil
2 teaspoons minced garlic
2 teaspoons minced fresh rosemary
1-1/2 pounds small thin carrots
3 small onions, quartered
3 bacon strips, chopped

Sprinkle roast with 1/8 teaspoon each of salt and pepper; place in a shallow roasting pan. With a sharp knife, cut 1/2-in.-deep slits in the roast; insert a garlic slice in each slit. Tie rosemary sprigs on top of roast with kitchen string.

In a small bowl, combine the oil, minced garlic and rosemary, and remaining salt and pepper. Place carrots and onions around roast; drizzle with oil mixture. Top with bacon.

Bake, uncovered, at 350° for 1 to 1-1/4 hours or until a meat thermometer reads 160°. Let stand for 10 minutes before slicing. **Yield:** 8-10 servings.

Editor's Note: If small thin carrots are unavailable, halve or quarter them lengthwise.

Paella

(Pictured at right)

A big pan of paella is the perfect choice when cooking for a crowd. All you need to round out the meal is fresh bread and a green salad.
—Jane Montgomery, Hilliard, Ohio

3 pounds uncooked skinless turkey breast, cubed
4 pounds uncooked chorizo, cut into 1-1/2-inch pieces *or* bulk spicy pork sausage
3 tablespoons olive oil
2 medium onions, chopped
1 medium sweet red pepper, chopped
4 garlic cloves, minced
1/2 teaspoon cayenne pepper
2 cups tomato puree
1 cup white wine *or* chicken broth
5 cups water
4 cups uncooked long grain rice
3-1/2 cups chicken broth
2 teaspoons salt
1 teaspoon dried thyme
3/4 teaspoon saffron threads *or* 2 teaspoons ground turmeric
1 bay leaf
2 pounds uncooked medium shrimp, peeled and deveined
3/4 cup pitted Greek olives
1/2 cup minced fresh parsley

In a large skillet, cook the turkey and chorizo in oil in batches until browned. Remove with a slotted spoon and keep warm.

In the same skillet, saute onions and red pepper until tender. Stir in garlic and cayenne; cook for 1-2 minutes or until garlic is golden brown. Stir in tomato puree and wine or broth. Bring to a boil; cook and stir for 2 minutes or until thickened.

Transfer to a soup kettle. Stir in the water, rice, broth, salt, thyme, saffron, bay leaf, turkey and sausage. Bring to a boil. Reduce heat; cover and simmer for 20 minutes or until rice is tender.

Add shrimp; cook for 2-3 minutes or until shrimp turn pink. Remove from the heat; discard bay leaf. Stir in olives and parsley. **Yield:** 24 servings (1 cup each).

What Is Paella?

PAELLA (pronounced pa-yay-ya) is a Spanish dish containing rice, meats and vegetables. The name comes from the pan in which it is authentically cooked.

Duck with Harvest Medley

Our Test Kitchen home economists created a balsamic vinegar reduction to enhance the fantastic flavors of duck and sweet potatoes in this elegant entree.

4 cups water
2 cups pearl onions
2 cups balsamic vinegar
1/4 cup maple syrup
2 tablespoons brown sugar
1 cup dried cherries
6 duck breasts with skin
  (5 ounces *each*)
1 tablespoon thinly sliced
  fresh sage leaves
2-1/2 teaspoons salt, *divided*
1 teaspoon pepper, *divided*
4 medium sweet potatoes,
  peeled and diced
1/2 cup chicken broth
1/4 cup white wine *or* additional
  chicken broth
1 teaspoon ground cumin
1/3 cup chopped pecans, optional
1 tablespoon minced fresh
  parsley

In a large saucepan, bring water to a boil. Add pearl onions; boil for 3 minutes. Drain and rinse in cold water; peel and set aside.

In another large saucepan, bring the vinegar, syrup and brown sugar to a boil. Reduce heat; simmer, uncovered, for 15 minutes or until liquid is nearly reduced by half. Add cherries; simmer 3-5 minutes longer. Remove from the heat; set aside.

Cut a pocket in each duck breast. Stuff with sage; sprinkle with 1-1/2 teaspoons salt and 1/2 teaspoon pepper. Place skin side down in a large skillet. Cook over medium-low heat for 10-12 minutes or until most of the duck fat has melted. Turn; cook for 2-3 minutes or until lightly browned. Reserve drippings.

Transfer duck to a 15-in. x 10-in. x 1-in. baking pan. Bake, uncovered, at 375° for 15-22 minutes or until meat reaches desired doneness (for medium, a meat thermometer should read 165°; well-done, 180°).

In the duck drippings, saute sweet potatoes and pearl onions for 6-8 minutes or until lightly browned. Stir in the broth, wine or additional broth, cumin, and remaining salt and pepper. Cook 3-5 minutes longer or until potatoes are tender. Stir in pecans if desired. Serve with duck and cherry sauce. Garnish with parsley. **Yield:** 6 servings.

GET TO KNOW DUCK

ALTHOUGH duck is considered to be a white meat, the breast meat is darker than chicken or turkey breast. Duck has a stronger flavor than chicken or turkey.

You'll likely need to order duck breasts from your butcher. They're available with or without skin.

Cranberry Brisket with Horseradish Mashed Potatoes

(Pictured at right)

The sweet and savory brisket is a great complement to the zesty potatoes. The rich color of the meat makes it a great holiday option.
— Racelle Schaefer
Studio City, California

1 fresh beef brisket (3 to 4 pounds)
1 can (16 ounces) whole-berry cranberry sauce
1 can (12 ounces) ginger ale
1/2 cup dried cranberries
1 envelope onion soup mix
8 medium potatoes, peeled and quartered
1/3 cup milk
1/4 cup butter, cubed
2 tablespoons prepared horseradish

Place brisket in a greased 13-in. x 9-in. x 2-in. baking dish. Combine the cranberry sauce, ginger ale, cranberries and soup mix; pour over meat. Cover and bake at 375° for 2 hours.

Uncover; bake 1 hour longer or until meat is tender, basting occasionally. Meanwhile, place potatoes in a Dutch oven; cover with water. Bring to a boil. Reduce heat; cover and simmer for 30-35 minutes or until tender.

Drain potatoes; mash with milk, butter and horseradish. Let brisket stand for 5 minutes; thinly slice across the grain. Serve meat and juices with potatoes. **Yield:** 8 servings (1-2/3 cups gravy).

Editor's Note: This is a fresh beef brisket, not corned beef.

Glazed Racks of Lamb

(Pictured on the cover)

Because of the cost, rack of lamb isn't an entree you make every day.
So when you do prepare it, you need a tried-and-true recipe like this one from our home economists.

2 frenched racks of lamb
  (1-1/2 pounds *each*)
1/2 cup honey
1/2 cup cherry preserves
2 teaspoons olive oil
1 teaspoon lime juice

Place the lamb on a greased foil-lined baking sheet. Drape a piece of heavy-duty foil over bones to prevent over-browning. In a small bowl, combine the honey, preserves, oil and lime juice. Set aside 1/2 cup. Spoon half of the remaining glaze over lamb.

Broil 4-6 in. from the heat for 10-12 minutes or until meat reaches de-sired doneness (for medium-rare, a meat thermometer should read 145°; medium, 160°; well-done, 170°), basting once with remaining glaze.

Remove lamb from the oven and loosely cover with foil. Let stand for 5 minutes before cutting. Brush with re-served glaze. **Yield:** 4 servings.

RACK OF LAMB LESSON

RACK OF LAMB is sold whole (seven to eight ribs) or is cut into rib chops. Oftentimes, rack of lamb is "frenched," which refers to when about 1-1/2-in. of the meat is removed from the bones, resulting in an elegant presentation.

Cherry-Chipotle Pork Medallions

Chipotle peppers give every bite of these pork medallions a bit of kick.
—Roxanne Chan, Albany, California

1 pork tenderloin (3/4 pound),
  cut into 1-inch slices
1/4 teaspoon sugar
1/4 teaspoon salt
1/4 teaspoon ground cinnamon
2 teaspoons olive oil
1/2 cup frozen pitted dark sweet
  cherries, thawed and halved
3 tablespoons orange juice
1 tablespoon sliced almonds
1 tablespoon orange
  marmalade
1 tablespoon red wine vinegar

1 to 1-1/2 teaspoons finely chopped chipotle
  peppers in adobo sauce
1 garlic clove, crushed
Thinly sliced green onions, optional

Flatten pork slices to 1/2-in. thickness. Combine the sugar, salt and cinnamon; sprinkle over meat. In a large skillet over medium heat, cook pork in oil in batches until juices run clear. Remove and keep warm.

Add the cherries, orange juice, almonds, marmalade, vinegar, chipotle peppers and garlic to the skillet. Return pork to the pan; heat through. Garnish with onions if de-sired. **Yield:** 2 servings.

Champagne Baked Ham

(Pictured at right)

Champagne, brown sugar and honey combine to make a beautiful, glossy glaze. The ham slices turn out delicious and juicy every time.
—Linda Foreman
Locust Grove, Oklahoma

   1 **boneless fully cooked ham
      (9 pounds)**
1-1/2 **cups champagne**
  3/4 **cup packed brown sugar**
4-1/2 **teaspoons honey**
  3/4 **teaspoon ground ginger**
  3/4 **teaspoon ground mustard**

Place ham on a rack in a shallow roasting pan. Score the surface of the ham, making diamond shapes 1/2 in. deep. Bake, uncovered, at 325° for 1-1/2 hours.

Meanwhile, in a small saucepan, combine the remaining ingredients. Bring to a boil; cook until glaze is reduced by half. Remove from the heat.

Baste ham with glaze; bake 30 minutes longer or until a meat thermometer reads 140°, basting twice with glaze. Let stand for 10 minutes before slicing. Serve with remaining glaze. **Yield:** 18 servings.

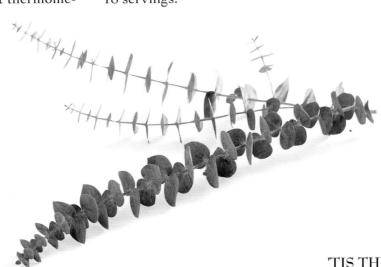

Meatball Rigatoni Alfredo

My kids love meatballs with rigatoni or spaghetti.
The cheesy Alfredo topping on this casserole is the crowning touch.
—Jennifer Ross, Clinton, Ohio

1 egg, lightly beaten
3/4 cup seasoned bread crumbs
1/3 cup water
1/4 cup grated Parmesan cheese
4-1/2 teaspoons minced fresh thyme
4-1/2 teaspoons minced fresh oregano
4-1/2 teaspoons minced fresh basil
1-1/2 teaspoons pepper
1/2 teaspoon salt
1-1/2 pounds ground beef
1 tablespoon vegetable oil
1 small onion, chopped
3 garlic cloves, minced
1/3 cup dry red wine *or* beef broth
1 can (28 ounces) crushed tomatoes
1 tablespoon minced fresh parsley
12 ounces uncooked rigatoni *or* large tube pasta

ALFREDO TOPPING:
1/4 cup butter, cubed
2 tablespoons all-purpose flour
2 cups half-and-half cream
1 cup grated Parmesan cheese, *divided*
1 teaspoon minced fresh thyme
1 teaspoon minced fresh oregano

In a large bowl, combine the first nine ingredients. Crumble beef over mixture and mix well. Shape into 1-1/2-in. balls. In a Dutch oven, brown meatballs in oil in batches; remove and keep warm.

Drain, reserving 1 tablespoon drippings. In the drippings, saute onion and garlic until tender. Add wine or broth; cook and stir for 3 minutes.

Return meatballs to the pan; stir in tomatoes and parsley. Bring to a boil. Reduce heat; cover and simmer for 25-30 minutes or until a meat thermometer reads 160° and meatballs are no longer pink.

Cook rigatoni according to package directions. Meanwhile, in a small saucepan, melt butter. Stir in flour until smooth; gradually add cream. Bring to a boil; cook and stir for 1-2 minutes or until thickened. Remove from the heat. Stir in 3/4 cup Parmesan cheese.

Drain rigatoni; place in a large bowl. Add meatballs and sauce; stir to coat. Transfer to a greased 13-in. x 9-in. x 2-in. baking dish.

Top with Alfredo sauce; sprinkle with thyme, oregano and remaining Parmesan cheese. Bake, uncovered, at 400° for 20-25 minutes or until bubbly. **Yield:** 6 servings.

Orange Roughy with Red Pepper Sauce

(Pictured at right)

A homemade roasted red pepper sauce beautifully tops flaky orange roughy fillets. The pecan garnish adds a bit of crunch.
—Joyce Mitchell, Kilmarnock, Virginia

SPICED PECANS:
>   2 tablespoons Worcestershire sauce
>   1 tablespoon butter
>   1 teaspoon vegetable oil
>   1 cup pecan halves
> 1/4 teaspoon salt
> 1/4 teaspoon dried thyme
> 1/4 teaspoon dried oregano
> 1/4 teaspoon cayenne pepper

RED PEPPER SAUCE:
> 1/4 cup white wine vinegar
> 1/4 cup lemon juice
>   2 tablespoons chopped shallots
> 3/4 cup roasted sweet red peppers, drained

FISH:
>   6 orange roughy *or* whitefish fillets (8 ounces *each*)
> 1/8 teaspoon pepper
>   1 cup all-purpose flour
> 3/4 cup butter, melted
>   2 tablespoons vegetable oil

In a small saucepan, combine the Worcestershire sauce, butter and oil; cook and stir until butter is melted. Stir in the pecans, salt, thyme, oregano and cayenne until blended; cook 3-4 minutes longer or until lightly toasted. Cool.

In another small saucepan, bring the vinegar, lemon juice and shallots to a boil; cook for 8-10 minutes or until sauce is reduced to 1/2 cup. In a blender, puree red peppers. Gradually stir puree into sauce; heat through. Keep warm.

Sprinkle fish fillets with pepper. Place flour and butter in separate shallow bowls. Dip fillets in flour, then in butter. In a large skillet over medium heat, fry fillets in oil in batches for 4-6 minutes on each side or until fish flakes easily with a fork. Serve with red pepper sauce; garnish with spiced pecans. **Yield:** 6 servings.

'TIS THE Season

Christmas Cookies & Candy

IT'S THE little things that make the holidays special, and nothing stirs child-like anticipation more than a pretty tray piled high with sweet treats.

With this dazzling assortment of Christmas cookies and candies, it's easier than ever to turn your kitchen into a winter wonderland of seasonal treats.

Watch faces light up with joy when you give a festive tin filled to the brim with sweet-and-salty Pecan Caramel Chews and the old-fashioned Honey Almond Nougats.

A plate full of irresistible Nutmeg Logs and Cranberry-White Chocolate Cookies makes the perfect surprise for dear old Santa.

And what better way to enjoy a cup of coffee with friends than by nibbling on Chocolate-Coated Candy Canes. (All recipes shown at right.)

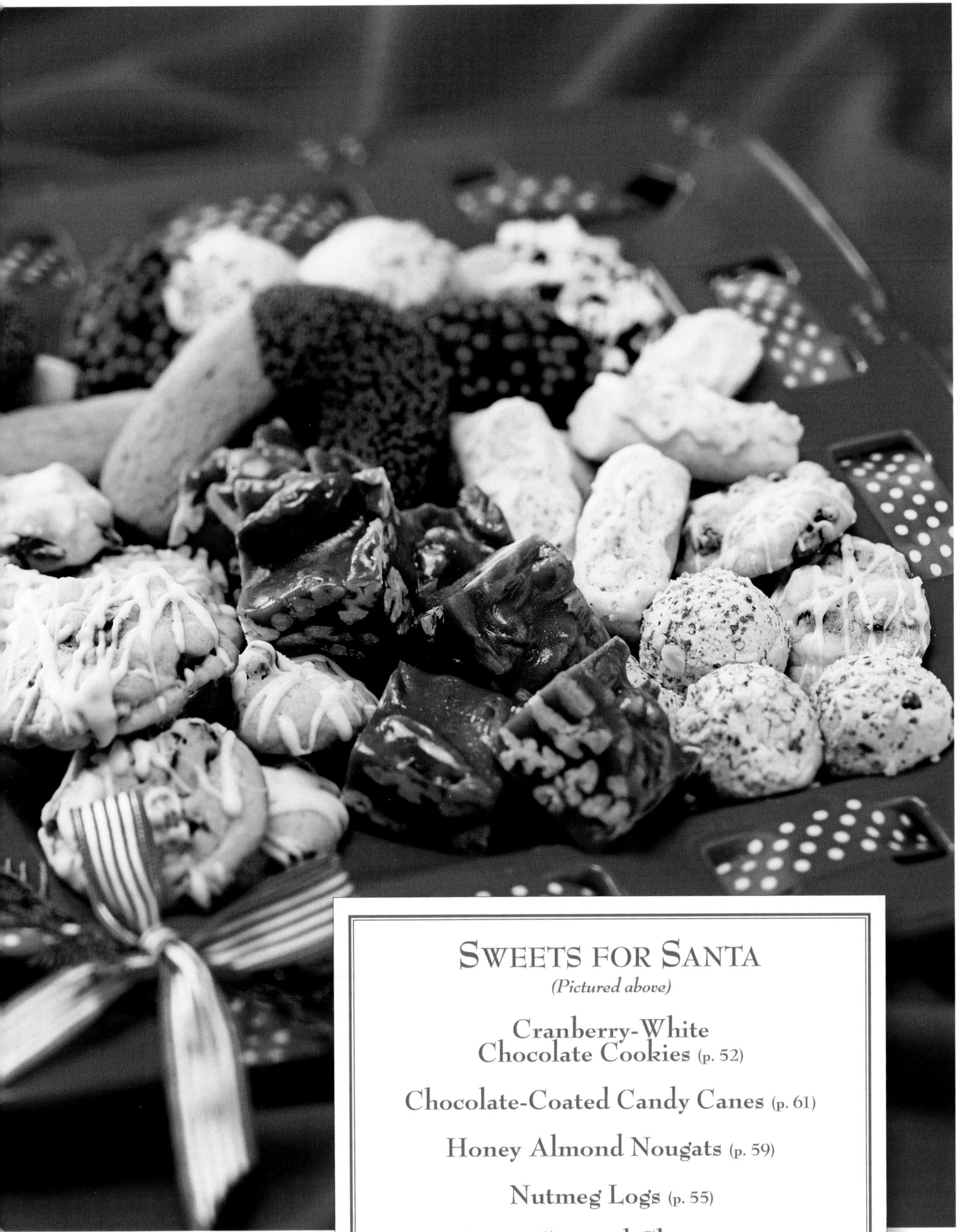

Sweets for Santa

(Pictured above)

Cranberry-White Chocolate Cookies

(Pictured on page 51)

*White chocolate and sweet cranberries make these chewy cookies irresistible,
while the red and white colors add a festive appearance to any cookie tray.*
—*Sherry Conley, Noel Hants County, Nova Scotia*

1 cup butter, softened
3/4 cup sugar
3/4 cup packed brown sugar
2 eggs
1/3 cup cranberry juice
1 teaspoon vanilla extract
3 cups all-purpose flour
2 teaspoons baking powder
1/2 teaspoon salt
2 cups dried cranberries
2 cups vanilla *or* white chips
GLAZE:
2 cups vanilla *or* white chips
2 tablespoons plus 1-1/2
teaspoons shortening

In a large bowl, cream butter and sugars until light and fluffy. Beat in the eggs, cranberry juice and vanilla. Combine the flour, baking powder and salt; gradually add to creamed mixture and mix well. Fold in cranberries and vanilla chips.

Drop by rounded teaspoonfuls 2 in. apart onto greased baking sheets. Bake at 350° for 10-12 minutes or until edges begin to brown. Cool for 2 minutes before removing to wire racks to cool completely.

For glaze, microwave vanilla chips and shortening at 70% power until melted; stir until smooth. Drizzle over cookies. **Yield:** about 7 dozen.

SWEET CANDY SUCCESS

FOLLOW these simple hints to create confectionery sensations!
- Measure and assemble all ingredients for a candy recipe before beginning. Do not substitute or alter the basic ingredients.
- Use heavy-gauge saucepans that are deep enough to allow candy mixtures to boil freely without boiling over.
- For safe stirring when preparing recipes with hot boiling sugar, use wooden spoons with long handles.
- Humid weather affects results when making candy that is cooked to a specific temperature or that contains egg whites. For best results, make candy on days when the humidity is less than 60%.
- When making chocolate-dipped candies, use shortening. Margarine contains some water, which will cause chocolate to "seize" or curdle, so it can't be used to coat candies.
- Store homemade candies in tightly-covered containers unless otherwise directed. Don't store more than one kind of candy in a single container.

Eggnog-Filled Cookie Cups

(Pictured at right)

No one can resist these yummy, little bites and their creamy eggnog-flavored filling. The mini desserts come together easily and look so fancy on a dessert platter.
—Melissa Jelinek
Menomonee Falls, Wisconsin

   1 package (3 ounces) cook-and-serve vanilla pudding mix
1-1/2 cups eggnog
  1/3 cup milk
   2 teaspoons rum extract, *divided*
   1 cup butter, softened
  1/2 cup packed brown sugar
   2 egg yolks
   2 cups all-purpose flour
  1/8 teaspoon salt
  1/4 cup sugar
  1/8 teaspoon ground allspice
  1/4 teaspoon ground nutmeg

In a small saucepan, combine the pudding mix, eggnog and milk. Cook and stir until mixture comes to a boil. Remove from the heat; stir in 1 teaspoon extract. Transfer to a small bowl. Cover surface of pudding with waxed paper; refrigerate until chilled.

In a large mixing bowl, cream the butter and brown sugar until light and fluffy. Beat in the egg yolks and remaining extract. Combine the flour and salt; gradually add to the creamed mixture and mix well.

In a small bowl, combine sugar and allspice. Shape dough into 1-in. balls; roll in sugar mixture. With floured fingers, press onto the bottom and up the sides of well-greased miniature muffin cups.

Bake at 350° for 10-15 minutes or until light golden brown. Immediately remove from the pans to wire racks to cool completely.

Just before serving, pipe or spoon pudding into cups. Sprinkle with nutmeg. Store in an airtight container in the refrigerator. **Yield:** 2-1/2 dozen.

Editor's Note: This recipe was tested with commercially prepared eggnog.

Pecan Caramel Chews

(Pictured on page 51)

My aunt gave me this recipe, and I think it's the best candy I've ever eaten.
It takes some time to make, but the end result is worth every minute.
—*Mary Kay Hilt, Gardner, Kansas*

1-1/2 teaspoons butter
  2 cups sugar
  1 cup light corn syrup
  3 cups heavy whipping cream,
    divided
Dash salt
  6 cups pecan halves
  1 teaspoon vanilla extract

Line a 13-in. x 9-in. x 2-in. pan with foil; butter the foil. Set aside. In a heavy saucepan, combine the sugar, corn syrup, 1 cup cream and salt. Bring to a boil over medium heat, stirring occasionally. Cook until a candy thermometer reads 234° (soft-ball stage).

Gradually stir in 1 cup cream. Cook until mixture returns to 234°. Gradually add remaining cream. Cook and stir until mixture reaches 240°.

Remove from the heat. Stir in pecans and vanilla. Quickly pour into prepared pan; cool completely.

Using foil, lift candy out of pan. Discard foil; cut candy into squares. **Yield:** 3-1/2 pounds.

Editor's Note: We recommend that you test your candy thermometer before each use by bringing water to a boil; the thermometer should read 212°. Adjust your recipe temperature up or down based on your test.

Santa's Surprise Cookies

Miniature Snickers candy bars are tucked inside these cookies, making it impossible to eat just one!
The dark chocolate drizzle makes them deliciously decadent, while adding such a pretty appearance.
—*Cheryl Smith, Jamestown, Pennsylvania*

  1 cup butter, softened
  1 cup creamy peanut butter
  1 cup sugar
  1 cup packed brown sugar
  2 eggs
  1 teaspoon vanilla extract
3-1/2 cups all-purpose flour
  1 teaspoon baking soda
  2 packages (11-1/2 ounces *each*)
    miniature Snickers candy
    bars
GLAZE:
  1 package (9-1/2 ounces) Dove
    dark chocolate candies
  1 teaspoon shortening

In a large bowl, cream the butter, peanut butter and sugars until light and fluffy. Beat in eggs and vanilla. Combine flour and baking soda; gradually add to creamed mixture and mix well. Cover and refrigerate for 1 hour or until easy to handle.

Roll dough into 1-1/4-in. balls. Press a candy bar into each; reshape balls. Place 2 in. apart on ungreased baking sheets.

Bake at 325° for 10-14 minutes or until edges are lightly browned. Cool for 2 minutes before removing to wire racks to cool completely.

In a microwave-safe bowl, melt chocolate candies and shortening; stir until smooth. Drizzle over cookies. Let stand until set. **Yield:** about 6 dozen.

Nutmeg Logs

(Pictured at right and on page 51)

The rich, buttery frosting on these mildly-spiced cookies will tempt young and old alike. The tasty morsels practically melt in your mouth.
—Jean Wysocki, Westminster, Colorado

1 cup butter, softened
3/4 cup sugar
1 egg
2 teaspoons vanilla extract
3 cups all-purpose flour
1 teaspoon ground nutmeg
1/4 teaspoon salt
FROSTING:
1/3 cup butter, softened
2 cups confectioners' sugar
1 teaspoon rum extract
1 teaspoon vanilla extract
2 to 3 tablespoons half-and-half cream
Ground nutmeg

In a large bowl, cream butter and sugar until light and fluffy. Beat in egg and vanilla. Combine the flour, nutmeg and salt; gradually add to creamed mixture and mix well.

Divide dough into 14 pieces. Shape each portion into a 12-in. x 1/2-in.-thick rope. Cut ropes into 2-in. pieces. Place 2 in. apart on greased baking sheets.

Bake at 350° for 9-12 minutes or until set and bottoms are lightly browned. Cool for 1 minute before removing to wire racks to cool completely.

For frosting, in a small bowl, beat butter until fluffy. Add the confectioners' sugar and extracts; beat until blended. Beat in enough cream to achieve desired consistency. Frost cookies. Sprinkle with nutmeg. Store in an airtight container in the refrigerator. **Yield:** 7 dozen.

Family Traditions

MY FRIENDS and I gather each year for a cookie exchange. The one rule is this: no drop cookies, bars or candies allowed. This really gets our creative juices flowing!

On the night of the party, everyone places one dozen of their cookies on a tray so everyone can taste them. The evening ends with a hilarious white-elephant gift exchange. Plus we all go home with a nice selection of cookies.
—Leslie Poertner, Germantown, Wisconsin

Triple-Chip Cinnamon Brownies

Being a huge chocolate-lover, these decadent brownies, featuring rich Kahlua flavor,
crunchy pecans and a heavenly cream cheese frosting, are among my favorites.
—*Carla Knibbs, Okotoks, Alberta*

1 egg, beaten
2/3 cup packed brown sugar
1/4 cup butter, melted
1/4 cup Kahlua
2 teaspoons vanilla extract
3/4 cup all-purpose flour
1/4 cup baking cocoa
1 teaspoon baking powder
1 teaspoon ground cinnamon
1/4 teaspoon salt
1/4 cup milk chocolate chips
1/4 cup semisweet chocolate chips
1/4 cup vanilla *or* white chips
1/4 cup chopped pecans
FROSTING:
1 package (3 ounces) cream
cheese, softened
1/4 cup butter, softened
1/2 cup confectioners' sugar
1 teaspoon ground cinnamon
1 teaspoon vanilla extract
2 to 3 teaspoons milk

In a large bowl, combine the egg, brown sugar, butter, Kahlua and vanilla. Combine the flour, cocoa, baking powder, cinnamon and salt; stir into egg mixture until blended. Fold in chips and pecans.

Transfer to a greased 9-in. square baking pan. Bake at 350° for 20-25 minutes or until a toothpick inserted near the center comes out clean. Cool on a wire rack.

For frosting, in a small mixing bowl, beat the cream cheese, butter and confectioners' sugar until light and fluffy. Add the cinnamon, vanilla and enough milk to achieve desired consistency. Spread over brownies. Store in the refrigerator. **Yield:** 2 dozen.

BAKE THE PERFECT BATCH

BAKING cookies can be a breeze with these handy tips.

- Keep cookies small and consistent in size by using a small kitchen scoop, such as a melon baller or teaspoon.
- For the most evenly baked and browned cookies, use shiny aluminum pans. Dark-coated, nonstick pans tend to cause the cookies to bake too quickly and burn. If the pans are thin, stack two to give the cookies some "insulation."
- Always place cookie dough on cold cookie sheets. If you don't let the cookie sheets cool, your cookie dough will spread too much from the heat of the cookie sheets.

Snowcapped Gingerbread Biscotti

(Pictured at right)

On Christmas morning, enjoy your coffee with this seasonal biscotti. Dipped in butterscotch and vanilla, the gingerbread-flavored treat is doubly delicious.
— Trisha Kruse, Eagle, Idaho

    1/3 cup butter, softened
      1 cup packed brown sugar
    1/4 cup molasses
      3 eggs
  3-1/4 cups all-purpose flour
      3 teaspoons ground cinnamon
      1 teaspoon ground nutmeg
    1/2 teaspoon baking powder
    1/2 teaspoon salt
    1/2 teaspoon ground allspice
    1/2 teaspoon ground cloves
      1 cup hazelnuts, toasted and
         chopped
    1/4 cup candied *or* crystallized
         ginger, finely chopped
      1 cup butterscotch chips, melted
      1 cup vanilla *or* white chips,
         melted

In a large bowl, cream the butter and brown sugar until light and fluffy. Beat in molasses. Add eggs, one at a time, beating well after each addition. Combine the flour, cinnamon, nutmeg, baking powder, salt, allspice and cloves; gradually add to creamed mixture and mix well. Stir in hazelnuts and ginger.

Divide dough in half. Cover and refrigerate for 30 minutes. On a lightly floured surface, shape dough into two 10-in. x 3-in. logs. Transfer to greased baking sheets. Bake at 350° for 20-25 minutes or until lightly browned and firm to the touch.

Transfer to a cutting board; cut diagonally with a sharp knife into 1/2-in. slices. Place cut side down on greased baking sheets. Bake for 7-9 minutes on each side or until lightly browned. Remove to wire racks to cool.

Dip biscotti halfway into melted butterscotch chips; shake off excess. Place on waxed paper until set. Dip butterscotch-coated ends partially into melted vanilla chips; shake off excess. Place on waxed paper until set. Store in an airtight container. **Yield:** 2-1/2 dozen.

Pumpkin Fudge

When you're tired of traditional chocolate fudge, whip up a batch of this seasonal alternative.
Every delicious piece captures the perfect balance of pumpkin and spice.
—*Marlene Fudge, Rushville, Indiana*

1 tablespoon plus 3/4 cup butter, *divided*
2 cups sugar
3/4 cup packed brown sugar
2/3 cup evaporated milk
1/2 cup canned pumpkin
1 teaspoon ground cinnamon
1/2 teaspoon pumpkin pie spice
1/4 teaspoon ground nutmeg
1 package (10 ounces) cinnamon baking chips
1 jar (7 ounces) marshmallow creme
1 cup chopped pecans
1 teaspoon vanilla extract

Line a 13-in. x 9-in. x 2-in. pan with foil and grease the foil with 1 tablespoon butter; set aside. Cube the remaining butter and place in a large saucepan; add the sugars, milk, pumpkin, cinnamon, pumpkin pie spice and nutmeg.

Bring to a boil over medium heat, stirring constantly. Reduce heat to low; cook and stir until a candy thermometer reads 238° (soft-ball stage).

Remove from the heat. Stir in cinnamon chips until melted. Stir in the marshmallow creme, pecans and vanilla. Transfer to prepared pan. Chill until firm.

Using foil, lift fudge out of pan. Discard the foil; cut fudge into 1-in. squares. Store in an airtight container in the refrigerator. **Yield:** 3 pounds.

Editor's Note: We recommend that you test your candy thermometer before each use by bringing water to a boil; the thermometer should read 212°. Adjust your recipe temperature up or down based on your test.

Frosted Chocolate Shortbread

These unique shortbread cookies have been a part of our family Christmas tradition for several years.
By changing the decorations or icing, you can enjoy the buttery morsels all year long.
—*Deb Nixon, Paris, Ontario*

1-3/4 cups butter, softened
1-1/2 cups confectioners' sugar
2-1/4 cups all-purpose flour
2/3 cup cornstarch
1/2 cup baking cocoa
Dash salt
FROSTING:
1-1/2 cups confectioners' sugar
2 tablespoons baking cocoa
2 tablespoons water
Colored sprinkles, optional

In a large bowl, cream butter and confectioners' sugar until light and fluffy. Combine the flour, cornstarch, cocoa and salt; gradually add to creamed mixture and mix well.

Press into an ungreased 9-in. square baking pan. Bake at 325° for 30-35 minutes or until center is set. Cool on a wire rack.

Cut into 1-1/2-in. x 1-in. squares. In a small bowl, whisk the confectioners' sugar, cocoa and water until smooth. Frost the cookies; decorate with the sprinkles if desired. **Yield:** 4-1/2 dozen.

Honey Almond Nougats

(Pictured at right and on page 51)

These festive nougats created by our Test Kitchen staff add a special touch to your offering of holiday treats. A blend of honey, cinnamon and almond flavors keep guests coming back for more.

1-1/2 teaspoons butter
  2/3 cup superfine sugar
    2 teaspoons cornstarch
  1/2 cup honey
    2 egg whites
    2 cups ground almonds
    1 teaspoon ground cinnamon
    1 cup finely chopped almonds

Grease a large bowl with the butter; set aside. In a large heavy saucepan over medium heat, combine the sugar, cornstarch and honey. Cook and stir until the sugar is dissolved and mixture comes to a boil. Cover mixture and boil for 1 minute. Uncover; cook, without stirring, until a candy thermometer reads 286° (soft-crack stage).

In a stand mixer, beat egg whites until stiff peaks form. With mixer running on high speed, carefully pour hot sugar mixture in a slow, steady stream into the mixing bowl. Beat on high for 10 minutes or until mixture holds its shape and is lukewarm, scraping sides of bowl occasionally.

Fold in almonds and cinnamon. Transfer to prepared bowl; cool to room temperature. Shape into 1-in. balls; roll balls in chopped almonds. Store in an airtight container. **Yield:** about 1 pound.

Editor's Note: We recommend that you test your candy thermometer before each use by bringing water to a boil; the thermometer should read 212°. Adjust your recipe temperature up or down based on your test.

Ginger-Cream Sandwich Cookies

It wouldn't be the holidays without a platter of these timeless favorites.
The sweet, creamy filling complements the tender ginger cookies wonderfully.
—*Donna Gonda, North Canton, Ohio*

1/2 cup butter, softened
3/4 cup sugar
2 eggs
2/3 cup molasses
1/2 cup milk
2-3/4 cups all-purpose flour
1-1/4 teaspoons ground cinnamon
1 teaspoon baking soda
1/2 teaspoon salt
1/2 teaspoon ground ginger
FILLING:
1/2 cup butter, softened
3 cups confectioners' sugar
1/4 cup molasses

1 tablespoon milk
1-1/4 teaspoons ground ginger

In a large bowl, cream butter and sugar until light and fluffy. Beat in the eggs, molasses and milk. Combine the flour, cinnamon, baking soda, salt and ginger; gradually add to creamed mixture and mix well (dough will be soft). Cover and refrigerate for at least 1 hour.

Drop by rounded tablespoonfuls 2 in. apart onto greased baking sheets. Bake at 375° for 8-10 minutes or until set. Remove to wire racks to cool.

In a small bowl, beat filling ingredients until smooth. Spread over bottoms of half of the cookies; top with remaining cookies. Store in the refrigerator. **Yield:** 2 dozen.

Iced Coconut-Orange Cookies

A favorite these iced cookies deliver the perfect amount of coconut and citrus flavors.
—*Jovina Cardellino, West Sunbury, Pennsylvania*

1/2 cup butter, softened
2/3 cup sugar
1 egg
3 tablespoons orange juice
1 tablespoon lemon juice
1 teaspoon grated orange peel
1/2 teaspoon grated lemon peel
1-3/4 cups all-purpose flour
1/4 teaspoon baking soda
1/4 teaspoon salt
1 cup flaked coconut

ICING:
1-1/3 cups confectioners' sugar
5 teaspoons orange juice
1 teaspoon lemon juice
1/2 teaspoon grated orange peel
1 drop yellow food coloring, optional

In a small bowl, cream butter and sugar until light and fluffy. Beat in egg. Beat in orange and lemon juices and peels. Combine the flour, baking soda and salt; gradually add to creamed mixture and mix well. Beat in coconut.

Drop by rounded teaspoonfuls 2 in. apart onto greased baking sheets. Bake at 350° for 10-12 minutes or until edges are lightly browned. Cool for 1 minute before removing to wire racks to cool completely. In a small bowl, beat the icing ingredients until smooth. Spread over cookies. Let stand until set. **Yield:** 3 dozen.

Chocolate-Coated Candy Canes

(Pictured at right and on page 51)

Shaped like candy canes, these sweet, cinnamon-flavored cookies are made extra-special when dipped in chocolate and decorated with sprinkles.
—*Edie DeSpain, Logan, Utah*

   1 cup butter, softened
3/4 cup sugar
1/4 cup confectioners' sugar
   2 egg yolks
   2 teaspoons vanilla extract
   2 cups all-purpose flour
   3 teaspoons ground cinnamon
   2 teaspoons baking powder
   2 teaspoons poppy seeds
1/4 teaspoon salt
  12 squares (1 ounce *each*)
     bittersweet chocolate, melted
**Red sprinkles, finely chopped
    pistachios *and/or* toasted flaked
    coconut, optional**

In a large bowl, cream butter and sugars until light and fluffy. Beat in egg yolks and vanilla. Combine the flour, cinnamon, baking powder, poppy seeds and salt; gradually add to creamed mixture and mix well.

Divide dough into 36 pieces; shape each into a 6-in. rope. Place 2 in. apart on greased baking sheets; curve the top of each cookie to form the handle of a candy cane.

Bake at 350° for 10-12 minutes or until edges are lightly browned. Cool for 2 minutes before removing to wire racks to cool completely.

Dip the handle of each cookie into melted chocolate; allow excess to drip off. Place on waxed paper; decorate with sprinkles, pistachios and/or toasted flaked coconut if desired. Let stand until set. Store in an airtight container. **Yield:** 3 dozen.

Cranberry Orange Pinwheels

The sweet-tart combination of orange and cranberries make these
Yuletide cookies a favorite. A batch of the colorful gems always goes over well with guests.
— Pat Habiger, Spearville, Kansas

  1 cup butter, softened
1-1/2 cups sugar
  2 eggs
  2 teaspoons grated orange peel
  3 cups all-purpose flour
1/2 teaspoon baking powder
1/2 teaspoon salt
  1 cup fresh *or* frozen
    cranberries, thawed
  1 cup chopped pecans
1/4 cup packed brown sugar

In a large bowl, cream butter and sugar until light and fluffy. Add eggs, one at a time, beating well after each addition. Beat in orange peel. Combine the flour, baking powder and salt; gradually add to creamed mixture and mix well.

Divide dough in half. Cover and refrigerate for 1 hour or until easy to handle. Meanwhile, in a food processor, combine the cranberries, pecans and brown sugar. Cover and process until finely chopped; set aside.

Roll out one portion of dough between two sheets of waxed paper to a 10-in. square. Remove top sheet; spread dough with half of the cranberry mixture to within 1/2 in. of edges. Roll up tightly jelly-roll style. Wrap in plastic wrap. Repeat with remaining dough and cranberry mixture. Refrigerate for 4 hours or overnight.

Unwrap rolls and cut into 1/4-in. slices. Place 2 in. apart on ungreased baking sheets. Bake at 375° for 8-10 minutes or until edges are lightly browned. Remove to wire racks. Store in an airtight container. **Yield:** 80 cookies.

Strawberry-Filled Cookies

A dab of strawberry jam in the center of these sweet bites makes them such a treat.
—Jennifer Eits, Omaha, Nebraska

2/3 cup butter, softened
  4 ounces cream cheese, softened
1-1/2 cups sugar
  1 egg
  1 teaspoon vanilla extract
  3 cups all-purpose flour
1-1/2 teaspoons baking powder
1/2 teaspoon salt
  6 tablespoons coarse sugar
  1 cup strawberry jam

In a large bowl, cream the butter, cream cheese and sugar until light and fluffy. Beat in egg and vanilla. Combine the flour, baking powder and salt; gradually add to creamed mixture and mix well. Cover and refrigerate for 1 hour or until easy to handle.

Place coarse sugar in a shallow bowl. Roll dough into 1-in. balls; roll in sugar. Place 2 in. apart on ungreased baking sheets. Using the end of a wooden spoon handle, make a 1/2-in. indentation in the center of each ball.

Bake at 375° for 9-11 minutes or until set. Press again into indentation with spoon handle. Remove to wire racks to cool. Spoon about 3/4 teaspoon strawberry jam into each cookie. **Yield:** about 5 dozen.

Coconut Graham Bars

(Pictured at right)

These rich, chocolaty bar cookies travel well and feed a lot of people so they're ideal for potlucks.
—Patty Van Zyl, Hospers, Iowa

2 cups graham cracker crumbs
1/2 cup sugar
1/2 cup butter, melted
2 cups flaked coconut
1 can (14 ounces) sweetened
   condensed milk
TOPPING:
1-1/2 cups packed brown sugar
6 tablespoons heavy whipping
   cream
1/4 cup butter, cubed
3/4 cup semisweet chocolate chips

In a small bowl, combine the graham cracker crumbs, sugar and butter. Press onto the bottom of a greased 13-in. x 9-in. x 2-in. baking pan. Bake at 350° for 8-10 minutes or until lightly browned.

Combine coconut and milk; spread over warm crust. Bake for 12-15 minutes or until edges are lightly browned. Cool on a wire rack.

In a large saucepan, combine the brown sugar, cream and butter. Bring to a boil over medium heat, stirring constantly. Boil for 1 minute. Remove from the heat; stir in chocolate chips until melted. Spread over coconut layer. Cool before cutting. **Yield:** 4-1/2 dozen.

Chocolate Peppermint Cookies

This recipe has been in our family at least 40 years.
Little ones like to help place the chocolate piece in the center of each cookie.
—Deborah Paugh, Fostoria, Ohio

3/4 cup butter, softened
1/2 cup sugar, *divided*
1 egg yolk
1 teaspoon vanilla extract
2 cups all-purpose flour
1/2 cup crushed peppermint
   candies
1/4 cup semisweet chocolate
   chunks

In a small bowl, cream butter and 1/4 cup sugar until light and fluffy. Beat in egg yolk and vanilla. Gradually add flour and mix well. Stir in crushed candies.

Roll dough into 1-in. balls; roll in remaining sugar. Place 2 in. apart on greased baking sheets. Lightly press a chocolate chunk into each ball.

Bake at 350° for 9-11 minutes or until edges are lightly browned. Remove to wire racks. **Yield:** about 2-1/2 dozen.

'TIS THE *Season*

Holiday Sweets From Around the World

THERE'S something about the holiday season that makes people nostalgic for the mouth-watering memories of days gone by.

At this time of year, cooks frequently reach for recipes that define their ancestry and that likely have been in their family for generations.

In this unique chapter, you can sample some traditional tastes of classic holiday desserts from around the world, such as Danish Christmas Cake (recipe shown at right).

Each impressive, great-tasting treat will surely become part of your own Christmas custom!

Dobostorte

(Pictured at right)

It takes some time to prepare a Hungarian seven-layer cake, but the effort is well worth it! Every forkful is moist and delicious.
—Susan Carn, Fremont, Ohio

6 eggs, *separated*
3/4 cup sugar
1 cup all-purpose flour
CHOCOLATE BUTTERCREAM:
1-3/4 cups semisweet chocolate chips
1/3 cup plus 2 tablespoons
    brewed coffee
1/3 cup plus 2 tablespoons sugar
7 egg yolks, beaten
1-1/4 teaspoons vanilla extract
1 cup butter, softened
CARAMEL TOPPING:
12 caramels
7 teaspoons evaporated milk

Place egg whites in a small mixing bowl; let stand at room temperature for 30 minutes. Meanwhile, using a pencil, draw an 8-in. circle on each of seven sheets of parchment paper. Place each sheet, pencil mark down, on a baking sheet; set aside.

In a large mixing bowl, beat egg yolks on high speed for 5 minutes or until thick and lemon-colored. Gradually beat in sugar. Sift flour twice; gradually add to yolk mixture and mix well (batter will be very thick).

With clean beaters, beat egg whites on medium until soft peaks form. Gradually fold into batter. Place 1/2 cup batter on one of the prepared baking sheets; using a small spatula, spread batter evenly into an 8-in. circle. Bake at 350° for 6-7 minutes or until cake

springs back when lightly touched (do not overbake).

Cool on a wire for 5 minutes; gently peel off parchment paper. Repeat with remaining batter and pans. When cool, stack cakes with waxed paper or paper towels in between. Gently smooth top and sides of stack. Refrigerate overnight if desired.

For buttercream, in a small saucepan, melt chips with coffee and sugar; stir until smooth. Remove from the heat. Add a small amount of mixture to egg yolks; return all to the pan, stirring constantly. Cook for 2 minutes or until mixture is thickened and reaches 160°, stirring constantly. Remove from the heat; stir in vanilla. Cool to room temperature.

In a large mixing bowl with a whisk attachment, beat butter until fluffy, about 5 minutes. Gradually beat in chocolate mixture. If necessary, refrigerate until frosting achieves spreading consistency.

Set aside one cake layer. Spread 1/4 cup frosting on each of the remaining cake layers; stack on a serving plate.

In a small saucepan, melt caramels with milk. Remove from the heat; pour evenly over reserved cake layer. Place on top of cake. Frost sides of cake and decorate the top with remaining frosting. **Yield:** 12 servings.

Zimtsterne

(Pictured at far right, top)

During December, homes and bakeries in Switzerland are filled with the aroma of classic cookies, such as these cinnamon stars. Our home economists share this version.

1 cup butter, softened
2 cups sugar
2 eggs
3 squares (1 ounce *each*) semisweet chocolate, melted and cooled
2-3/4 cups all-purpose flour
1/3 cup ground cinnamon

In a large mixing bowl, cream butter and sugar until light and fluffy. Beat in eggs and chocolate. Combine flour and cinnamon; gradually add to creamed mixture and mix well. Wrap dough in plastic wrap; refrigerate for 1 hour or until easy to handle.

On a lightly floured surface, roll out dough to 1/4-in. thickness. Cut with a floured 2-in. star-shaped cookie cutter. Place 1 in. apart on ungreased baking sheets. Chill and reroll scraps if desired.

Bake at 350° for 9-11 minutes or until edges are firm. Remove to wire racks. **Yield:** about 5 dozen.

Julgrot

This rice pudding is a traditional addition to our Scandinavian-style smorgasbord on Christmas Day. The recipe has been in the family for years.
—Linda Orvik, Fargo, North Dakota

2 cups water
1/2 cup uncooked long grain rice
1/2 teaspoon salt
2 cups milk
2 eggs
1/2 cup sugar
1/2 cup raisins
1/2 teaspoon vanilla extract
Dash ground nutmeg
1 blanched almond

In a heavy saucepan, combine the water, rice and salt. Bring to a boil. Reduce heat; cover and simmer for 10-13 minutes or until almost tender.

Add milk; return to a boil. In a large bowl, combine the eggs and sugar; gradually stir in 1 cup hot rice mixture. Return all to the pan, stirring constantly.

Remove from the heat; stir in the raisins, vanilla and nutmeg. Transfer to a greased shallow 1-1/2-qt. baking dish.

Bake, uncovered, at 350° for 30-35 minutes or until a knife inserted near the center comes out clean. Top with the almond. Serve warm. Refrigerate leftovers. **Yield:** 8 servings.

Family Traditions

BEFORE serving Scandinavian rice pudding, we place a whole almond on top. According to legend, whoever gets the almond in their bowl will be blessed with good fortune in the coming year.
—Linda Orvik, Fargo, North Dakota

Chocolate Lebkuchen

(Pictured at right, bottom)

Having lived in Germany, I try to keep my German cooking as authentic as possible. These lovely lebkuchen are a Christmas custom.
—Cathy Lemmon, Helena, Montana

1 cup plus 2 tablespoons
   all-purpose flour
1/4 cup sugar
Dash salt
1/3 cup cold butter
   3 tablespoons water
   1 teaspoon vanilla extract
TOPPING:
1/4 cup butter, softened
1/4 cup sugar
   1 egg
   1 tablespoon canola oil
2/3 cup quick-cooking oats
1/2 cup all-purpose flour
1/3 cup ground almonds
1/3 cup ground hazelnuts
1/4 cup baking cocoa
   1 teaspoon baking powder
1/2 teaspoon ground cinnamon
1/4 teaspoon *each* ground cloves,
   cardamom and allspice
1/4 cup finely chopped candied
   lemon peel
1/4 cup finely chopped candied
   orange peel
GLAZE:
   6 squares (1 ounce *each*)
   semisweet chocolate,
   chopped
   2 squares (1 ounce *each*)
   unsweetened chocolate,
   chopped
1/4 cup butter, cubed

In a small bowl, combine the flour, sugar and salt; cut in butter until mixture resembles coarse crumbs. Combine water and vanilla; gradually add to crumb mixture, tossing with a fork until dough forms a ball.

On a lightly floured surface, roll out dough to 1/16-in. thickness. Cut with a floured 2-1/2-in. round cookie cutter. Place on ungreased baking sheets. Bake at 325° for 8-10 minutes or until set. Remove from pans to wire racks to cool.

For topping, in a small mixing bowl, cream butter and sugar until light and fluffy. Beat in egg and oil. Combine the oats, flour, nuts, cocoa, baking powder and spices; gradually add to creamed mixture and mix well. Fold in candied peels.

Drop a rounded tablespoonful of topping on each cookie; gently press down. Place 2 in. apart on ungreased baking sheets. Bake at 325° for 13-16 minutes or until set. Remove from pans to wire racks to cool.

In a microwave-safe bowl, melt chocolate and butter; stir until smooth. Dip each cookie halfway in chocolate; allow excess to drip off. Place on waxed paper; let stand until set. Store in airtight containers. **Yield:** about 1-1/2 dozen.

Makowiec

During the holidays, poppy seed swirl loaves make an appearance in many Polish homes. This recipe comes from our Test Kitchen.

1 pound poppy seeds (about 2-1/2 cups)
1/2 cup chopped almonds
2 tablespoons butter
3/4 cup sugar
1/2 cup chopped candied citron
1 egg
1/4 cup chopped candied orange peel
1/4 cup honey
1 teaspoon grated lemon peel
1 teaspoon vanilla extract
2 egg whites

DOUGH:
2 packages (1/4 ounce *each*) active dry yeast
1/4 cup warm water (110° to 115°)
4 to 4-1/2 cups all-purpose flour
1 cup confectioners' sugar
1/2 teaspoon salt
3/4 cup cold butter
1/2 cup sour cream
2 eggs
2 egg yolks
2 teaspoons grated lemon peel
1 teaspoon vanilla extract

GLAZE:
1 cup confectioners' sugar
1 tablespoon lemon juice

Place poppy seeds in a small saucepan and cover with water. Bring to a boil. Remove from the heat; let stand until cool. Strain through a fine mesh strainer.

Place poppy seeds and almonds in a food processor; cover and process until blended. In a large skillet, melt butter. Add sugar and poppy seed mixture; cook and stir over low heat for 10 minutes. Remove from the heat. Transfer to a large bowl; cool to room temperature.

Stir in the citron, egg, orange peel, honey, lemon peel and vanilla. In a small mixing bowl, beat egg whites on high speed until stiff peaks form. Gradually fold into poppy seed mixture; set aside.

In a small bowl, dissolve yeast in warm water; let stand for 5 minutes. In a large bowl, combine 3 cups flour, confectioners' sugar and salt; cut in butter until crumbly. Add the sour cream, eggs, egg yolks, lemon peel, vanilla and yeast mixture; mix well. Stir in enough remaining flour to form a soft dough.

Turn onto a floured surface; knead until smooth and elastic, about 6-8 minutes. Divide dough in half. Roll each portion into a 14-in. x 12-in. rectangle. Spread poppy seed filling over each rectangle to within 1/2 in. of edges. Roll up jelly-roll style, starting with a long side; pinch seams to seal and tuck ends under.

Place loaves seam side down on greased baking sheets. Cover and let rise until doubled, about 45 minutes.

Bake at 350° for 30-35 minutes or until golden brown. Remove from pans to wire racks. Cool for 15 minutes. Combine glaze ingredients; drizzle over loaves. **Yield:** 2 loaves (14 slices each).

CANDIED CITRON CLUES

CITRON is a shrub native to India that yields a citrus-like fruit. Its thick peel is often candied and used in baked goods, such as fruitcake. During the holiday season, look for it in your grocery store near other candied fruits.

Cannoli Cheesecake

(Pictured at right)

Combining two of our favorite desserts, this is a traditional holiday treat in my Italian family. We're always certain to pass down the recipe to the next generation.
— *Marie McConnell*
Las Cruces, New Mexico

3 cartons (15 ounces *each*) ricotta cheese
1-1/2 cups sugar
1/2 cup all-purpose flour
3 teaspoons vanilla extract
2 teaspoons grated orange peel
7 eggs, lightly beaten
1/3 cup miniature semisweet chocolate chips
1/4 cup chopped pistachios

Place a greased 9-in. springform pan on a double thickness of heavy-duty foil (about 18 in. square). Securely wrap foil around pan; set aside.

In a large mixing bowl, beat ricotta cheese and sugar until blended. Beat in the flour, vanilla and orange peel. Add eggs; beat on low speed just until combined. Pour into prepared pan; sprinkle with chocolate chips. Place in a large baking pan; add 1 in. of hot water to larger pan.

Bake at 350° for 65-75 minutes or until center is almost set. Remove pan from water bath. Cool on a wire rack for 10 minutes. Carefully run a knife around edge of pan to loosen; cool 1 hour longer.

Refrigerate overnight. Sprinkle with pistachios. Remove sides of pan before slicing. **Yield:** 12 servings.

'TIS THE *Season*

Quick & Easy Yuletide Desserts

ONE OF the great joys of Christmas is making tempting treats for family and friends. But with the hustle and bustle of the season, finding time to create those delicious goodies seems almost impossible.

Thankfully, this assortment of no-fuss desserts can put some time back into your holiday schedule. From sweet finales that require only a touch of "dressing up" to time-saving desserts with make-ahead convenience, you'll delight in this chapter's showstopping selections that only look like you spent hours in the kitchen.

Adorned with elegant store-bought truffles and wrapped in a ribbon of chopped hazelnuts, surprisingly easy Truffle-Topped Cake will make jaws drop. (Recipe shown at right.)

ELEGANT & EASY
(Pictured above)

Truffle-Topped Cake (p. 76)

Truffle-Topped Cake

(Pictured on page 75)

This eye-catching dessert created by the Taste of Home Test Kitchen staff will be the talk of the party—especially if guests find out how easy it is to make. Store-bought truffles and chopped hazelnuts add holiday pizzazz to an ordinary boxed cake mix.

1 package (18-1/4 ounces)
    yellow cake mix
1 cup butter, softened
1 jar (12-1/4 ounces) caramel
    ice cream topping
3 tablespoons milk
1-1/2 teaspoons vanilla extract
6 cups confectioners' sugar
3/4 cup chopped hazelnuts
Assorted truffles

Prepare and bake cake according to package directions, using two greased 9-in. square baking pans. Cool cakes for 10 minutes before removing them from pans to wire racks to cool completely.

For frosting, in a large bowl, beat the butter until light and fluffy. Beat in the caramel topping, milk and vanilla until smooth. Gradually add the confectioners' sugar; beat until smooth.

Place one cake layer on a serving plate; spread with 1 cup frosting. Top with remaining cake layer. Frost top and sides of cake with remaining frosting. Press hazelnuts into sides of cake. Top cake with truffles. **Yield:** 12 servings.

Editor's Note: This recipe was tested with Ferrero Rocher truffles.

Pecan-Peach Ice Cream Cake

Everyone will be pleasantly surprised by the taste of peaches in this pretty winter dessert. It's a nice change of pace from the usual chocolate treats.
— Teri Rasey-Bolf, Cadillac, Michigan

2-1/4 cups crushed pecan
    shortbread cookies, *divided*
1 cup chopped pecans, toasted,
    divided
1/4 cup butter, melted
1 loaf (10-3/4 ounces) frozen
    pound cake, thawed and cubed
1 carton (1-3/4 quarts) peach *or*
    vanilla ice cream, softened
1 cup peach preserves

In a small bowl, combine 2 cups cookie crumbs, 1/2 cup pecans and butter. Press onto the bottom of a greased 9-in. springform pan.

Top with half of the cake cubes, ice cream and preserves. Repeat layers. Sprinkle with remaining cookie crumbs and pecans. Cover and freeze for several hours or overnight. Let stand at room temperature for 10 minutes before cutting. **Yield:** 12 servings.

Coconut Chiffon Pie

(Pictured at right)

I like to garnish slices of this smooth, silky pie with coconut shavings.
—Kristine Fry, Fennimore, Wisconsin

1 unbaked pastry shell
  (9 inches)
1 envelope unflavored gelatin
1/4 cup cold water
1/2 cup sugar
1/4 cup all-purpose flour
1/2 teaspoon salt
1-1/2 cups milk
3/4 teaspoon vanilla extract
1/4 teaspoon almond extract
1 cup heavy whipping cream,
  whipped
1 cup flaked coconut

Line unpricked pastry shell with a double thickness of heavy-duty foil. Bake at 450° for 8 minutes. Remove foil; bake 5 minutes longer. Cool on a wire rack.

Sprinkle gelatin over cold water; let stand for 1 minute. In a small saucepan, combine the sugar, flour and salt. Gradually stir in milk until smooth. Cook and stir over medium-low heat until mixture comes to a boil; cook and stir 1 minute longer or until thickened.

Remove from the heat. Whisk in gelatin mixture until dissolved. Transfer to a mixing bowl. Refrigerate until slightly thickened, about 30 minutes. Add extracts; beat on medium speed for 1 minute. Fold in whipped cream and coconut. Spread into pie crust. Refrigerate for at least 3 hours before serving. Garnish as desired. **Yield:** 6-8 servings.

FRESH COCONUT CURLS

ADD extra holiday dazzle to Coconut Chiffon Pie by decorating the top with wide strips of fresh coconut. Coconut curls are wider than store-bought flaked coconut and lend a more elegant appearance to desserts. Creating the attractive garnish yourself is easier than you might think.

- Start with a split coconut. To loosen the coconut meat, place the broken coconut shells on a baking sheet. Bake for about 10 minutes at 350°. Remove them from the oven and let cool.
- Pry the coconut meat from the shell with a sturdy paring knife. Using a vegetable peeler, peel off long strips of coconut from the meat.
- If you prefer to toast the shavings before using as a garnish, place on a baking sheet and bake at 350° until lightly toasted. Let cool before using.

Eggnog Cheese Pie

Crunched for time? Then this make-ahead dessert from our Test Kitchen is for you!
Eggnog lends the creamy cheesecake filling delicious holiday flair. Plus,
because the pie chills overnight, you have time to wrap a few presents or send out those last few cards.

1-1/4 cups crushed chocolate
    wafers (about 30 wafers)
   3 tablespoons butter, melted
FILLING:
   1 package (8 ounces) cream
    cheese, softened
 1/2 cup sugar
   2 tablespoons all-purpose flour
   2 eggs
   1 cup eggnog
 1/4 teaspoon rum extract
TOPPING:
   1 cup heavy whipping cream
   2 tablespoons eggnog
   1 tablespoon confectioners'
    sugar
 1/4 teaspoon rum extract

In a small bowl, combine wafer crumbs and butter. Press onto the bottom and up the sides of a greased 9-in. pie plate. Bake at 350° for 8 minutes. Cool on a wire rack.

In a small bowl, beat the cream cheese, sugar and flour until smooth. Add eggs; beat on low speed until combined. Beat in eggnog and extract. Pour into crust.

Bake at 325° for 45-55 minutes or until center is almost set. Cool on a wire rack. Refrigerate overnight.

In a small bowl, beat cream until soft peaks form. Add the eggnog, confectioners' sugar and extract; beat until stiff peaks form. Cut pie into slices; dollop with topping. **Yield:** 6-8 servings.

Editor's Note: This recipe was tested with commercially prepared eggnog.

Peppermint Brownie Sandwich

This is a really fun dessert to serve at holiday parties.
I love that this rich, decadent treat calls for only three ingredients!
—Lisa Varner, Greenville, South Carolina

   1 package fudge brownie mix
    (8-inch square pan size)
   2 pints peppermint ice cream,
    softened
Whipped cream and peppermint
  candies, optional

Line two 9-in. cake pans with parchment paper; coat with cooking spray and set aside. Prepare brownie batter according to package directions. Pour into prepared pans.

Bake at 350° for 20-25 minutes or until a toothpick inserted near the center comes out clean. Cool for 10 minutes before removing from pans to wire racks to cool completely.

Remove parchment paper. Place one brownie layer in an ungreased 9-in. springform pan. Spread with ice cream. Place remaining brownie layer, crumb side down, over ice cream. Cover and freeze for 4 hours or until firm.

Remove from the freezer 15 minutes before serving. Remove sides of pan. Garnish with whipped cream and peppermint candies if desired. **Yield:** 12 servings.

Raspberry-Fudge Frozen Dessert

(Pictured at right)

This frozen specialty always receives a big "thumbs up" from all that taste it. Everyone compliments the combination of vanilla, raspberry and chocolate fudge flavors.
—Sue Kroening, Mattoon, Illinois

2 cups vanilla ice cream, slightly softened
1/2 cup chopped pecans, toasted
2 cups raspberry sherbet *or* sorbet, slightly softened
2 cups chocolate fudge ice cream, slightly softened
1 package (10 ounces) frozen sweetened raspberries, thawed
2 cups (12 ounces) semisweet chocolate chips
1/4 cup butter, cubed
1/2 cup light corn syrup
1/2 cup water
Fresh raspberries, optional

Line the bottom and sides of a 9-in. x 5-in. x 3-in. loaf pan with plastic wrap. Combine vanilla ice cream and pecans; spread into prepared pan. Freeze for 30 minutes.

Spread raspberry sherbet over vanilla ice cream. Freeze for 30 minutes. Spread chocolate ice cream over the top. Cover and freeze for 8 hours or until firm.

Mash and strain raspberries, reserving 1/4 cup juice (discard seeds and save remaining raspberry juice for another use). In a microwave-safe bowl, melt chocolate chips and butter; stir until smooth. Whisk in the corn syrup, water and reserved raspberry juice; cool.

Remove dessert from the freezer 10 minutes before serving. Using plastic wrap, remove loaf from pan; discard plastic wrap. Using a serrated knife, cut ice cream into 12 slices. Spoon chocolate sauce onto dessert plates; top with a slice of the dessert. Garnish with fresh raspberries if desired. **Yield:** 12 servings.

Almond Bars

(Pictured at far right)

These cake-like snacks look adorable on a tray of assorted desserts.
The melt-in-your-mouth flavor means they are usually the first to disappear.
—Cheryl Newendorp, Pella, Iowa

1 cup butter, softened
1 cup almond paste
2-1/4 cups sugar, *divided*
2 eggs
1 teaspoon almond extract
2 cups all-purpose flour
1/2 cup slivered almonds

In a large bowl, cream the butter, almond paste and 2 cups sugar. Add eggs and extract; beat well. Add flour; beat just until moistened.

Spread into a greased 13-in. x 9-in. x 2-in. baking dish. Sprinkle with remaining sugar; top with almonds.

Bake at 350° for 30-35 minutes or until a toothpick inserted near the center comes out clean. Cool on a wire rack. Cut into squares. Store bars in the refrigerator. **Yield:** 4-1/2 dozen.

Candy Bar Brownie Trifle

Even something as simple as a trifle can make an extraordinary ending to a holiday meal.
It comes together quickly—and disappears even faster. You and your guests will love digging into
layers of brownie, chocolate pudding, whipped topping, Snickers candy bars and caramel.
—Adriane Louie, Jackson, Mississippi

1 package fudge brownie mix
 (13-inch x 9-inch pan size)
1 package (3.9 ounces) instant
 chocolate pudding mix
1 package (11-1/2 ounces)
 miniature Snickers candy
 bars, refrigerated
1 carton (8 ounces) frozen
 whipped topping, thawed
1 jar (12 ounces) caramel ice
 cream topping

Prepare and bake brownies according to package directions. Cool on a wire rack. Prepare pudding according to package directions. Crush candy bars; set aside.

Cut brownies into 1-in. cubes; place half of the cubes in a 3-qt. trifle bowl or large glass serving bowl; press down lightly. Top with half of the whipped topping, pudding, caramel topping and crushed candy bars; repeat layers. Cover and refrigerate until serving. **Yield:** 16 servings.

Nutty Chocolate Cake

(Pictured at right)

*The creamy, almond-flavored filling
tucked between layers of rich,
chocolate cake makes this impressive
indulgence a family favorite.
It's a relatively simple way
to "wow" your guests.*
—Linda DuVal
Colorado Springs, Colorado

1 package (18-1/4 ounces)
    chocolate cake mix
1 can (8 ounces) almond paste
1/2 cup butter, softened
1/2 cup heavy whipping cream
2 cups (12 ounces) semisweet
    chocolate chips
1 cup (8 ounces) sour cream
Dash salt
1/2 cup sliced almonds, toasted

Prepare and bake cakes according to
package directions, using two greased
9-in. round baking pans. Cool for 10
minutes before removing from pans to
wire racks to cool completely.

For filling, in a small bowl, beat almond paste and butter until smooth.
Gradually beat in cream until fluffy.

Cut each cake horizontally in half; spread filling over bottom layers. Replace top layers.

In a large microwave-safe bowl, melt chocolate chips; stir
until smooth. Stir in sour cream and salt. Spread over the
top of each cake. Sprinkle with almonds. Refrigerate leftovers. **Yield:** 2 cakes (8 servings each).

EASY, ELEGANT CAKES

NEED an outstanding cake for the holidays but don't have a lot of time? Try one of these tricks for dressing up a plain cake:

- For Black Forest Torte, prepare a chocolate cake mix according to the package directions, using a 13-in. x 9-in. x 2-in. baking pan; cool. Spoon a 21-ounce can of cherry pie filling over the top of the cake. Spread 4 cups of thawed whipping topping over the pie filling. Refrigerate at least 2 hours.
- For Angel Food Ice Cream Cake, slice a prepared angel food cake into thirds horizontally. Place the bottom layer on a serving plate. Spread 1/2 quart softened ice cream (in the flavor of your choice) over cake; top with middle cake layer. Spread with the remaining 1/2 quart ice cream; add top cake layer. Freeze for 2 to 3 hours before serving. Serve with sweetened whipped cream, sliced fresh fruit or any flavor ice cream topping.
- Make your favorite cake mix in a fluted tube pan; cool. Just before serving, set on a serving platter and fill the center with assorted sliced fresh fruit.

Dark Chocolate Fondue

*With just a hint of cinnamon and almond flavor, this smooth chocolate sauce is ideal
for dipping sliced fruit, cake pieces and marshmallows.
If you happen to have any leftover—which is rare—it's delicious served over vanilla ice cream.
—Shannon Abdollmohammadi, Woodinville, Washington*

2 cups (12 ounces) semisweet chocolate chips
1/2 cup heavy whipping cream
2 tablespoons sugar
2 tablespoons sweetened condensed milk
2 teaspoons ground cinnamon
1/4 teaspoon almond extract
Assorted fresh fruit and pound cake cubes

In a small saucepan, melt the chocolate chips with the cream, sugar, milk and cinnamon. Remove from the heat; stir in extract.

Transfer to a small fondue pot and keep warm. Serve with fruit and cake cubes. **Yield:** 1-1/2 cups.

White Chocolate Dream Torte

(Pictured at right)

*For a sensational alternative
to dark chocolate desserts,
turn to this luscious torte. A white
chocolate, cheesecake-like filling is
surrounded by tender ladyfingers. With
very little effort, you can create a
stunning ending to your holiday dinner.*
— Bethany Irwin
Traverse City, Michigan

1 package (8 ounces) cream
  cheese, softened
1/3 cup sugar
4 squares (1 ounce *each*) white
  baking chocolate, melted and
  cooled
1-1/2 teaspoons vanilla extract,
  divided
1 carton (16 ounces) frozen
  whipped topping, thawed,
  divided
2 packages (3 ounces *each*)
  ladyfingers, split
3/4 cup vanilla *or* white chips

In a large bowl, beat cream cheese and sugar until smooth. Beat in white chocolate and 1 teaspoon vanilla. Fold in half of the whipped topping.

Arrange ladyfingers on the bottom and around the edge of an ungreased 9-in. springform pan. Spread half of the cream cheese mixture evenly over ladyfingers on bottom of pan. Arrange the remaining ladyfingers over the cream cheese mixture to resemble the spokes of a wheel. Sprinkle with vanilla chips.

Spread with remaining cream cheese mixture. Combine remaining whipped topping and vanilla; spread over the top. Cover and refrigerate for at least 2 hours. Remove sides of pan before slicing. **Yield:** 12 servings.

'Tis the Season

Gifts from the Kitchen

THERE'S no better way to express your sentiment to someone special at Christmas than by giving that person a gift made with your own hands.

Yuletide treats are always well received…even by those hard-to-shop-for folks!

Tired taste buds will rise and shine when waffles, muffins or bagels are topped with creamy Cinnamon Espresso Butter.

White Chocolate Peppermint Crunch is better than any store-bought variety. So why not make your own? It's quick and delicious!

For something more savory, Herbed Vinegar, Tortellini Bean Soup Mix and Herb Mix for Dipping Oil are sure to satisfy. (All recipes are shown at right.)

HOMEMADE FROM THE HEART
(Clockwise from top left)

Herbed Vinegar (p. 90)

Tortellini Bean Soup Mix (p. 86)

Herb Mix for Dipping Oil (p. 91)

Cinnamon Espresso Butter (p. 87)

White Chocolate Peppermint Crunch (p. 88)

Tortellini Bean Soup Mix

(Pictured on page 85)

I like to give mixes for Christmas gifts. One year, I gave this soup mix in a jar
and included a kettle, a mug and a pint of my home-canned tomatoes.
— Doris Simmons, Browning, Illinois

1 cup dried great northern beans
1/4 cup dried lentils
1/4 cup dried green split peas
3/4 cup uncooked dried tricolor
    tortellini
1 tablespoon dried parsley flakes
1 tablespoon chicken bouillon
    granules
2 teaspoons dried minced garlic
1 teaspoon dried thyme
1/2 teaspoon salt
ADDITIONAL INGREDIENTS:
8 cups water
1 can (49-1/2 ounces) chicken
    broth
1 can (14-1/2 ounces) diced
    tomatoes, drained
2 medium carrots, chopped

2 celery ribs, chopped
Grated Parmesan cheese, optional

In a 3-cup jar or container with a tight-fitting lid, layer the beans, lentils and peas. In a small resealable plastic bag, combine the tortellini, parsley, bouillon, garlic, thyme and salt. Place bag in jar. Replace lid and store in a cool dry place. **Yield:** 1 batch (about 2-1/4 cups).

   To prepare soup: Remove the bag of tortellini and seasonings; set aside. Rinse the beans, lentils and peas; drain. Place in a Dutch oven. Add 8 cups of water. Bring to a boil. Reduce heat; cover and simmer for 45-60 minutes or until the beans are tender.

   Stir in the tortellini and seasonings, broth, tomatoes, carrots and celery. Bring to a boil. Reduce heat; simmer, uncovered, for 8-10 minutes or until pasta and vegetables are tender. Serve with Parmesan cheese if desired. **Yield:** 15 servings (3-3/4 quarts).

A GUIDE FOR GIVING GIFTS FROM THE KITCHEN

AFTER taking the time to make a homemade gift, think about packaging it in a pretty way. Here are some ideas:

- Include a copy of the recipe, especially for mixes that require additional ingredients. Be sure to indicate storage requirements for perishable items.
- Be on the lookout at rummage sales, flea markets and discount stores for jars and bottles in various shapes and sizes. They work well for dried mixes as well as for prepared foods, such as jams, jellies and flavored vinegars. You may even want to consider tying a festive spreader or serving spoon on top.
- Attractive metal tins work well for packaging snack mixes and cookies.
- Inexpensive glass pie plates, dinner plates and serving platters are perfect for pies, cakes and cookies.
- A loaf of bread tied to a cutting board with a kitchen towel is always appreciated.
- Use coffee mugs or teapots to present coffee and tea blends.
- If gifting cutout cookies with an unusual shape, attach a clean cutter as well.

Buffalo-Style Snack Mix

(Pictured at right)

*Corn chips and peanuts are a
fun way to dress up ordinary popcorn.
The hot sauce adds a bit of kick
that no one can resist.*
— Deirdre Dee Zosha
Milwaukee, Wisconsin

2-1/2 quarts popped popcorn,
    divided
  2 cups corn chips
  1 cup dry roasted peanuts
1/4 cup butter, cubed
  2 tablespoons Louisiana-style
    hot sauce
  1 teaspoon celery seed

In a large bowl, combine 2 cups popcorn, corn chips and peanuts. In a small saucepan, melt butter; add hot sauce and celery seed. Remove from the heat. Pour over popcorn mixture and toss to coat.

Transfer to a greased 15-in. x 10-in. x 1-in. baking pan. Bake at 350° for 10-15 minutes or until crisp. Place in a large bowl; add remaining popcorn and toss to coat. Store in an airtight container. **Yield:** 2-1/2 quarts.

Cinnamon Espresso Butter

(Pictured on page 85)

*I've used this tasty butter on everything from bagels to biscotti!
I like to use a teaspoon of espresso powder for the instant coffee granules.*
— Diane Hixon, Niceville, Florida

  2 teaspoons instant coffee
    granules
  2 teaspoons water
1/2 teaspoon vanilla extract
1/2 cup butter, softened
  1 tablespoon confectioners' sugar
  1 teaspoon ground cinnamon

In a small bowl, combine the coffee granules, water and vanilla. In another small bowl, cream the butter, confectioners' sugar and cinnamon until light and fluffy. Add coffee mixture; beat until smooth. Store in the refrigerator for up to 1 month. **Yield:** 1/2 cup.

White Chocolate Peppermint Crunch

(Pictured on page 84)

This is my favorite confection to make at Christmas. Not only is it easy, it's delicious as well.
I often fill small bags with the crunchy candy to place in gift baskets.
—Nancy Shelton, Boaz, Kentucky

2 tablespoons butter, *divided*
1 pound white candy coating
1 tablespoon canola oil
1 cup crushed peppermint
   candies *or* candy canes

Line a baking sheet with foil and grease the foil with 1 tablespoon butter; set aside. In a microwave-safe bowl or heavy saucepan, melt the candy coating. Stir in oil and remaining butter until smooth. Stir in peppermint candies.

Pour onto the prepared baking sheet, spreading to desired thickness. Refrigerate for 30 minutes or until firm. Break into pieces. Store in an airtight container in the refrigerator. **Yield:** about 1-1/2 pounds.

Flavorful Pizza Sauce

I could never find the right pizza sauce recipe to please me.
So I experimented with my own version until I got it just right. I think you'll enjoy it!
—Cheryl Williams, Evington, Virginia

2 cans (8 ounces *each*) tomato
   sauce
1 can (12 ounces) tomato paste
4 teaspoons Worcestershire
   sauce
1 tablespoon dried parsley flakes
1 tablespoon Italian seasoning
1-1/2 teaspoons garlic powder
1 teaspoon sugar
1 teaspoon dried basil
1 teaspoon dried oregano
3/4 teaspoon salt
1/4 teaspoon pepper

In a large bowl, combine all of the ingredients. Transfer to a storage container. Cover and refrigerate for up to 1 week. **Yield:** about 2-1/2 cups.

Banana-Walnut Mini Loaves

(Pictured at right)

We have many walnut trees in Pennsylvania. You have to collect and crack a lot of nuts for a pound of meat. Oh, how great the baked goods taste!
—Lee Sauers, Mifflinburg, Pennsylvania

1/2 cup butter, softened
  1 cup sugar
  2 eggs
1-1/3 cups mashed ripe bananas
       (2 to 3 medium)
1-3/4 cups all-purpose flour
  2 teaspoons ground cardamom
  1 teaspoon baking soda
1/2 teaspoon ground cinnamon
1/2 teaspoon ground nutmeg
1/2 cup chopped black walnuts
CINNAMON SPREAD:
  1 package (8 ounces) cream
     cheese, softened
  3 tablespoons confectioners'
     sugar
1/2 teaspoon ground cinnamon

In a large bowl, cream butter and sugar. Add eggs, one at a time, beating well after each addition. Beat in bananas. Combine the flour, cardamom, baking soda, cinnamon and nutmeg; gradually add to banana mixture. Fold in walnuts.

Pour batter into six greased 4-1/2-in. x 2-1/2-in. x 1-1/2-in. loaf pans. Bake at 350° for 22-26 minutes or until a toothpick inserted near the center comes out clean. Cool for 10 minutes before removing from pans to wire racks to cool completely.

In a small bowl, combine the spread ingredients. Serve with bread. Refrigerate leftovers. **Yield:** 6 loaves (4 slices each) and 1 cup spread.

Herbed Vinegar

(Pictured on page 84)

This herb vinegar from our Test Kitchen would be a great addition to your favorite salad dressing or could be used in place of vinegar in any recipe. The terrific flavors of tarragon and basil really shine through.

1/2 cup minced fresh basil
1/4 cup minced fresh tarragon
2 cups white wine vinegar
**Fresh basil *and/or* tarragon sprigs,
    optional**

Place basil and tarragon in a small glass bowl. In a small saucepan, heat vinegar just until simmering; pour over herbs. Cool to room temperature. Cover and let stand in a cool dark place for 5 days.

Strain and discard herbs. Pour vinegar into a sterilized jar or decorative bottle. Add basil and/or tarragon sprigs if desired. Store in a cool dark place for up to 6 months. **Yield:** 2 cups.

Chocolate Quick Bread

*My husband and I both enjoy cooking, but the baking is left to me.
Our sons loved this chocolaty quick bread when they were little...and still do as grownups!*
—Melissa Mitchell-Wilson, Wichita, Kansas

1-3/4 cups all-purpose flour
1/2 cup baking cocoa
1/2 teaspoon baking powder
1/2 teaspoon baking soda
1/2 teaspoon salt
1/2 cup butter, softened
1 cup sugar
2 eggs
1 cup buttermilk
**1/2 cup miniature semisweet
    chocolate chips**
1/3 cup chopped pecans

In a large bowl, combine the flour, cocoa, baking powder, baking soda and salt. In a large mixing bowl, cream butter and sugar until light and fluffy. Add eggs, one at a time, beating well after each addition. Add buttermilk; mix well. Stir into dry ingredients just until moistened. Fold in chocolate chips and pecans.

Pour into a greased 9-in. x 5-in. x 3-in. loaf pan. Bake at 350° for 55-60 minutes or until a toothpick inserted near the center comes out clean. Cool for 10 minutes before removing from pan to a wire rack to cool completely. **Yield:** 1 loaf (16 slices).

Herb Mix for Dipping Oil

(Pictured at right and on page 85)

Our home economists combine a blend of herbs to create this mouthwatering mix. Plumping the herbs in water before stirring them into olive oil enhances the flavor.

1 tablespoon dried minced garlic
1 tablespoon dried rosemary, crushed
1 tablespoon dried oregano
2 teaspoons dried basil
1 teaspoon crushed red pepper flakes
1/2 teaspoon salt
1/2 teaspoon coarsely ground pepper
ADDITIONAL INGREDIENTS (for each batch):
1 tablespoon water
1/2 cup olive oil
1 French bread baguette (10-1/2 ounces)

In a small bowl, combine the first seven ingredients. Store in an airtight container in a cool dry place for up to 6 months. **Yield:** 3 batches (1/4 cup total).

To prepare dipping oil: In a small microwave-safe bowl, combine 4 teaspoons herb mix with water. Microwave, uncovered, on high for 10-15 seconds. Drain excess water. Transfer to a shallow serving plate; add oil and stir. Serve with bread. **Yield:** 1/2 cup per batch.

DIPPING OIL GIFT IDEA

WHEN giving Herb Mix for Dipping Oil as a gift, supply the recipient with all of the fixings (as shown on page 85).

Place one batch of the Herb Mix into a small mesh bag; close bag. Use a new, clean kitchen towel to tie a loaf of bread onto a bottle of olive oil. Drape the mesh bag over the top of the bottle. Make a copy of the recipe so they know how to prepare the dipping oil.

Grandma's Stollen

When I was a child, my grandmother always prepared stollen at Christmas and Easter.
This recipe makes four loaves, which are great to share with family and friends.
—Kathy Green, Layton, New Jersey

1-1/2 cups chopped almonds
1-1/2 cups chopped candied citron
1-1/2 cups red candied cherries
   3/4 cup chopped candied pineapple
   3/4 cup golden raisins
   3/4 cup brandy
    7 to 8 cups all-purpose flour
   1/2 cup sugar
    2 packages (1/4 ounce *each*)
      active dry yeast
    2 teaspoons salt
1-1/2 cups milk
1-1/2 cups butter, cubed
    3 eggs
   1/4 cup confectioners' sugar

In a large bowl, combine the almonds, citron, cherries, pineapple and raisins. Stir in brandy. Cover and let the mixture stand for several hours or overnight, stirring occasionally.

In another large bowl, combine 4 cups flour, sugar, yeast and salt. In a small saucepan, heat milk and butter to 120°-130°. Add to dry ingredients; beat just until moistened. Add eggs; beat until smooth. Stir in enough of the remaining flour to form a soft dough.

Turn onto a floured surface; knead until smooth and elastic, about 6-8 minutes. Place in a very large greased bowl, turning once to grease top. Cover and let rise in a warm place until doubled, about 1 hour.

Punch dough down; turn onto a floured surface. Knead fruit mixture into dough (knead in more flour if necessary). Divide into fourths. Roll each portion into a 10-in. x 8-in. oval. Fold a long side over to within 1 in. of opposite side; press edges lightly to seal. Place on greased baking sheets. Cover and let rise until doubled, about 30 minutes.

Bake at 350° for 35-40 minutes or until golden brown. Remove to wire racks to cool. Sprinkle with confectioners' sugar. **Yield:** 4 loaves (12 slices each).

STORING SWEET YEAST BREADS

DO YOU THINK you don't have time to give oven-fresh yeast breads to friends and neighbors? Yeast breads actually keep very well at room temperature or in the refrigerator or freezer. So you can make them when time allows and then distribute them as gifts when appropriate.

Place completely cooled sweet yeast breads in airtight containers or resealable plastic bags; keep at room temperature for 2 to 3 days. Breads containing perishable items should be refrigerated.

For longer storage, unfrosted breads can be frozen for up to 3 months. Thaw at room temperature. When completely defrosted, frost, glaze or dust with confectioners' sugar as desired.

Raspberry Truffle Pie

(Pictured at right)

*A special dessert like this creamy pie
is perfect for the holidays.
The raspberry sauce pairs well
with the chocolate filling.*
—*Suzy Moore, Milwaukie, Oregon*

1-1/4 cups graham cracker crumbs
1/4 cup sugar
1 tablespoon baking cocoa
1/4 cup butter, melted

FILLING:
4 squares (1 ounce *each*)
semisweet chocolate
2 tablespoons milk
1 package (8 ounces) cream
cheese, softened
3 tablespoons sugar
1/3 cup raspberry liqueur
1-3/4 cups heavy whipping cream

RASPBERRY SAUCE:
2 cups fresh raspberries
1/2 cup sugar
1/4 cup raspberry liqueur

In a bowl, combine the graham cracker crumbs, sugar, cocoa and butter; press onto the bottom and up the sides of a greased 9-in. pie plate. Bake at 375° for 8-10 minutes or until lightly browned. Cool on a wire rack.

For filling, in a small saucepan, melt chocolate with milk; stir until smooth. Remove from the heat; set aside to cool.

In a large bowl, beat the cream cheese and sugar until smooth. Gradually beat in the liqueur and cooled chocolate mixture just until combined. In a small bowl, beat cream until stiff peaks form; fold into the chocolate mixture. Pour into crust. Cover and refrigerate for at least 4 hours.

For sauce, place raspberries and sugar in a blender; cover and process until blended. Press mixture through a fine meshed sieve; discard seeds. Stir in liqueur. Serve sauce with pie. **Yield:** 8 servings (1-3/4 cups sauce).

Granola Honey Braid

I guarantee that one slice of this sweet, tender bread will not be enough...
despite your good intentions. I copied the recipe from my sister, who often made it for Sunday dinners.
Now my family and I enjoy it on any day and at any time of year.
— Kathy Rairigh, Milford, Indiana

1 package (1/4 ounce) active
   dry yeast
1/4 cup warm water (110° to 115°)
1 cup warm milk (110° to 115°)
1/4 cup butter, cubed
2 eggs, lightly beaten
1/4 cup honey
1 teaspoon salt
2 cups granola without raisins,
   crushed
3-3/4 to 4-1/4 cups all-purpose flour
FILLING:
1-1/2 cups granola without raisins,
   crushed
2/3 cup honey
1/3 cup plus 2 tablespoons butter,
   softened
GLAZE:
3/4 cup confectioners' sugar
1/4 cup honey
2 tablespoons butter, softened
1 to 2 teaspoons milk, optional

In a large bowl, dissolve the yeast in warm water. Add the milk, butter, eggs, honey and salt; mix well. Add the granola and 2 cups of flour; beat on medium speed for 3 minutes. Stir in enough of the remaining flour to form a soft dough. Do not knead. Cover and let rise in a warm place until doubled, about 1 hour.

Punch dough down; turn onto a well-floured surface. Roll into an 18-in. x 12-in. rectangle. Combine filling ingredients; spread over dough. Cut lengthwise into three strips. Roll up each strip jelly-roll style, beginning at a long side; pinch edges and ends to seal well.

Place ropes seam side down on a well-greased baking sheet. Braid ropes together (do not stretch); seal ends. Cover and let rise until doubled, about 1 hour.

Bake at 350° for 25-30 minutes or until golden brown. Remove to a wire rack. Combine glaze ingredients; frost warm braid. Cool before slicing. **Yield:** 1 loaf (24 slices).

Hot Buttered Rum Mix

(Pictured at right)

*I offered this comforting, hot drink
to guests at one of my "Bunco" gatherings.
I like to keep a batch in the freezer
for easy entertaining.*
—*Carol Beyerl*
East Wenatchee, Washington

1 cup butter, softened
2 cups confectioners' sugar
1 cup plus 2 tablespoons
    packed brown sugar
2 cups vanilla ice cream,
    softened
1-1/2 teaspoons ground cinnamon
1/2 teaspoon ground nutmeg
1 teaspoon rum extract
ADDITIONAL INGREDIENT
   (for each serving):
   3/4 cup boiling water

In a large bowl, cream the butter and sugars until light and fluffy. Add the ice cream, cinnamon, nutmeg and extract; mix well. Transfer mixture to a freezer container; freeze overnight. **Yield:** 3-1/2 cups.

  To prepare hot drink: Dissolve 3-4 tablespoons of mix in boiling water; stir well. **Yield:** 14-18 servings.

Cranberry Lime Curd

*When I was visiting a friend in California, she made this fruity curd for brunch.
It was so tasty and refreshing that I brought the recipe home with me.*
—*Billie Schneider, Tarkio, Missouri*

1 can (16 ounces) whole-berry
    cranberry sauce
4 eggs
1/2 cup lime juice
1/2 cup sugar
1/2 cup butter, softened
2 teaspoons grated lime peel

In a blender, combine the cranberry sauce, eggs, lime juice, sugar and butter; cover and process until smooth. Transfer to a large saucepan. Cook and stir over low heat until mixture is thickened and reaches 160°.

  Strain mixture and discard the pulp. Stir in the lime peel. Transfer to a storage container; cover and refrigerate for up to 1 week. **Yield:** 3 cups.

'TIS THE *Season*

Christmas Friendship Luncheon

THERE'S no better time to show your appreciation for your closest chums than during the holiday season. You can offer a delicious soup, salad and sandwich lunch with ease.

Give a grown-up taste twist to classic grilled cheese and tomato soup by preparing Roasted Red Pepper Bisque and comforting Grilled Cheese Supreme.

The rich, creamy soup pairs well with the grilled cheese sandwiches, which also showcase mushrooms, tomatoes, onions and avocado.

In Spinach Festival Salad, a zesty balsamic vinaigrette dressing nicely coats greens, vegetables and turkey. (All recipes shown at right.)

Then settle in for an afternoon of fun and fellowship!

LADIES LUNCHEON
(Pictured above)

Roasted Red Pepper Bisque (p. 99)

Grilled Cheese Supreme (p. 100)

Spinach Festival Salad (p. 98)

Spinach Festival Salad

(Pictured on page 96)

I first whipped up this salad for my sister before we headed out for a day of shopping.
Now I'm asked to make it for her whenever she comes over.
—Malinda Smith, Stone Mountain, Georgia

1 medium sweet yellow pepper
1 medium sweet red pepper
1/2 pound sliced deli turkey,
   cut into strips
1 package (6 ounces) fresh
   baby spinach
2 plum tomatoes, sliced
2 green onions, sliced
1/2 cup crumbled tomato and
   basil feta cheese
3 pepperoncinis, sliced
2 tablespoons grated Romano
   cheese
1 to 2 garlic cloves, minced
1 teaspoon Italian seasoning
1/2 teaspoon crushed red pepper
   flakes
1/2 teaspoon pepper
3/4 cup balsamic vinaigrette

Broil peppers 4 in. from the heat until skins blister, about 5 minutes. With tongs, rotate peppers a quarter turn. Broil and rotate until all sides are blistered and blackened. Immediately place peppers in a bowl; cover and let stand for 15-20 minutes.

Meanwhile, in a salad bowl, combine the turkey, spinach, tomatoes, onions, feta cheese, pepperoncinis, Romano cheese, garlic and seasonings.

Peel off and discard charred skin from peppers. Remove stems and seeds. Slice peppers; add to salad and toss to combine. Serve with vinaigrette. **Yield:** 6 servings.

Editor's Note: Look for pepperoncinis (pickled peppers) in the pickle and olive section of your grocery store.

Broiled Shrimp Canapes

The crisp toast contrasts nicely with the mild-flavored shrimp topping in these savory snacks.
To save time, assemble the topping the day before and chill until ready to use.
—Jeff Johnston, Janesville, Wisconsin

10 slices day-old white bread
1/4 cup butter, melted
1-1/2 teaspoons minced fresh thyme
1/2 pound cooked medium shrimp,
   peeled, deveined and chopped
1/2 cup shredded Swiss cheese
1/2 cup seasoned bread crumbs
1/3 cup mayonnaise

Using a 1-1/2-in. round cookie cutter, cut out four circles from each slice of bread. Place on a baking sheet. Combine butter and thyme; brush over bread circles. Bake at 400° for 5 minutes or until lightly browned.

In a small bowl, combine the shrimp, Swiss cheese, bread crumbs and mayonnaise (mixture will be dry and crumbly). Place 2 teaspoonfuls on each bread circle; press down gently. Broil 6-8 in. from the heat for 2-3 minutes or until hot and bubbly. Serve warm. **Yield:** 40 appetizers.

Roasted Red Pepper Bisque

(Pictured at right and on page 97)

Folks are sure to comment about the awesome roasted red pepper flavor in this velvety soup. It's a fantastic first course for special occasions or alongside sandwiches at a casual gathering.
—*Mary Ann Zettlemaier*
Chelsea, Michigan

8 medium sweet red peppers
1 large onion, chopped
2 tablespoons butter
3 cups chicken broth, *divided*
2 cups half-and-half cream
1/2 teaspoon salt
1/2 teaspoon white pepper
6 tablespoons shredded
   Parmesan cheese, *divided*

Broil peppers 4 in. from the heat until skins blister, about 5 minutes. With tongs, rotate peppers a quarter turn. Broil and rotate until all sides are blistered and blackened. Immediately place peppers in a large bowl; cover and let stand for 15-20 minutes.

Peel off and discard charred skin. Remove stems and seeds; set peppers aside.

In a large saucepan, saute onion in butter until tender; cool slightly. In a blender, combine onion mixture, 2 cups broth and roasted peppers; cover and process until smooth. Return to the pan.

Stir in cream and remaining broth; heat through (do not boil). Stir in salt and pepper. Sprinkle each serving with 1 tablespoon Parmesan cheese. **Yield:** 6 servings (2 quarts).

Grilled Cheese Supreme

(Pictured on page 97)

Buttery rye holds a bevy of veggies, cheese and avocado in these
full-flavored sandwiches. I've also prepared them on my outdoor grill.
—*Billie Moss, Walnut Creek, California*

12 slices hearty rye bread
12 teaspoons mayonnaise
18 slices cheddar cheese
3 small tomatoes, thinly sliced
1-1/2 cups sliced fresh mushrooms
6 thin slices sweet onion
1 medium ripe avocado, peeled and cut into 12 wedges
12 teaspoons butter, softened

Spread six slices of bread with mayonnaise, 1 teaspoon on each; layer with a cheese slice, tomatoes, mushrooms, a second cheese slice, onion, avocado and remaining cheese. Spread remaining bread with remaining mayonnaise; place on top.

Butter outsides of sandwiches. Toast on a heated griddle for 2-3 minutes on each side or until bread is lightly browned and cheese is melted. **Yield:** 6 servings.

SWEET ONION SECRETS

SWEET ONIONS have a high water content, which makes them more mild than other onions. So they're ideal for eating raw in sandwiches and salads. Varieties include Vidalia, Walla Walla and Bermuda.

Select onions that are free of bruises and wrinkles. Store them in a cool, dry place for 4 to 6 weeks. Cut onions should be wrapped, refrigerated and used within a few days.

Bacon-Wrapped Meatballs

These hearty appetizers are a hit at whatever party I serve them.
The appealing aroma while baking is irresistible.
—*Pamela Shank, Parkersburg, West Virginia*

2 eggs, beaten
2 tablespoons milk
3/4 cup shredded Parmesan cheese
1/4 cup seasoned bread crumbs
1/2 teaspoon salt
1/4 teaspoon pepper
1 pound lean ground beef
24 bacon strips, cut in half widthwise

In a large bowl, combine the eggs, milk, Parmesan cheese, bread crumbs, salt and pepper. Crumble beef over mixture and mix well. Shape into 1-in. balls.

In a large skillet, cook bacon over medium heat until partially cooked but not crisp. Remove to paper towels to drain. Wrap a piece of bacon around each meatball; secure with a wooden toothpick.

Place meatballs on a greased rack in a shallow baking pan. Bake at 375° for 8 minutes. Turn; bake 3-5 minutes longer or until meat is no longer pink and bacon is crisp. **Yield:** 4 dozen.

Fruit 'n' Almond-Stuffed Brie

(Pictured at right)

Our friends enjoy this special appetizer as part of all our Christmas celebrations. An apricot filling and a raspberry topping make it more special than the usual Brie cheese spread.
— Douglas Wasdyke
Effort, Pennsylvania

2/3 cup sliced almonds
1/3 cup chopped dried apricots
1/4 cup brandy
1 sheet frozen puff pastry, thawed
1 round (8 ounces) Brie *or* Camembert cheese, rind removed
1 egg, beaten
RASPBERRY SAUCE:
1/2 cup sugar
1 tablespoon cornstarch
1/2 cup cold water
2 cups fresh *or* frozen raspberries
Assorted crackers

In a small saucepan with high sides, combine the almonds, apricots and brandy. Cook and stir over medium-low heat until liquid is almost evaporated. Remove from the heat; set aside.

On a lightly floured surface, roll puff pastry into an 11-in. x 9-in. rectangle. Cut cheese in half horizontally; place bottom half in the center of pastry. Spread with half of the almond mixture. Top with remaining cheese and almond mixture.

Fold pastry around cheese; trim excess dough. Pinch edges to seal. Place seam side down on ungreased baking sheet. Brush with egg. Bake at 375° for 30-35 minutes or until puffed and golden brown.

In a small saucepan, combine the sugar, cornstarch and water until smooth; add raspberries. Bring to a boil over medium heat, stirring constantly. Cook and stir for 1 minute or until slightly thickened. Strain and discard seeds. Transfer sauce to a small pitcher or bowl; serve with stuffed Brie and crackers. **Yield:** 8 servings.

Gingerbread Star Tree

(Pictured at far right)

Our home economists created this impressive, tasty cookie tree.
Guests can nibble on the gingerbread cookies as they talk and mingle.

DOUGH:
1-1/3 cups packed brown sugar
1-1/3 cups molasses
 2 cups cold butter, cubed
 2 eggs, beaten
 8 cups all-purpose flour
 3 tablespoons ground ginger
 2 tablespoons ground cinnamon
 4 teaspoons baking soda
 2 teaspoons ground allspice
 2 teaspoons ground cloves
 1 teaspoon salt
 1 teaspoon ground cardamom

ROYAL ICING AND DECORATIONS:
7-1/2 cups confectioners' sugar, *divided*
 6 tablespoons meringue powder, *divided*
 10 tablespoons warm water, *divided*
Edible glitter
Candy of your choice
Dark chocolate and white candy coating, melted

EQUIPMENT:
Pencil
Ruler
Waxed paper
Scissors
Cookie cutters—round (2-1/2 inches, 2 inches and 1-1/2 inches) and star-shaped (3 inches, 2 inches and 1 inch)
#101 petal pastry tip

To create star templates: With a pencil and ruler, draw five-pointed stars on sheets of waxed paper, labeling each template with its dimensions. Draw an 8-1/2-in. star, 8-in. star, 7-1/2-in. star, 7-1/4-in. star, 6-3/4-in. star, 6-in. star and 4-1/2-in. star. Cut out with scissors and set aside.

To make dough: In a large saucepan over medium heat, bring brown sugar and molasses just to a boil, stirring constantly. Remove from the heat; stir in butter until melted. Stir in eggs until blended. Combine the remaining dough ingredients; stir into brown sugar mixture. Divide dough into four portions.

On a lightly floured surface, roll out each portion to 1/4-in. thickness. Using templates, cut one 8-1/2-in. star, two 8-in. stars, one 7-1/2-in. star, two 7-1/4-in. stars, one 6-3/4-in. star, two 6-in. stars and one 4-1/2-in. star. Place on greased baking sheets. Bake at 325° for 12-15 minutes or until set. Remove to wire racks to cool.

Cut two circles using a floured 2-1/2-in. round cookie cutter. Cut 12 circles using a floured 2-in. round cookie cutter. Cut two circles using a floured 1-1/2-in. round cookie cutter. Cut remaining dough using floured star-shaped cookie cutters. Reroll scraps. Place cut-outs on greased baking sheets. Bake at 325° for 10-12 minutes or until set. Remove to wire racks to cool.

For one batch of icing: In a large mixing bowl, combine 3-3/4 cups confectioners' sugar, 3 tablespoons meringue powder and 5 tablespoons water; beat on low speed just until combined. Beat on high for 4-5 minutes or until stiff peaks form. Keep icing covered at all times with a damp cloth. If necessary, beat again on high speed to restore texture.

To assemble: With icing and round cookies, make six large sandwich cookies and one small sandwich cookie. Let stand for 15 minutes or until set.

Place the 8-1/2-in. star on a serving plate. Spread a small amount of icing onto center of star; top with an 8-in. star. Spread a small amount of icing onto center of star; top with a large sandwich cookie. Spread a small amount of icing onto sandwich cookie; top with remaining 8-in. star. Let stand for 15 minutes or until set.

Repeat with remaining icing, sandwich cookies and stars, building tree using the largest stars and sandwich cookies first. After each star is added, let stand for 15 minutes or until set.

To decorate: Prepare a second batch of icing. Cut a small hole in the corner of a pastry or plastic bag; insert #101 petal tip. Fill bag with icing. Decorate tree as desired with icing, edible glitter and candy. Decorate a 2-in. star cookie as desired; secure on the treetop with icing.

To decorate small star cookies: Dip cookies in melted candy coating; place on waxed paper and let stand until set. Sprinkle white cookies with edible glitter. Leave some cookies plain if desired. Gently place cookies onto tree branches and on the serving platter. **Yield:** 1 gingerbread tree and 3 dozen small star cookies.

Editor's Note: Meringue powder and edible glitter are available from Wilton Industries. Call 1-800/794-5866 or visit *www.wilton.com*.

Spiced Hot Chocolate

(Pictured above)

*When my family needs to warm up on a cold morning or evening,
I head to the kitchen to make this hot cocoa. The spices are very well balanced.*
—*Hannah Barringer, Loudon, Tennessee*

  1 cup sugar
1/2 cup baking cocoa
1/2 teaspoon salt
1/2 teaspoon ground cinnamon
1/2 teaspoon ground nutmeg
1/2 teaspoon ground cloves
  8 cups milk
2/3 cup water
  1 teaspoon vanilla extract
Miniature marshmallows, optional

In a 3-qt. microwave-safe dish, combine the first six ingredients. Whisk in milk and water until smooth. Microwave, uncovered, on high for 3-4 minutes or until mixture comes to a boil.

Stir in vanilla. Ladle into mugs; serve with marshmallows if desired. **Yield:** 2-1/2 quarts.

Editor's Note: This recipe was tested in a 1,100-watt microwave.

Mushroom Tartlets

I first helped my mom make these appetizers when I was just eleven years old.
Now as a military wife, I serve these tarts all over the world!
—Jennie McComsey, Hanscom AFB, Massachusetts

1 package (8 ounces) cream
   cheese, softened
1/2 cup butter, softened
1-1/2 cups all-purpose flour
FILLING:
1 pound fresh mushrooms,
   finely chopped
2 tablespoons butter
1 package (3 ounces) cream
   cheese, cubed
1/2 teaspoon salt
1/4 teaspoon dried thyme

In a small mixing bowl, beat cream cheese and butter until light and fluffy. Add flour; beat until mixture forms a ball. Cover and refrigerate for 1 hour.

For filling, in a large skillet, saute mushrooms in butter. Drain and pat dry. Return to the pan; stir in cream cheese until melted. Stir in salt and thyme; set aside.

On a lightly floured surface, roll dough to 1/16-in. thickness; cut into 2-1/2-in. circles. Press onto the bottoms and up the sides of greased miniature muffin cups. Place a rounded teaspoonful of filling in each cup.

Bake at 350° for 12-17 minutes or until edges are lightly browned. Remove from pans to wire racks. Serve warm. **Yield:** about 3 dozen.

Chili Corn Dip

This recipe came from friends who live in Australia.
The unusual "Down Under" dip goes over big here in the North East.
—Judy Ward, Centereach, New York

2 cans (16 ounces *each*) whole
   kernel corn, drained
1 medium onion, finely
   chopped
1/2 to 1 teaspoon chili powder
1 tablespoon butter
1 cup (4 ounces) shredded
   cheddar cheese
1/2 pound sliced bacon, cooked
   and crumbled
2 tablespoons sour cream
Pepper to taste
Tortilla chips

Place the corn in a food processor; cover and process until coarsely chopped. In a large skillet, saute the onion and chili powder in butter for 2 minutes or until the onion is tender. Add the corn and cheddar cheese; cook and stir until the cheese is melted.

Remove from the heat; stir in the bacon, sour cream and pepper. Serve warm with tortilla chips. **Yield:** 3 cups.

Friendship Bookmark Favors

(Pictured at right)

WHETHER you've had them for many years or only a few months, friends play an important role in every chapter of your life.

So when you gather with your girlfriends over the holidays, let them know just how special they are by crafting Friendship Bookmark Favors.

Begin by cutting a 24-in. length of black cotton cording. Thread a 2-in.-long eye pin onto one end of cording.

Add colored beads and form the end of the eye pin into a loop.

Add a jump ring and star charm onto the end of the eye pin. Fold cording back and tie both strands in an overhand knot to secure.

Add a colored bead or beads to the other end of the cording. Fold the cording back; tie an overhand knot.

Trim ends of cording close to the knot. Add a drop of clear nail polish or glue to the cut ends of the cording to prevent fraying.

Tuck each bookmark into a journal, adding an inscription in the journal if desired.

GIVING *Thanks*

It's Thanksgiving...a time to gather with friends
and family for down-home delicious dishes.
Whether you're hosting a formal sit-down dinner
for four or a crowd-pleasing, casual buffet,
you'll fall for the mouthwatering menus featured here.
Pumpkin pie may be a mainstay on this time-honored holiday.
But why not add a little spice with a host of recipes
for other pleasing pies and tarts?

GIVING *Thanks*

Bountiful Thanksgiving Buffet

WHEN you're expecting a large group of people at your house on Thanksgiving Day, a buffet is the easiest way to serve your breathtaking bounty.

Slice Always-Tender Roasted Turkey in the kitchen. Then bring the platter to the table, along with plenty of Make-Ahead Turkey Gravy.

Your guests will clamor for hearty helpings of traditional dishes like Apple-Walnut Sausage Stuffing, Duo Mashed Potatoes and Creamy Spinach Bake.

For a refreshing side dish, set out a big bowl of Candied Pecan Pear Salad. (All recipes are shown at right.)

When folks are ready for dessert, have them head to a separate sideboard where they can find Gooey Caramel Apple Bars (p. 115) and hot coffee.

FULL-FLAVORED FARE
(Clockwise from top right)

Duo Mashed Potatoes (p. 112)

Creamy Spinach Bake (p. 113)

Always-Tender Roasted Turkey (p. 111)

Make-Ahead Turkey Gravy (p. 114)

Apple-Walnut Sausage Stuffing (p. 116)

Candied Pecan Pear Salad (p. 112)

THANKSGIVING DINNER TIMELINE

A Few Weeks Before:

- Prepare two grocery lists—one for non-perishable items to purchase now and one for perishable items to purchase a few days before Thanksgiving.
- Order a fresh turkey or buy and freeze a frozen turkey (22 to 24 pounds).
- Bake the Farmhouse Bread and let cool. Freeze each loaf in a large, heavy-duty resealable plastic bag.

Five Days Before:

- Thaw the frozen turkey in a pan in the refrigerator. (Allow at least 24 hours of thawing for every 5 pounds.)
- Make Giving Thanks Gourds (page 117).

Two Days Before:

- Buy remaining grocery items, including the fresh turkey if you ordered one.
- Prepare the base for Make-Ahead Turkey Gravy. Strain; discard wings and vegetables. Cover and refrigerate.

The Day Before:

- If desired, bake the Always-Tender Roasted Turkey. Let stand 15 minutes before carving. Pour drippings into a measuring cup and skim fat. Place sliced turkey in a roasting pan; pour drippings over the top. Cool completely, then cover and refrigerate.
- For the Apple-Walnut Sausage Stuffing, slice the celery, chop the onion and cook the sausage. Refrigerate in separate containers. Cube the bread; store in an airtight container at room temperature.
- Make the candied pecans for the salad; cool and store in an airtight container at room temperature. Prepare the dressing; chill.
- Steam the spinach for Creamy Spinach Bake. Place in a covered airtight container and refrigerate.
- Bake the Gooey Caramel Apple Bars. Cool; cover and store at room temperature.
- Set your buffet table.

Thanksgiving Day:

- In the morning, thaw the three Farmhouse Bread loaves.
- Skim fat from the Make-Ahead Turkey Gravy cooking liquid. Return cooking liquid to the refrigerator.
- Peel and cube the russet and sweet potatoes for Duo Mashed Potatoes. Place in a bowl of cold water and chill.
- Roast the turkey if you didn't do so the day before.
- If you roasted the turkey the day before, cover and reheat the sliced meat in the drippings at 350° for 45-65 minutes.
- Make the Apple-Walnut Sausage Stuffing and bake.
- Assemble the Creamy Spinach Bake and cook as directed.
- Prepare Duo Mashed Potatoes.
- If desired, wrap the bread in foil and reheat in a 350° oven for 15-20 minutes. Slice and serve with butter.
- If you roasted the turkey today, cover the cooked turkey and let stand for 15 minutes before carving.
- Prepare Make-Ahead Turkey Gravy.
- Assemble the salad; drizzle with dressing just before serving.
- Serve the Gooey Caramel Apple Bars.

Always-Tender Roasted Turkey

(Pictured at right and on page 109)

For years I prepared my Thanksgiving turkey only to have it turn out dry. That's when I decided to give this recipe a try. Baking the bird in an oven bag keeps it moist and tender... and there's no basting involved.
—Shirley Bedzis, San Diego, California

1/4 **cup butter, softened**
6 **garlic cloves, minced**
1 **turkey (22 to 24 pounds)**
2 **teaspoons salt**
2 **teaspoons pepper**
2 **tablespoons all-purpose flour**
1 **turkey-size oven roasting bag**
4 **celery ribs, coarsely chopped**
2 **medium onions, sliced**

In a small bowl, combine butter and garlic. Pat turkey dry. Carefully loosen skin of turkey; rub butter mixture under the skin. Sprinkle salt and pepper over skin of turkey and inside cavity. Skewer turkey openings; tie drumsticks together.

Place flour in oven bag and shake to coat. Place the bag in a roasting pan; add celery and onions. Place turkey,

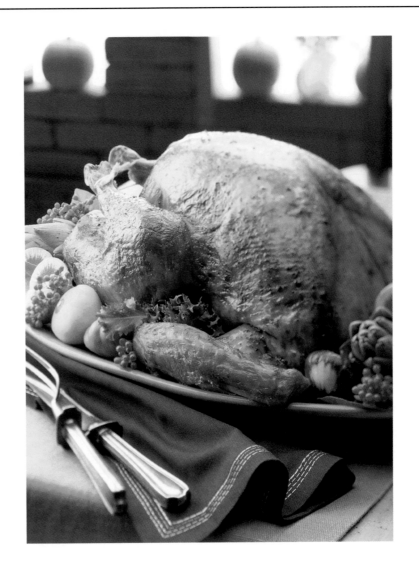

breast side up, over vegetables. Cut six 1/2-in. slits in top of bag; close bag with tie provided.

Bake at 350° for 3-1/2 to 4 hours or until a meat thermometer reads 180°. Let stand for 15 minutes before carving. Skim fat and thicken drippings if desired.

If preparing turkey the day before, pour drippings into a measuring cup; skim fat. Arrange slices in an ungreased shallow roasting pan; pour drippings over turkey. Cool completely. Cover and refrigerate overnight.

The next day, bake at 350° for 45-65 minutes or until heated through. **Yield:** 22-24 servings.

Duo Mashed Potatoes

(Pictured at far right and on page 109)

*For families who like traditional mashed potatoes as well as sweet potato casseroles,
you can't go wrong with our Test Kitchen's recipe, which features both kinds of "spuds."*

6 pounds russet potatoes (about
  9 large), peeled and cubed
6 pounds sweet potatoes (about
  9 large), peeled and cubed
2 packages (8 ounces *each*)
  cream cheese, cubed
2/3 to 1 cup half-and-half cream
5 teaspoons minced fresh sage
5 teaspoons minced fresh thyme
1 teaspoon salt
1/2 teaspoon pepper

Place russet and sweet potatoes in a soup kettle; cover with water. Bring to a boil. Reduce heat; cover and simmer for 15-20 minutes or until tender. Drain.

In a large mixing bowl, mash the potatoes with cream cheese, cream and seasonings until potatoes reach desired consistency. **Yield:** 24 servings (3/4 cup each).

Candied Pecan Pear Salad

(Pictured on page 108)

*For special occasions, I like to dress up packaged salad greens with sweet pears,
crunchy pecans and a slightly tart pomegranate dressing.*
—Douglas Wasdyke, Effort, Pennsylvania

1 teaspoon butter
1/2 cup chopped pecans
1-1/4 teaspoons sugar
1/4 teaspoon ground cinnamon
1 cup pomegranate seeds, *divided*
1/2 cup raspberry vinegar
1 tablespoon Dijon mustard
1 tablespoon honey
1/4 teaspoon salt
1/8 teaspoon pepper
1 cup olive oil
1 large pear
1 teaspoon lemon juice
3 packages (5 ounces *each*)
  spring mix salad greens
1/2 cup crumbled blue cheese

In a small heavy skillet, melt butter. Add pecans; cook over medium heat until toasted, about 4 minutes. Sprinkle with sugar and cinnamon; cook and stir for 2-4 minutes or until sugar is melted. Spread on foil to cool.

For dressing, in a blender, combine 1/2 cup pomegranate seeds, vinegar, mustard, honey, salt and pepper; cover and process until smooth. While processing, gradually add oil in a steady stream.

Cut pear into thin slices; sprinkle with lemon juice. In a salad bowl, combine the greens, pears, blue cheese and candied pecans. Drizzle with dressing and toss to coat. Sprinkle with remaining pomegranate seeds. Serve immediately. **Yield:** 12 servings (1 cup each).

Creamy Spinach Bake

(Pictured at right and on page 109)

This creamy, comforting side dish wonderfully rounds out Thanksgiving dinner. Just a little of this rich casserole goes a long way.
—Jennifer Bley, Austin, Texas

  3 packages (9 ounces *each*)
    fresh baby spinach
  1 small red onion, chopped
  1 tablespoon butter
  1 package (8 ounces) cream
    cheese, cubed
  1 cup (8 ounces) sour cream
1/2 cup half-and-half cream
1/3 cup plus 3 tablespoons grated
    Parmesan cheese, *divided*
  3 garlic cloves, minced
1/8 teaspoon pepper
  2 cans (14 ounces *each*)
    water-packed artichoke
    hearts, rinsed, drained and
    chopped
  1 tablespoon snipped fresh dill
1/4 teaspoon seasoned salt
  8 butter-flavored crackers,
    coarsely crushed

Place half of the spinach in a steamer basket; place in a large saucepan over 1 in. of water. Bring to a boil; cover and steam for 3-4 minutes or just until wilted. Transfer to a bowl. Repeat with remaining spinach; set aside.

In a large saucepan, saute onion in butter until tender. Reduce heat to low; stir in the cream cheese, sour cream, half-and-half, 1/3 cup Parmesan cheese, garlic and pepper. Cook and stir until cream cheese is melted. Stir in the artichokes, dill, seasoned salt and spinach.

Transfer to an ungreased 2-qt. baking dish. Sprinkle with cracker crumbs and remaining Parmesan cheese. Bake, uncovered, at 350° for 20-25 minutes or until edges are bubbly. **Yield:** 12 servings (1/2 cup each).

Make-Ahead Turkey Gravy

(Pictured on page 109)

As far as my family is concerned, I can never have enough homemade gravy on hand for Thanksgiving dinner! They drape it over their turkey, potatoes and stuffing. The base for this flavorful gravy is made with turkey wings and can be prepared in advance.
—*Linda Fitzsimmons, Fort Edward, New York*

 2 turkey wings (1-1/2 to
    2 pounds)
 2 medium onions, quartered
 2 cans (one 49 ounces, one
    14-1/2 ounces) reduced-
    sodium chicken broth, *divided*
 2 medium carrots, cut into
    2-inch pieces
 2 celery ribs with leaves,
    cut into 2-inch pieces
 4 fresh thyme sprigs
1/2 cup plus 2 tablespoons
    all-purpose flour
 1 tablespoon butter
1/4 teaspoon pepper

Place turkey wings and onions in a greased 13-in. x 9-in. x 2-in. baking dish. Bake, uncovered, at 400° for 1-1/4 hours, turning once.

Transfer wings and onions to a Dutch oven. Add the large can of broth, carrots, celery and thyme. Bring to a boil. Reduce heat; simmer, uncovered, for 45 minutes.

Strain; discard wings and vegetables. Skim fat from cooking liquid. Add enough remaining broth to measure 3-1/2 cups; set aside.

In a large saucepan, whisk flour and remaining broth until smooth. Gradually stir in cooking liquid. Bring to a boil; cook and stir for 2 minutes or until thickened. Stir in butter and pepper. **Yield:** 4-1/4 cups.

Editor's Note: The base for the gravy can be made two days in advance. Strain; discard wings and vegetables. Cover and refrigerate. When ready to use, skim the fat and continue with the recipe as directed.

IT'S ALL GRAVY

FOR some folks, gravy is a side dish in itself! If your family favors gravy on all of their Thanksgiving fare, double the recipe for Make-Ahead Turkey Gravy. To keep it warm for a buffet, serve it in a slow cooker.

Gooey Caramel Apple Bars

(Pictured at right)

Instead of assembling plenty of pies when feeding a crowd at Thanksgiving, our home economists suggest you bake a batch of these caramel apple bars.

 5 cups all-purpose flour
1-1/4 teaspoons sugar
1-1/4 teaspoons salt
1-1/4 cups butter-flavored
    shortening
 3 eggs
1/4 cup cold water
 2 tablespoons plus 1-1/2
    teaspoons white vinegar
FILLING:
10-1/2 cups sliced peeled tart apples
    (about 12 medium)
 1 cup sugar
 1 cup packed brown sugar
1/2 cup all-purpose flour
1-3/4 teaspoons ground cinnamon
1/2 teaspoon salt
1/2 teaspoon ground nutmeg
1/3 cup heavy whipping cream
1/3 cup butter, cubed
 1 cup chopped walnuts
1-1/2 teaspoons vanilla extract

In a large bowl, combine the flour, sugar and salt. Cut in shortening until mixture resembles coarse crumbs. In a small bowl, whisk the eggs, water and vinegar; gradually add to flour mixture, tossing with a fork until dough forms a ball.

Divide dough in half so that one portion is slightly larger than the other; wrap each in plastic wrap. Refrigerate for 1 hour or until easy to handle.

Roll out larger portion of dough between two sheets of waxed paper into a 17-in. x 12-in. rectangle. Transfer to an ungreased 15-in. x 10-in. x 1-in. baking pan. Press pastry onto the bottom and up the sides of pan; trim pastry even with top edges of pan.

In a large bowl, combine the apples, sugars, flour, cinnamon, salt and nutmeg. Stir in cream. In a Dutch oven, melt butter. Add apple mixture; cook over medium heat for 8-10 minutes or until apples are slightly tender. Stir in walnuts and vanilla. Spoon into crust.

Roll out remaining pastry; place over filling. Trim and seal edges. Cut slits in top. Bake at 375° for 35-40 minutes or until crust is golden brown and filling is bubbly. Cool on a wire rack. Cut into bars. **Yield:** 2 dozen.

Apple-Walnut Sausage Stuffing

(Pictured on page 109)

Coming from an Italian family, I like to use lots of herbs and seasonings in my cooking.
This treasured stuffing features Parmesan cheese, apples and walnuts.
—Pamela Hewitt, Laguna Niguel, California

5 celery ribs, thinly sliced
2 medium onions, chopped
3 teaspoons rubbed sage
2 teaspoons dried thyme
1 cup butter, cubed
3/4 cup grated Parmesan cheese
1/3 cup minced fresh parsley
1 teaspoon salt
1/2 teaspoon pepper
1 pound bulk Italian sausage
16 cups cubed day-old bread
5 medium tart apples, peeled
and thinly sliced

1 can (14-1/2 ounces) chicken broth
1-1/2 cups chopped walnuts

In a large skillet, saute the celery, onions, sage and thyme in butter until vegetables are tender. Transfer to a very large bowl; cool slightly. Stir in the Parmesan cheese, parsley, salt and pepper; set aside.

In the same skillet, cook sausage over medium heat until no longer pink; drain. Add to celery mixture. Add the bread cubes, apples, broth and walnuts; toss to coat.

Transfer to a greased 3-qt. baking dish (dish will be full). Cover and bake at 350° for 25 minutes. Uncover; bake 10-15 minutes longer or until heated through and lightly browned. **Yield:** 16 servings (3/4 cup each).

Farmhouse Bread

This lovely loaf is loaded with nutritious grains so we can indulge in slice after slice.
—Judy Cook, Branson, Missouri

2 packages (1/4 ounce *each*)
active dry yeast
2-1/4 cups warm water (110° to
115°)
1 can (12 ounces) evaporated
milk
1/4 cup canola oil
3 tablespoons honey
2 cups quick-cooking oats
2 cups whole wheat flour
1/2 cup cornmeal
1 tablespoon salt
4-1/2 to 5 cups bread flour

In a large bowl, dissolve yeast in warm water. Add the milk, oil, honey, oats, whole wheat flour, cornmeal, salt and 2 cups bread flour. Beat until smooth. Stir in enough remaining bread flour to form a soft dough.

Turn onto a floured surface; knead until smooth and elastic, about 6-8 minutes. Place in a greased bowl, turning once to grease top. Cover and let rise in a warm place until doubled, about 1 hour.

Punch dough down. Turn onto a lightly floured surface; divide into thirds. Shape into loaves. Place in three greased 9-in. x 5-in. x 3-in. loaf pans. Cover and let rise until doubled, about 30 minutes.

Bake at 375° for 30-35 minutes or until golden brown. Remove from pans to wire racks to cool. **Yield:** 3 loaves (16 slices each).

Giving Thanks Gourds

(Pictured above)

EXPRESS your appreciation for everything you've been given this Thanksgiving season by imprinting your sentiments on a brightly colored batch of pretty pumpkins.

First, gather gourds in a variety of shapes and sizes. Think of all you're thankful for, such as health, family, food and friends. Write the words on pumpkins with a black permanent marker.

Using a Creative Versa-Tool™ or a wood-burning tool, trace over the letters, allowing the tip of the tool to darken the shell of the pumpkin. (See Engraving Gourds at right.) When finished, use a damp paper towel to remove any visible marker lines.

The gourds can be prepared several weeks in advance. Use them to decorate mantels, sideboards and your buffet table.

At the end of your Thanksgiving dinner, encourage guests to take a gourd or two home with them.

ENGRAVING GOURDS

AFTER writing on the pumpkins with permanent marker, trace over the letters with a wood-burning tool. (We used the Creative Versa-Tool™ from Walnut Hollow®.) The tip of the tool gets extremely hot so it's important to keep it away from you, other people and anything on your work surface. Be sure to read the instructions that come with the tool.

Thanksgiving Dinner For Four

IF YOU HAVE reservations about planning an elegant, sit-down dinner for your party of four this Thanksgiving, let the menu featured here provide you with some inspiration!

Stuffed Game Hens are a fun and fancy way to welcome your family to the table. With just six ingredients, this easy yet elegant entree is one you'll come to rely on all year long.

Such a special occasion calls for dressed-up dishes like Brussels Sprouts in Lemon Sauce and Port Wine Cranberry Sauce.

Remember to pass a basket of oven-fresh Buttery Whole Wheat Dinner Rolls—alongside a dish of Garlic-Chive Whipped Butter. (All recipes shown at right.)

CLASSY CUISINE

(Pictured above)

Stuffed Game Hens (p. 122)

Brussels Sprouts in Lemon Sauce (p. 122)

Port Wine Cranberry Sauce (p. 126)

Buttery Whole Wheat Dinner Rolls (p. 124)

Garlic-Chive Whipped Butter (p. 124)

THANKSGIVING MENU PLANNER

A Few Weeks Before:

- Prepare two grocery lists—one for non-perishable items to purchase now and one for perishable items to purchase a few days before Thanksgiving Day.
- Purchase four frozen Cornish game hens; keep in your freezer at home.
- Bake Buttery Whole Wheat Dinner Rolls and let cool. Freeze in a single layer in large, heavy-duty resealable plastic bags.

Two Days Before:

- Buy remaining grocery items.
- Place Cornish hens in a shallow pan; thaw in the refrigerator.
- Make Garlic-Chive Whipped Butter. Place in a covered container and chill.

The Day Before:

- Toast the sliced almonds for the Brussels Sprouts in Lemon Sauce; store in an airtight container.
- Chop the pecans for the Pumpkin Praline Creme Brulee; store at room temperature in an airtight container. Bake the creme brulee; cover and refrigerate.
- For Cranberry Wild Rice, toast the pine nuts; cover and store at room temperature. Make the rice; cool and chill in a covered container.
- Prepare base for Gingered Pumpkin Bisque; process in a blender. Cover and refrigerate.
- Make Port Wine Cranberry Sauce. Place in an airtight container; chill.

- Set the table.
- Make the centerpiece on page 127.

Thanksgiving Day:

- In the morning, thaw Buttery Whole Wheat Dinner Rolls.
- Peel, cube and seed butternut squash for Apple Butternut Squash. Place in a bowl; cover with water and chill.
- Two hours before dinner, remove the creme brulee ramekins from the refrigerator and place on a baking sheet. Let stand at room temperature for 15 minutes. Sprinkle with brown sugar and broil as directed. Sprinkle with pecans. Return to the refrigerator.
- Bake the Stuffed Game Hens.
- Roll the napkins and secure with Cabbage Leaf Napkin Rings (page 127).
- Make Apple Butternut Squash.
- Prepare the Brussels Sprouts in Lemon Sauce.
- Place Gingered Pumpkin Bisque in a saucepan; stir in cream and vanilla. Heat through but do not boil. Garnish as directed.
- If desired, wrap the rolls in foil and reheat in a 350° oven for 15 minutes. Serve the rolls with the Garlic-Chive Whipped Butter.
- Make Cranberry Wild Rice.
- Reheat Port Wine Cranberry Sauce if desired or serve cold.
- Serve the Pumpkin Praline Creme Brulee for dessert.

Gingered Pumpkin Bisque

(Pictured at right)

*Every spoonful of this pretty
pumpkin soup hints of autumn.
Impress guests by serving it as the
first course at your sit-down dinners.*
—Patricia Kile
Elizabethtown, Pennsylvania

1/3 cup chopped shallots
1/4 cup chopped onion
  1 teaspoon minced fresh
    gingerroot
  1 tablespoon canola oil
  2 tablespoons all-purpose flour
  1 can (14-1/2 ounces) chicken
    broth
1/3 cup apple cider *or* juice
3/4 cup plus 2 tablespoons
    canned pumpkin
  2 tablespoons plus 1-1/2
    teaspoons maple syrup
1/8 teaspoon dried thyme
1/8 teaspoon ground cinnamon
1/8 teaspoon pepper
Dash ground cloves
1/2 cup heavy whipping cream *or*
    half-and-half cream
1/4 teaspoon vanilla extract
Additional heavy whipping cream,
  optional
Fresh thyme sprigs, optional

In a small saucepan, saute the shallots, onion and ginger in oil until tender. Stir in the flour until blended; cook and stir for 2 minutes or until golden brown. Gradually stir in the broth and cider. Bring to a boil; cook and stir for 2 minutes or until thickened.

Stir in the pumpkin, syrup and seasonings. Return to a boil. Reduce heat; cover and simmer for 10 minutes. Remove from the heat; cool slightly.

In a blender, process soup until smooth. Return to the pan. Stir in cream and vanilla; heat through (do not boil). If desired, drizzle individual servings with additional cream and garnish with thyme sprigs. **Yield:** 4 servings.

Stuffed Game Hens

(Pictured on page 119)

I like to delight dinner guests with this simply elegant entree.
The combination of mushrooms, pears and basil is surprisingly delicious.
—Jerry Huff, Oakland, California

1/2 pound fresh mushrooms,
    chopped
2 medium pears, peeled and
    chopped
4 teaspoons minced fresh basil
1 teaspoon dill weed
1/2 cup olive oil
4 Cornish game hens
    (20 ounces *each*)

In a large bowl, combine the mushrooms, pears, basil and dill. Brush the oil over outsides of hens and inside cavities; stuff with the mushroom mixture. Tie the legs together with kitchen string.

Place breast side up on a rack in a shallow roasting pan. Bake, uncovered, at 350° for 1-3/4 to 2 hours or until a meat thermometer reads 180° for hens and 165° for stuffing, basting occasionally with pan juices. **Yield:** 4 servings.

Brussels Sprouts in Lemon Sauce

(Pictured on page 119)

I've been making this wonderful dish for more than 20 years.
I can't even remember where I got the recipe, but it's a great one all people enjoy!
—Mary Ann Morgan, Cedartown, Georgia

1 pound fresh *or* frozen
    brussels sprouts
1/4 cup butter, cubed
2/3 cup mayonnaise
2 tablespoons lemon juice
1/2 teaspoon celery salt
1/4 cup shredded Parmesan
    cheese
1/4 cup sliced almonds, toasted

If using fresh brussels sprouts, trim and cut an X in the core end of each. In a large saucepan, bring 1 in. of water and sprouts to a boil. Reduce heat; cover and simmer for 10-12 minutes or until tender.

Meanwhile, in a small saucepan, melt butter over low heat. Whisk in the mayonnaise, lemon juice and celery salt until smooth; heat through (do not boil).

Drain brussels sprouts and place in a serving bowl. Drizzle with lemon sauce. Sprinkle with Parmesan cheese and almonds. **Yield:** 4 servings.

Cranberry Wild Rice

(Pictured at right)

*Nuts are a wonderful source of protein
and nutrition, so I look for ways
to include them in many of my dishes.
The addition of cranberries
makes it perfect for fall.*
—*Dawn Bryant, Hershey, Nebraska*

  4 cups water
3/4 cup uncooked wild rice
  1 small red onion, chopped
1/2 cup chopped dried
    cranberries
  3 garlic cloves, minced
  1 teaspoon dried thyme
  1 tablespoon olive oil
  2 tablespoons pine nuts,
    toasted

In a large saucepan, bring water and
rice to a boil. Reduce heat; simmer, uncovered, for 50-60 minutes or until rice
is tender.

In a large skillet, saute the onion,
cranberries, garlic and thyme in oil until onion is tender. Drain rice if needed;
stir in onion mixture and pine nuts.
Yield: 4 servings.

Family Traditions

WE GROW a huge garden and can hundreds of
jars a year. After our family enjoys Thanksgiving
dinner, we fill boxes with home-canned goods from
our pantry for everyone to take home. It's a great
feeling to know their cupboards are stocked with
the fruits of our labor.

—*Randy and Susan Peterson*
Ridgeway, Ohio

Buttery Whole Wheat Dinner Rolls

(Pictured on page 118)

Whether served plain or with butter, these whole grain rolls are tender and delicious.
—Angela Coffman, Stewartsville, Missouri

1 tablespoon active dry yeast
3/4 cup warm water (110° to 115°)
1/3 cup sugar
1/3 cup nonfat dry milk powder
4 tablespoons butter, softened, *divided*
1 egg
1 teaspoon salt
2 cups whole wheat flour
1/2 to 1 cup bread flour

In a small bowl, dissolve yeast in warm water. Add the sugar, milk powder, 2 tablespoons butter, egg, salt and whole wheat flour. Beat until smooth. Stir in enough bread flour to form a soft dough (dough will be sticky).

Turn onto a floured surface; knead until smooth and elastic, about 6-8 minutes. Place in a greased bowl, turning once to grease top. Cover and let rise in a warm place until doubled, about 1 hour.

In a shallow microwave-safe bowl, melt remaining butter. Punch dough down. Turn onto a lightly floured surface; divide into 16 pieces. Shape each into a ball; roll in melted butter. Place 2 in. apart on greased baking sheets. Cover and let rise until doubled, about 30 minutes.

Bake at 375° for 8-10 minutes or until golden brown. Remove from pans to wire racks. **Yield:** 16 rolls.

Garlic-Chive Whipped Butter

(Pictured on page 118)

Looking for a way to dress up ordinary bread or dinner rolls? Set out a bowl of this creamy garlic butter from our Test Kitchen!

1/2 cup butter, softened
1/4 cup grated Parmesan cheese
1 tablespoon minced chives
1 to 2 garlic cloves, minced

In a small mixing bowl, beat all ingredients until blended. Refrigerate until serving. **Yield:** 1/2 cup.

WHIPPED BUTTER ROSETTES

ADD an elegant touch to your table by using Garlic-Chive Whipped Butter to create butter rosettes. Blend the ingredients as directed; chill for 10-15 minutes. Line a baking sheet with parchment paper. Spoon the butter mixture into a pastry bag fitted with a star-shaped tip. Squeeze the butter out onto the prepared pan to create small rosettes. Refrigerate until ready to serve.

Pumpkin Praline Creme Brulee

(Pictured at right)

The crunchy pecans are a nice contrast to the creamy custard in this recipe from our home economists. This dessert adds elegance to any meal.

6 **egg yolks**
1/4 **cup maple syrup**
1 **cup heavy whipping cream**
1/2 **cup canned pumpkin**
1/4 **teaspoon ground cinnamon**
1/4 **teaspoon vanilla extract**
1/8 **teaspoon ground ginger**
4 **teaspoons brown sugar**
1/4 **cup chopped pecans, toasted**

In a small bowl, whisk egg yolks and syrup. In a small saucepan, heat cream over medium heat until bubbles form around sides of pan. Remove from the heat; stir a small amount of hot cream into egg yolk mixture. Return all to the pan, stirring constantly. Stir in the pumpkin, cinnamon, vanilla and ginger.

Transfer to four 6-oz. ramekins or custard cups. Place cups in a baking pan; add 1 in. of boiling water to pan. Bake, uncovered, at 325° for 25-30 minutes or until centers are just set (mixture will jiggle). Remove ramekins from water bath; cool for 10 minutes. Cover and refrigerate for at least 4 hours.

Two hours before serving, place ramekins on a baking sheet. Let stand at room temperature for 15 minutes. Sprinkle with brown sugar. Broil 8 in. from the heat for 4-7 minutes or until sugar is caramelized. Sprinkle with the pecans. Refrigerate until chilled. **Yield:** 4 servings.

Port Wine Cranberry Sauce

(Pictured on page 118)

This crimson-colored sauce from our Test Kitchen has just the right amount of tartness to complement poultry, pork and game.

1 package (12 ounces) fresh *or* frozen cranberries
1-1/4 cups sugar
1/4 cup port wine *or* grape juice
2 teaspoons cornstarch
2 tablespoons cold water

In a small saucepan, combine the cranberries, sugar and wine or grape juice. Cook over medium heat for 10-12 minutes or just until the berries begin to pop. Combine cornstarch and water until smooth; stir into cranberry mixture.

Bring to a boil; cook and stir for 2 minutes or until the berries pop and sauce is thickened. Serve warm or cold. Refrigerate leftovers. **Yield:** 2 cups.

Apple Butternut Squash

Our home economists created this creamy side dish that pairs apple butter and butternut squash. The mild flavor would work well with any entree.

1 medium butternut squash, peeled, seeded and cubed
1/4 cup apple butter
1 tablespoon heavy whipping cream
1/4 teaspoon salt
1/4 teaspoon ground cinnamon

Place squash in a large saucepan and cover with water; bring to a boil. Reduce heat; cover and simmer for 15-20 minutes or until tender. Drain.

In a large mixing bowl, mash squash with apple butter, cream, salt and cinnamon until blended. **Yield:** 5 servings.

Editor's Note: This recipe was tested with commercially prepared apple butter.

Gorgeous Greens

(Pictured at right)

WHEN autumn arrives, so do the brilliant fall colors of orange, gold, rust and more.

But consider going green this Thanksgiving by fashioning the arrangement featured here.

Instead of pumpkins, grab hold of white gourds in assorted sizes. Your grocer's produce section is the source for flowering kale and sprigs of fresh rosemary and sage.

A bounty of white and muted green flowers rounds out the centerpiece. We used hydrangea, licorice vine, millet, blue thistle, tallow berry, dusty miller and hypericum.

For natural napkin rings, make the Cabbage Leaf Napkin Rings as instructed below.

CABBAGE LEAF NAPKIN RINGS

WHY buy napkin rings to go with the "gourd-eous" centerpiece above when you can make your own natrual variety? Start by folding a square dinner napkin in half to make a rectangle. Roll up tightly, starting from a short side; set aside.

1. Slightly overlap the stem ends of two ornamental cabbage leaves; wrap craft wire around the ends to secure.

2. Wrap the leaves around the rolled napkin, overlapping the leaves on top. Use a wooden skewer to make small holes in and out of the leaves. Remove the skewer; insert a small twig in and out of the holes.

GIVING *Thanks*

Pleasing Pies & Tarts

NOTHING warms the house or stirs the memory on Thanksgiving Day like the aroma of freshly baked pies and tarts. For many families, the holiday dinner wouldn't be complete without serving a certain variety!

The delectable desserts featured here showcase seasonal produce like apples, pears, pumpkins and nuts.

For a delicious twist on an American classic, delve into a wedge of Cherry-Apple Lattice Pie, or indulge in a piece of Walnut-Streusel Pumpkin Pie.

To lend your menu a more casual feel, Rustic Pear Tart adds simplistic beauty and unbelievable flavor to any meal. (All recipes shown at right.)

Save Room for Dessert!

(Top to bottom)

Cherry-Apple Lattice Pie (p. 132)

Rustic Pear Tart (p. 130)

Walnut-Streusel Pumpkin Pie (p. 134)

Rustic Pear Tart

(Pictured on page 129)

*People can never get enough of this pie's sugar-crusted top and scrumptious filling
that features ripe, sweet pears, dried cherries and crunchy walnuts.*
—*Lisa Varner, Greenville, South Carolina*

1 sheet refrigerated pie pastry
4 cups thinly sliced peeled
   fresh pears
1/4 cup dried cherries
1 teaspoon vanilla extract
4 tablespoons sugar, *divided*
4 teaspoons cornstarch
1 teaspoon ground cinnamon
1/2 teaspoon ground ginger
1/4 cup chopped walnuts
1 egg white
1 tablespoon water

On a lightly floured surface, roll out the pastry into a 14-in. circle. Transfer to a parchment paper-lined baking sheet; set aside.

In a large bowl, combine the pears, cherries and vanilla. Combine 3 tablespoons sugar, cornstarch, cinnamon and ginger; sprinkle over pear mixture and stir gently to combine. Spoon over pastry to within 2 in. of edges; sprinkle with walnuts. Fold edges of pastry over filling, leaving center uncovered.

Beat egg white and water; brush over folded pastry. Sprinkle with remaining sugar. Bake at 375° for 35-40 minutes or until crust is golden and filling is bubbly. Using parchment paper, slide tart onto a wire rack to cool. **Yield:** 6-8 servings.

Rum-Raisin Pumpkin Pie

*When you want a welcome alternative to the usual holiday dessert fare, I recommend this spin on traditional
pumpkin pie. The combination of pumpkin, raisins and rum gives each piece rich and delicious flavor.*
—*Gertrudis Miller, Evansville, Indiana*

1/2 cup raisins
1/4 cup rum
1/4 cup boiling water
2 eggs
3/4 cup packed brown sugar
1 tablespoon all-purpose flour
1/2 teaspoon salt
1/2 teaspoon ground ginger
1/2 teaspoon ground cinnamon
1/4 teaspoon ground nutmeg
1/4 teaspoon ground cloves
1 can (15 ounces) solid-pack
   pumpkin
1 cup evaporated milk
1 unbaked pastry shell (9 inches)

Place raisins and rum in a small bowl. Cover with boiling water; let stand for 5 minutes.

Meanwhile, in a large bowl, combine the eggs, brown sugar, flour, salt and spices. Stir in pumpkin and raisin mixture. Gradually add milk. Pour into pastry shell.

Bake at 400° for 35-40 minutes or until a knife inserted near the center comes out clean (cover the edges with foil during during the last 15 minutes if necessary to prevent overbrowning). Cool on a wire rack. Refrigerate leftovers. **Yield:** 6-8 servings.

Caramel Nut Tart

(Pictured at right)

A nut-lover's dream, this ooey-gooey tart adds that something special to your dessert offerings. Its candy bar-like taste makes it hard to eat just one slice.
—Donna Urban
Glenolden, Pennsylvania

1-1/4 cups all-purpose flour
1/8 teaspoon salt
1 package (3 ounces) cold cream cheese
1/4 cup cold butter
2 to 3 tablespoons ice water

FILLING:
1/3 cup butter, cubed
1/3 cup packed brown sugar
2 tablespoons light corn syrup
1-1/2 cups mixed nuts
1/2 teaspoon vanilla extract

In a small bowl, combine flour and salt; cut in cream cheese and butter until mixture resembles coarse crumbs. Gradually add water, tossing with a fork until dough forms a ball.

Roll out dough into a 10-in. circle. Press onto the bottom and up the sides of an ungreased 9-in. fluted tart pan with a removable bottom; trim edges.

Line unpricked pastry with a double layer of heavy-duty foil. Bake at 450° for 8 minutes. Remove foil; bake 5 minutes longer. Cool on a wire rack. Reduce heat to 400°.

For the filling, in a small heavy saucepan, combine the butter, brown sugar and corn syrup. Bring to a boil over medium heat, stirring constantly. Remove from the heat; stir in nuts and vanilla. Spread into crust.

Place tart pan on a baking sheet. Bake for 15-20 minutes or until bubbly. Cool on a wire rack. **Yield:** 10 servings.

STORING PIES

COOL fruit pies at least 1 hour before serving. They can be kept at room temperature for 1 day. For longer storage, cover and refrigerate for up to 5 days.

Cool meringue-topped and custard pies on a wire rack for 1 hour, then chill at least 3 hours before serving. Custard and cream pies can be stored in the refrigerator for up to 3 days.

Cherry-Apple Lattice Pie

(Pictured on page 129)

Whether you're a fan of apple or cherry pie, this succulent combination features the best
of both desserts. It's one pie you'll want to serve every Thanksgiving.
—LeAnn Sager, Fairmont, Minnesota

1/2 cup dried cherries
1/4 cup unsweetened apple juice
2 tablespoons plus 1/2 cup sugar, *divided*
2-1/4 teaspoons ground cinnamon, *divided*
2 tablespoons cornstarch
6 cups thinly sliced peeled tart apples
1 teaspoon vanilla extract
1 package (15 ounces) refrigerated pie pastry
1 egg white

In a small microwave-safe bowl, combine the cherries and apple juice. Cover and microwave on high until heated through; set aside.

In a small bowl, combine 2 tablespoons sugar and 1/4 teaspoon cinnamon; set aside for topping. In a large bowl, combine cornstarch with the remaining sugar and cinnamon. Stir in the apples, vanilla and reserved cherry mixture.

Line a 9-in. deep-dish pie plate with bottom crust; trim pastry even with edge of plate. Add filling. With remaining pastry, make a lattice crust. Seal and flute edges. Beat egg white until foamy; brush over lattice top. Sprinkle with reserved cinnamon-sugar.

Cover edges loosely with foil. Bake at 450° for 15 minutes. Reduce heat to 350° and remove foil. Bake 30-45 minutes longer or until crust is golden brown and filling is bubbly. Cool on a wire rack. **Yield:** 8 servings.

Oatmeal Pecan Pie

For a delightful twist on a Southern favorite, look no further!
The addition of oats gives the pie a delicious, chewy texture.
—Sue Draheim, Waterford, Wisconsin

2 eggs
1/2 cup sugar
1/2 cup packed brown sugar
3/4 cup corn syrup
1/2 cup milk
1/4 cup butter, melted
1 teaspoon vanilla extract
Dash salt
2 cups pecan halves
3/4 cup quick-cooking oats

1/2 cup flaked coconut
1 unbaked pastry shell (9 inches)

In a large bowl, whisk the eggs and sugars. Gradually whisk in the corn syrup, milk, butter, vanilla and salt. Stir in pecans, oats and coconut. Pour into pastry shell.

Bake at 350° for 45-50 minutes or until a knife inserted near the center comes out clean (cover edges loosely with foil if necessary to prevent overbrowning). Cool on a wire rack. **Yield:** 8 servings.

Butternut Squash Pie

(Pictured at right)

This creamy squash pie bakes up rich and flavorful. The leaf-shaped cut-outs add an impressive touch.
—Mary Ellen Solesbee
Greer, South Carolina

Pastry for single-crust pie
   (9 inches)
1-1/4 cups sugar
4-1/2 teaspoons cornstarch
   1 tablespoon ground cinnamon
   3 cups mashed cooked
      butternut squash
1/2 cup butter, softened
   2 eggs
1/4 cup water
   3 teaspoons vanilla extract
Whipped cream, optional

Line a 9-in. pie plate with pastry; trim and flute edges. Cut out the scraps with a leaf-shaped cookie cutter for garnish if desired; place on a baking sheet and set aside.

In a large mixing bowl, combine the sugar, cornstarch and cinnamon. Add the squash, butter, eggs, water and vanilla; beat just until smooth. Pour into crust.

Cover the edges loosely with foil. Bake at 350° for 15 minutes. Remove the foil. Bake 35-40 minutes longer or until a knife inserted near the center comes out clean. Bake leaf cutouts for 5-7 minutes or until golden brown.

Cool pie and cutouts on a wire rack for 1 hour. Refrigerate pie until chilled. Garnish with pastry leaves and whipped cream if desired. **Yield:** 6-8 servings.

Walnut-Streusel Pumpkin Pie

(Pictured on page 129)

With its sweet, nutty topping and thin cream cheese layer, this extra-special pumpkin pie is sure to become a new-found family favorite.
—*Deborah Paulson, Deer Park, Washington*

Pastry for single-crust pie
    (9 inches)
     1 can (15 ounces) solid-pack
       pumpkin
     1 can (14 ounces) sweetened
       condensed milk
   1/2 cup sugar
   1/2 cup packed dark brown sugar
     2 eggs
     1 tablespoon all-purpose flour
1-1/2 teaspoons ground cinnamon
   1/2 teaspoon salt
   1/2 teaspoon ground nutmeg
   1/4 teaspoon ground ginger
CREAM CHEESE FILLING:
     1 package (8 ounces) cream
       cheese, softened
   1/4 cup sugar
   1/2 teaspoon vanilla extract
     1 egg, lightly beaten

TOPPING:
   1/2 cup old-fashioned oats
   1/2 cup packed dark brown sugar
   1/2 cup chopped walnuts
   1/4 cup all-purpose flour
   1/2 teaspoon ground cinnamon
   1/2 teaspoon ground nutmeg
   1/4 cup cold butter

Line a 9-in. deep-dish pie plate with pastry; trim and flute edges. Set aside.

In a large bowl, beat the pumpkin, milk, sugars, eggs, flour, cinnamon, salt, nutmeg and ginger until blended. Pour into crust.

In a small bowl, beat the cream cheese, sugar and vanilla until smooth. Add egg; beat on low speed just until combined. Gently spread over pumpkin layer.

In a small bowl, combine the oats, brown sugar, walnuts, flour, cinnamon and nutmeg; cut in butter until crumbly. Sprinkle over filling.

Cover edges loosely with foil. Bake at 400° for 15 minutes. Reduce heat to 350°; bake 50-55 minutes longer or until a knife inserted near the center comes out clean. Remove foil. Cool on a wire rack. Refrigerate leftovers. **Yield:** 10 servings.

PROTECTING PASTRY EDGES FROM OVERBROWNING

THE EDGES of a pie pastry often brown before the rest of the pie is thoroughly baked. To protect the edges, fold a 12-in. piece of foil into quarters. Place the folded corner toward you. Measure 3-3/4 in. up each adjacent side and cut out an arc joining the two sides. Discard the center.

Unfold the remaining foil and place it over the unbaked pie. Trim corners if necessary. Gently crimp the foil around the edge of the crust to secure. Bake as directed.

Chocolate Hazelnut Tart

(Pictured at right)

A slice of this rich, nutty tart is divine. Impressive, yet easy to prepare, it's the ideal fall dessert.
—*Gilda Lester*
Wilmington, North Carolina

6 tablespoons butter, softened
2 tablespoons cream cheese, softened
1/3 cup confectioners' sugar
1 teaspoon grated lemon peel
1 cup all-purpose flour
FILLING:
4 eggs
3/4 cup sugar
1/2 cup chocolate syrup
1/4 cup dark corn syrup
1 cup chopped hazelnuts, toasted
1 cup (6 ounces) miniature semisweet chocolate chips
Whipped cream and chocolate shavings, optional

In a small mixing bowl, beat the butter, cream cheese, confectioners' sugar and lemon peel until creamy. Beat in flour just until combined.

Shape dough into a disk. Wrap in plastic wrap; refrigerate for 30 minutes or until easy to handle.

Roll dough into an 11-in. circle. Press onto the bottom and up the sides of an ungreased 9-in. fluted tart pan with a removable bottom. Bake at 350° for 18-22 minutes or until lightly browned. Cool on a wire rack.

In a small bowl, combine the eggs, sugar, chocolate syrup and corn syrup. Pour into crust. Combine hazelnuts and chocolate chips; sprinkle over filling. Place pan on a baking sheet. Bake for 25-30 minutes or until center is almost set (center will set when cool). Cool on a wire rack.

Garnish with whipped cream and chocolate shavings if desired. Refrigerate leftovers. **Yield:** 12 servings.

Layered Caramel-Pear Tart

Baking this dazzling dessert in a springform pan instead of a tart pan gives it a more rustic, charming appearance. The combination of pears, caramel and pecans simply shouts fall.
—*Darlia Schaefer, Lincoln, Arkansas*

1/2 cup butter, softened
1/3 cup sugar
1 teaspoon vanilla extract
1 cup all-purpose flour
FILLING:
1 package (8 ounces) cream
cheese, softened
1/4 cup sugar
3 tablespoons caramel ice
cream topping
TOPPING:
2-1/4 cups sliced peeled fresh pears
1/2 cup chopped pecans
1/3 cup sugar
1/4 teaspoon ground cinnamon
1/4 teaspoon apple pie spice
Additional caramel ice cream
topping, optional

In a small bowl, cream the butter, sugar and vanilla. Gradually beat in the flour until blended. Press onto the bottom and 1-1/2 in. up the sides of a greased 9-in. springform pan; set aside.

In a small mixing bowl, beat the cream cheese, sugar and caramel topping until smooth. Spread evenly into crust. Arrange pear slices over filling. Combine the pecans, sugar, cinnamon and apple pie spice; sprinkle over pears.

Place pan on a baking sheet. Bake at 450° for 10 minutes. Reduce heat to 400°; bake 12-16 minutes longer or until edges are golden brown. Cool on a wire rack. Refrigerate for at least 1 hour before serving.

Remove sides of pan before slicing. Drizzle with additional caramel topping if desired. **Yield:** 12 servings.

Pecan Meringue Pie

The flavor of sweet pecans really shines through in this luscious dinner finale. People rave about the heavenly meringue crust.
—*Anne Powers, Munford, Alabama*

3 egg whites
1/4 teaspoon cream of tartar
1 cup sugar
1 teaspoon vanilla extract
1 cup graham cracker crumbs
1 cup chopped pecans
TOPPING:
1 cup heavy whipping cream
3 tablespoons sugar
1/2 teaspoon vanilla extract

Place egg whites in a large mixing bowl; let stand at room temperature for 30 minutes. Add cream of tartar; beat on medium speed until soft peaks form. Gradually beat in sugar, 1 tablespoon at a time, on high until stiff peaks form. Fold in the vanilla, cracker crumbs and pecans.

Spread onto the bottom and up the sides of a greased 9-in. pie plate. Bake at 350° for 25-30 minutes or until lightly browned. Cool on a wire rack.

For topping, in a small bowl, beat cream until it begins to thicken. Add sugar and vanilla; beat until stiff peaks form. Spread over cooled meringue shell. Store in the refrigerator. **Yield:** 6-8 servings.

Upside-Down Apple Cheese Pie

(Pictured at right)

When you want to serve something different for dessert, turn to my unique treat. The cheesecake-like pie features slices of tart apples and a delectable caramelized topping.
—Lisa Dilworth
Grand Rapids, Michigan

2/3 cup chopped pecans
1/2 cup packed brown sugar
3 tablespoons butter, melted
Pastry for double-crust pie (9 inches)
1 package (8 ounces) cream cheese, softened
1/2 cup shredded cheddar cheese
1 tablespoon plus 1 cup sugar, *divided*
1 teaspoon vanilla extract
4 cups thinly sliced peeled tart apples
1/4 cup all-purpose flour
2 tablespoons lemon juice
2 teaspoons ground cinnamon
1/2 teaspoon ground ginger

In a small bowl, combine the pecans, brown sugar and butter; spread into a greased 9-in. pie plate. Roll out one pastry to fit the pie plate; place over pecan mixture. Trim pastry even with edge of plate.

In a small mixing bowl, combine the cream cheese, cheddar cheese, 1 tablespoon sugar and vanilla; spread over the pastry. In large bowl, combine the apples, flour, lemon juice, cinnamon, ginger and remaining sugar; pour over the cheese mixture.

Roll out remaining pastry to fit top of pie; place over filling. Trim, seal and flute edges. Cut slits in top.

Bake at 375° for 45-50 minutes or until golden brown. Cool for 5 minutes before inverting onto a serving plate. Serve warm. **Yield:** 6-8 servings.

EASTER
Gatherings

*If you don't have plans to head somewhere warm
for Easter, don't worry! You can take your taste buds
on a flavorful trip with our Mediterranean-inspired dinner
starring Marinated Grilled Lamb. For meals throughout
the sunny season, showcase spring vegetables
in a selection of delicious side dishes.
From sweet to savory, delightful muffins
and scones round out menus around the clock.*

Breathtaking Easter Brunch

ARE YOU reluctant to have friends and family over for a formal, sit-down Easter dinner? Why not host a more casual brunch instead?

A bit of bubbly in Champagne Punch will add some spark to your celebration.

Wine 'n' Cheese Strata and Sausage-Filled Crepes are enticing entrees that are sure to satisfy.

Store-bought sausage just can't compare to homemade Turkey Sausage Patties.

And Mixed Fruit with Lemon-Basil Dressing is a fresh, sweet addition to the meal. (All recipes shown at right.)

EARLY-DAY DINING
(Clockwise from top right)

Turkey Sausage Patties (p. 146)

Champagne Punch (p. 144)

Sausage-Filled Crepes (p. 144)

Wine 'n' Cheese Strata (p. 142)

Mixed Fruit with Lemon-Basil Dressing (p. 146)

Wine 'n' Cheese Strata

(Pictured on page 141)

*Although I typically serve this strata for breakfast and brunch, it also makes
a nice light lunch or dinner. The hint of wine makes it special.*
—*Cheryl Schmitt, Clarinda, Iowa*

11 cups cubed day-old French
    bread
 1 cup (4 ounces) shredded
    Swiss cheese
 1 cup (4 ounces) shredded
    Monterey Jack cheese
 1 cup diced fully cooked ham
 3 green onions, sliced
 6 eggs
 2 cups milk
1/4 cup white wine *or* chicken
    broth
1-1/2 teaspoons Dijon mustard
1/8 teaspoon pepper
 1 cup (8 ounces) sour cream
1/4 cup shredded Parmesan
    cheese

Place bread cubes in a greased 13-in. x 9-in. x 2-in. baking dish; top with Swiss and Monterey Jack cheeses, ham and onions. In a large bowl, whisk the eggs, milk, wine or broth, mustard and pepper. Pour over the top. Cover and refrigerate overnight.

Remove from the refrigerator 30 minutes before baking. Cover and bake at 325° for 40-45 minutes or until a knife inserted near the center comes out clean and a thermometer reads 160°. Let stand for 10 minutes before cutting.

Meanwhile, in a small saucepan, combine sour cream and Parmesan cheese; cook and stir over low heat until warm. Serve with strata. **Yield:** 12 servings.

PLANNING YOUR BRUNCH MENU

BRUNCH is a great way to entertain, especially with these tips:

- Because brunch falls between breakfast and lunch, plan your menu to include dishes from each meal.
- Think about how much oven space you have by preparing cold dishes as well as hot items.
- Appeal to all palates by offering an assortment of both sweet and savory recipes.
- Guests with dietary restrictions will appreciate vegetarian, low-fat or low-sugar options.
- Don't prepare too many dishes requiring last-minute work. Do-ahead dishes (like Wine 'n'

Cheese Strata, above) are invaluable.

- Scrambled eggs, pancakes and made-to-order pancakes work best for a smaller gathering than for a crowd.
- For easy serving, pre-slice dishes like quiche, rolls and pastries before bringing them to the table.
- When setting the buffet table, leave room in front of serving dishes so guests can set down their plates while serving themselves.
- Brunch beverages include coffee, tea, punch, juice and milk. For alcoholic options, consider champagne, Bloody Marys and Mimosas.

Hot Cross Buns

(Pictured at right)

I've been known to make hot cross buns throughout the year, not just at Easter. My husband loves them toasted and topped with butter.
— Trudy Williams
Shannonville, Ontario

1 package (1/4 ounce) active dry yeast
1/4 cup warm water (110° to 115°)
3/4 cup warm milk (110° to 115°)
1/2 cup sugar
1/4 cup butter, melted
1-1/4 teaspoons salt
1 teaspoon ground cinnamon
1/2 teaspoon ground nutmeg
1/4 teaspoon ground cloves
1 egg
1 egg yolk
3-1/2 to 4 cups all-purpose flour
1/2 cup dried currants *or* raisins
1/4 cup chopped mixed candied peel
GLAZE:
2 tablespoons sugar
2 tablespoons water
ICING:
1/2 cup confectioners' sugar
2 teaspoons water

In a large mixing bowl, dissolve yeast in warm water. Add the milk, sugar, butter, salt, cinnamon, nutmeg, cloves, egg, egg yolk and 2 cups flour. Beat until smooth. Stir in the currants, candied peel and enough of the remaining flour to form a soft dough.

Turn onto a floured surface; knead until smooth and elastic, about 6-8 minutes. Place in a greased bowl, turning once to grease top. Cover and let rise in a warm place until doubled, about 1 hour.

Punch dough down. Turn onto a lightly floured surface; divide into 18 pieces. Shape each into a roll. Place 2 in. apart on greased baking sheets. Cover and let rise until doubled, about 30 minutes.

Bake at 400° for 12-15 minutes or until golden brown. Meanwhile, for glaze, combine sugar and water in small saucepan. Cook and stir over medium heat until sugar is dissolved. Place wire racks over waxed paper; place buns on racks. Brush with warm glaze; cool.

For icing, combine confectioners' sugar and water in a small bowl. Transfer to a small resealable plastic bag; cut a small hole in a corner of bag. Pipe a cross on top of each bun. **Yield:** 1-1/2 dozen.

Sausage-Filled Crepes

(Pictured on page 141)

I first made these hearty crepes 30 years ago when my children were young.
It's still one of their favorites and is always requested on special occasions.
—Karen Collins, Westminster, Colorado

3 eggs
1 cup milk
1 tablespoon canola oil
1 cup all-purpose flour
FILLING:
   1 pound bulk pork sausage
1/4 cup chopped onion
   1 package (3 ounces) cream
      cheese, cubed
1/2 cup shredded cheddar cheese
1/4 teaspoon dried marjoram
1/2 cup sour cream
1/4 cup butter, softened
Minced fresh parsley

In a small mixing bowl, combine the eggs, milk and oil. Add flour and mix well. Cover and refrigerate for 1 hour.

Heat a lightly greased 8-in. nonstick skillet; pour 3 tablespoons batter into the center of skillet. Lift and tilt pan to coat bottom evenly. Cook until top appears dry; turn and cook 15-20 seconds longer. Remove to a wire rack. Repeat with remaining batter, greasing skillet as needed. When cool, stack crepes with waxed paper or paper towels in between.

For filling, in a large skillet, cook the sausage and onion over medium heat until meat is no longer pink; drain. Add the cheeses and marjoram. Cook and stir until the cheese is melted.

Spoon about 2 tablespoons of filling down the center of each crepe. Roll up and place seam side down in a greased 13-in. x 9-in. x 2-in. baking dish.

Cover and bake at 375° for 40 minutes. Combine sour cream and butter; spoon over crepes. Bake, uncovered, for 5 minutes or until edges are lightly browned and sauce is heated through. Sprinkle with parsley. **Yield:** 8 servings.

Champagne Punch

(Pictured on page 141)

A blend of four fruit juices pairs well with bubbly champagne in this
party-pleasing punch. Add a strawberry garnish if desired for a festive touch.
—Amy Short, Lesage, West Virginia

4 cups orange juice
1 cup ruby red grapefruit juice
1/2 cup lemon juice
1/2 cup lime juice
2 bottles (750 milliliters *each*)
   champagne, chilled

In a 2-qt. pitcher, combine the juices. Refrigerate until chilled. Just before serving, stir in champagne. Serve in champagne glasses. **Yield:** 12 servings (3 quarts).

Granola Yogurt Parfaits

(Pictured at right)

I love this recipe because the granola and flavored yogurt can be made the day before. The next morning, just roll out of bed and assemble the parfaits in pretty glasses!
—*Laureen Pittman*
Riverside, California

4 cups (32 ounces) plain yogurt
1/2 cup orange juice
1/4 cup honey
1-1/2 teaspoons vanilla extract
4 teaspoons grated orange peel

GRANOLA:

1-1/2 cups old-fashioned oats
3/4 cup chopped walnuts
3 tablespoons dark brown sugar
3 tablespoons honey
2 tablespoons canola oil
1 teaspoon vanilla extract
1/4 teaspoon salt
3/4 cup dried cranberries

Line a strainer with four layers of cheesecloth or one coffee filter and place over a bowl. Place yogurt in prepared strainer; cover yogurt with edges of cheesecloth. Refrigerate for 8 hours or overnight.

Remove yogurt from cheesecloth and discard liquid from bowl. In another bowl, combine the yogurt, orange juice, honey, vanilla and orange peel. Cover and refrigerate until serving.

For granola, in a large bowl, combine oats and walnuts. Combine the brown sugar, honey, oil, vanilla and salt; pour over oat mixture and toss to coat. Transfer to a greased 15-in. x 10-in. x 1-in. baking pan.

Bake at 300° for 25-30 minutes or until golden brown, stirring twice. Cool on a wire rack. Transfer to a large bowl; stir in cranberries. Store in an airtight container.

To serve, alternate layers of yogurt and granola in six parfait glasses. **Yield:** 6 servings.

Turkey Sausage Patties

(Pictured on page 141)

I developed this recipe as a way to deter my husband from eating pork sausage.
The mixture also works well for making meatballs and burgers.
— *Yvonne Woodruff, Sacramento, California*

2 eggs
2/3 cup seasoned bread crumbs
1 small onion, finely chopped
2 tablespoons Worcestershire sauce
3 garlic cloves, minced
2 teaspoons garlic salt
2 teaspoons dried thyme
2 teaspoons ground cumin
1/2 teaspoon crushed red pepper flakes
1/2 teaspoon pepper
1/8 teaspoon ground nutmeg
2 pounds lean ground turkey
5 teaspoons canola oil, *divided*

In a large bowl, combine the first 11 ingredients. Crumble turkey over mixture and mix well. Shape into thirty 2-1/2-in. patties.

Heat 1 teaspoon oil in a large skillet over medium heat. Cook patties in batches over medium heat for 2-3 minutes on each side or until meat is no longer pink, using remaining oil as needed. **Yield:** 2-1/2 dozen.

Mixed Fruit with Lemon-Basil Dressing

(Pictured on page 141)

A slightly savory dressing really complements the sweet fruit in this salad. I also use the dressing on greens.
— *Dixie Terry, Goreville, Illinois*

2 tablespoons lemon juice
1/2 teaspoon sugar
1/4 teaspoon salt
1/4 teaspoon ground mustard
1/8 teaspoon onion powder
Dash pepper
6 tablespoons olive oil
4-1/2 teaspoons minced fresh basil
1 cup cubed fresh pineapple
1 cup sliced fresh strawberries
1 cup sliced peeled kiwifruit
1 cup cubed seedless watermelon
1 cup fresh blueberries
1 cup fresh raspberries

In a blender, combine the lemon juice, sugar, salt, mustard, onion powder and pepper; cover and process for 5 seconds. While processing, gradually add the oil in a steady stream. Stir in the basil.

In a large bowl, combine the fruit. Drizzle with dressing and toss to coat. Refrigerate until serving. **Yield:** 8 servings.

Raspberry-Rhubarb Coffee Cake

(Pictured at right)

Sweet raspberries and tart rhubarb are perfect partners in this classic coffee cake. I enjoy a piece alongside a glass of milk for a mid-morning snack.
—Carol Ross, Anchorage, Alaska

1 cup sugar
1/3 cup cornstarch
3 cups chopped fresh *or* frozen rhubarb
1 cup fresh *or* frozen raspberries, mashed
2 teaspoons lemon juice

BATTER:
3/4 cup butter-flavored shortening
1-1/2 cups sugar
3 eggs
3 cups all-purpose flour
1-1/2 teaspoons baking powder
3/4 teaspoon baking soda
1-1/2 cups (12 ounces) sour cream

TOPPING:
1/2 cup all-purpose flour
1/2 cup sugar
1/2 cup quick-cooking oats
1/2 teaspoon ground cinnamon
1/4 cup cold butter
1/2 cup flaked coconut
1/2 cup chopped walnuts

In a large saucepan, combine sugar and cornstarch; stir in rhubarb and raspberries. Bring to a boil over medium heat; cook for 2 minutes or until thickened, stirring constantly. Remove from the heat. Stir in lemon juice. Cool slightly.

In a large mixing bowl, cream shortening and sugar. Beat in eggs. Combine the flour, baking powder and baking soda; add to creamed mixture alternately with sour cream. Spread two-thirds of the batter into a greased 13-in. x 9-in. x 2-in. baking dish. Top with rhubarb mixture. Drop remaining batter by tablespoonfuls over filling.

In a small bowl, combine the flour, sugar, oats and cinnamon. Cut in butter until crumbly. Stir in coconut and walnuts. Sprinkle over batter.

Bake at 350° for 60-65 minutes or until a toothpick inserted near the center comes out clean. Cool on a wire rack. **Yield:** 12 servings.

Chocolate Chip Pancakes

These feather-light pancakes dotted with chocolate chips are one of my family's favorite breakfasts.
For even more chocolate flavor, I sometimes stir 2 tablespoons baking cocoa into the batter.
—Michelle Harbour, Lebanon, Tennessee

1 cup all-purpose flour
1/2 cup confectioners' sugar
2 teaspoons baking powder
1/4 teaspoon salt
1 egg, lightly beaten
2/3 cup milk
1/4 cup butter, melted
1/4 cup miniature semisweet
   chocolate chips
Chocolate syrup and whipped
   cream, optional

In a small bowl, combine the flour, confectioners' sugar, baking powder and salt. Combine the egg, milk and butter; stir into dry ingredients just until moistened. Stir in the chocolate chips.

Pour batter by 1/4 cupfuls onto a greased hot griddle; turn when bubbles form on top. Cook until the second side is golden brown. Serve with chocolate syrup and whipped cream if desired. **Yield:** 8 pancakes.

Creamy Fruit Dip in Lemon Shells

Since my husband and I host most of our family's holiday gatherings, I'm always
trying new recipes. Guests especially enjoy this creamy, citrus fruit dip.
—Erin Martinez, Kendall Park, New Jersey

4 ounces cream cheese,
   softened
1 cup (8 ounces) sour cream
3 tablespoons lemonade
   concentrate
1 tablespoon honey
2 to 3 medium lemons
Assorted fresh fruit

In a small mixing bowl, beat the cream cheese, sour cream, lemonade concentrate and honey until smooth. Cover and refrigerate for at least 1 hour.

Cut lemons in half lengthwise; scoop out pulp (discard or save for another use). Spoon dip into lemon shells. Serve with fresh fruit. **Yield:** 1-3/4 cups.

LOVELY LEMON SHELLS

TO MAKE the lemon shells for the Creamy Fruit Dip (above), gently squeeze the juice from each lemon half. With a sharp knife, cut the membrane at each end to loosen pulp from the shell. With your fingertips, pull up the membrane at one end and pull away from the shell.

Easy-Going Easter Flowers

(Pictured at right)

AFTER the bleak days of winter, a burst of color on your Easter buffet table is a welcome sight.

You don't need formal training in flower arranging to design the informal arrangement shown here.

Like most folks, your cupboards are overflowing with glass vases. Search out straight-sided ones in assorted shapes and sizes.

Wrap double-sided tape around the middle of each vase. Cut a band of sheet or reindeer moss to fit around each vase and place over the tape.

Wrap natural raffia around the center of the moss; tie ends in a knot or small bow. Fill the vases with water.

Because the height of centerpieces is not a concern on buffet tables, we chose to fill the moss-covered vessels with long-stemmed runnuculus.

Blooming between March and July, runnuculus have a long vase life and come in spectacular shades.

EASTER *Gatherings*

Elegant Easter Feast

DON'T have plans to head somewhere warm for Easter? Not to worry. You can take your taste buds on a flavorful trip!

For folks living in cold climates, it's time to head outdoors and make Marinated Grilled Lamb. The mild, Greek-style marinade infuses every moist and tender slice.

Loaded with plenty of produce, Roasted Asparagus with Leeks and Mashed Parsnips 'n' Potatoes are no ordinary sides.

Famished families agree a meal is only complete when people pass a basket of homemade bread like Dill Loaves. (All recipes are shown at right.)

Round out the meal with Mediterranean-inspired dishes like Olive Tapenade, Stuffed Eggplant Dip, Hearty Tabbouleh and Tuscan Tossed Salad.

LOVELY LAMB DINNER

(Pictured above)

Marinated Grilled Lamb (p. 158)

Mashed Parsnips 'n' Potatoes (p. 154)

Roasted Asparagus with Leeks (p. 154)

Dill Loaves (p. 156)

EASTER DINNER TIMELINE

A Few Weeks Before:
- Prepare two grocery lists—one for non-perishable items to purchase now and one for perishable items to purchase a few days before Easter.
- Order a leg of lamb from your butcher.
- Bake Dill Loaves; cool. Freeze in heavy-duty resealable plastic bags.

Two Days Before:
- Buy remaining grocery items, including the leg of lamb.
- Set the table.
- If desired, make the Simple Spring Centerpiece on page 159.

The Day Before:
- Prepare Hearty Tabbouleh; cover and refrigerate.
- Dice the green pepper, celery, onion and carrot for the Stuffed Eggplant Dip; cover tightly and chill.
- Make the Olive Tapenade. Store in an airtight container in the refrigerator.
- Bake the Pineapple Cheesecake; chill.
- For Tuscan Tossed Salad, make the dressing; cover and refrigerate. Bake the croutons; let cool and store in a resealable plastic bag at room temperature.

Easter Day:
- In the morning, thaw Dill Loaves at room temperature.
- Marinate the leg of lamb for Marinated Grilled Lamb.
- Peel and cut potatoes and parsnips for Mashed Parsnips 'n' Potatoes. Place in a bowl of cold water; cover and chill.
- Make the topping for Pineapple Cheesecake. Remove sides of springform pan; spread topping over cheesecake. Chill.
- Assemble the Tuscan Tossed Salad; cover and refrigerate.
- A couple of hours before dinner, prepare the Stuffed Eggplant Dip; cover and chill. Brush the eggplant shells with lemon; tightly wrap with plastic wrap and refrigerate.
- Just before guests arrive, reheat the eggplant dip; spoon into eggplant shells and serve with pita bread wedges. Set out Olive Tapenade and baguette slices.
- Grill the leg of lamb.
- Boil the parsnips and potatoes and assemble Mashed Parsnips 'n' Potatoes.
- Prepare the Roasted Asparagus with Leeks.
- Set out Hearty Tabbouleh and Tuscan Tossed Salad.
- Slice Dill Loaves and serve with butter.
- Serve the Pineapple Cheesecake and coffee for dessert.

Pineapple Cheesecake

(Pictured at right)

*With its make-ahead convenience,
this fruit-topped cheesecake
often appears on my holiday menus.
It never fails to impress guests.*
—*Lorraine Caland*
Thunder Bay, Ontario

1-1/4 cups graham cracker crumbs
1/4 cup sugar
1/3 cup butter, melted
FILLING:
   3 packages (8 ounces *each*)
     cream cheese, softened
1-1/2 cups (12 ounces) sour cream
   3/4 cup sweetened condensed
     milk
   1/4 cup sugar
   5 eggs, *separated*
   3 teaspoons vanilla extract
   3 to 4 teaspoons grated orange
     peel
TOPPING:
   1/4 cup sugar
   4 tablespoons cold water,
     divided
   1 can (20 ounces) crushed
     pineapple, drained
   1 tablespoon cornstarch

In a small bowl, combine the graham cracker crumbs, sugar and butter. Press onto the bottom of a greased 10-in. springform pan; set aside.

In a large mixing bowl, beat the cream cheese, sour cream, milk and sugar until smooth. Beat in egg yolks on low speed just until blended. Add vanilla and orange peel; beat just until blended. In a small mixing bowl, beat egg whites until stiff peaks form; fold into cream cheese mixture. Pour over the crust.

Place pan on a baking sheet. Bake at 325° for 70-75 minutes or until center is almost set. Cool on a wire rack for 10 minutes. Carefully run a knife around edge of pan to loosen; cool 1 hour longer. Cover and refrigerate for at least 6 hours or overnight.

For topping, combine sugar and 2 tablespoons water in a small saucepan. Bring to a boil over medium heat; cook for 2 minutes. Stir in pineapple. In a small bowl, combine cornstarch and remaining water until smooth; stir into pineapple mixture. Bring to a boil; cook and stir for 2 minutes or until thickened. Cool completely.

Remove sides of springform pan; spread topping over cheesecake. Store in the refrigerator. **Yield:** 12 servings.

Mashed Parsnips 'n' Potatoes

(Pictured on page 151)

*Parsnips add a slightly sweet flavor to mashed potatoes in this recipe
from our Test Kitchen. Flecks of thyme provide a bit of color.*

   5 large potatoes (about 2-1/2
      pounds), peeled and
      quartered
   7 medium parsnips, peeled and
      cut into 1/2-inch slices
 1/2 cup half-and-half cream
 1/4 cup butter, cubed
   1 tablespoon minced fresh
      thyme *or* 1/4 teaspoon dried
      thyme
   1 teaspoon salt
   1 teaspoon grated lemon peel

Place potatoes and parsnips in a Dutch
oven and cover with water. Bring to a
boil. Reduce heat; cover and cook for
15-20 minutes or until tender. Drain.

Place vegetables in a large mixing bowl. Add the
cream, butter, thyme, salt and lemon peel; beat until
smooth. **Yield:** 10 servings.

Parsnip Snippet

PARSNIPS are root vegetables that resemble a white
or pale yellow carrot. They add a sweetness and nutty flavor to recipes.

Purchase parsnips that are free from cracks and blemishes. Avoid large parsnips because they may be tough.

You can store unwashed parsnips in a perforated plastic bag in the refrigerator crisper drawer for up to 2
weeks. Before using, wash, trim ends and root tops; peel.

Roasted Asparagus with Leeks

(Pictured on page 151)

*No vegetable says "Spring!" quite like asparagus. In this recipe, our home economists
combine the pretty green spears with leeks. Crushed red pepper adds a little zest.*

   3 pounds fresh asparagus,
      trimmed
  12 medium leeks (white portion
      only), halved lengthwise
4-1/2 teaspoons olive oil
1-1/2 teaspoons dill weed
 1/2 teaspoon salt

 1/2 teaspoon crushed red pepper flakes
 1/4 teaspoon pepper

Place asparagus and leeks in an ungreased 15-in. x 10-in. x
1-in. baking pan. Combine the remaining ingredients; pour
over vegetables.

Bake at 400° for 20-25 minutes or until tender, stirring
occasionally. **Yield:** 12 servings.

Tuscan Tossed Salad

(Pictured at right)

*I like to let this salad sit awhile
to allow the flavors to blend.
Serve it in a pretty, clear trifle dish
and you'll have a stunning
side dish on the table.*
—Elaine Sweet, Dallas, Texas

1 loaf (1 pound) focaccia bread,
  cut into 1-inch cubes
1 tablespoon plus 1/4 cup olive
  oil, *divided*
1/2 cup balsamic vinegar
1/3 cup minced fresh basil
  4 anchovy fillets, rinsed and
  chopped
  2 garlic cloves, minced
1/4 teaspoon salt
1/4 teaspoon pepper
  1 package (5 ounces) spring
  mix salad greens
  3 large yellow *or* red tomatoes,
  seeded and chopped
  3 cups grape tomatoes
  2 medium cucumbers, peeled,
  seeded and diced
1/2 cup pitted Greek olives,
  halved
1/2 cup chopped celery
1/2 cup chopped red onion
  1 jar (7 ounces) roasted sweet
  red peppers, drained and
  sliced

Place bread cubes in a single layer on a baking sheet; drizzle with 1 tablespoon oil. Bake at 400° for 5-7 minutes or until lightly toasted. Cool on a wire rack.

For dressing, in a jar with a tight-fitting lid, combine the vinegar, basil, anchovies, garlic, salt, pepper and remaining oil; shake well. In a large bowl, combine the greens, tomatoes, cucumbers, olives, celery, onion and red peppers.

In a 3-qt. trifle bowl or deep salad bowl, layer a third of the bread cubes and a third of the greens mixture; drizzle with a third of the dressing. Repeat layers twice. Cover and refrigerate until serving. **Yield:** 16 servings.

Dill Loaves

(Pictured on page 151)

I've been depending on this recipe for more than 20 years.
I often shape the dough into rolls and use them for sandwiches.
— Barbara Jean Robo, Joplin, Montana

2 packages (1/4 ounce *each*)
   active dry yeast
1 cup warm water (110° to
   115°)
2 cups (16 ounces) 4% cottage
   cheese
2 tablespoons butter
1/4 cup finely chopped onion
4 teaspoons dill seed
2 teaspoons salt
2 eggs
5 to 5-1/2 cups all-purpose
   flour

In a large mixing bowl, dissolve yeast in warm water. In a small saucepan, heat cottage cheese and butter to 110°-115°; add to yeast mixture. Add onion, dill seed, salt, eggs and 4 cups flour; beat until smooth. Stir in enough remaining flour to form a firm dough (dough will be sticky).

Turn onto a floured surface; knead until smooth and elastic, about 6-8 minutes. Place in a greased bowl, turning once to grease top. Cover and let rise in a warm place until doubled, about 1 hour.

Turn onto a lightly floured surface; divide dough in half. Shape into two round loaves. Place on greased baking sheets. Cover and let rise until doubled, about 45 minutes.

Bake at 350° for 30-35 minutes or until golden brown. Remove from pans to wire racks to cool. **Yield:** 2 loaves (9 slices each).

Hearty Tabbouleh

This traditional Turkish bulgur salad from our Test Kitchen is filled with tomatoes,
green onions and cucumber. It's nicely seasoned with fresh mint and lemon juice.

1-1/4 cups bulgur
1-1/2 cups boiling water
1 small cucumber, diced
1 large tomato, seeded and
   diced
4 green onions, sliced
1 cup (4 ounces) crumbled feta
   cheese
1 can (2-1/4 ounces) sliced ripe
   olives, drained
1/4 cup lemon juice
1/4 cup olive oil

2 tablespoons minced fresh parsley
1 tablespoon minced fresh mint
1 tablespoon grated lemon peel
2 garlic cloves, minced
1 teaspoon salt
1/2 teaspoon pepper

Place bulgur in a small bowl; stir in water. Cover and let stand for 30 minutes or until water is absorbed.

Drain the bulgur and squeeze dry; cool completely. Transfer to a large bowl; stir in the remaining ingredients. Cover and refrigerate for at least 1 hour before serving. **Yield:** 8 servings.

Stuffed Eggplant Dip

(Pictured at right)

This dip is popular with family and friends, especially when we can feature our homegrown vegetables. Serving it in eggplant shells makes for a fun presentation.
— Marcia Marcoux
Charlton, Massachusetts

1 large eggplant
1 tablespoon lemon juice
1 medium green pepper, diced
2 celery ribs, diced
1 medium onion, diced
1 medium carrot, diced
1/4 cup olive oil
2 large tomatoes, chopped
2 tablespoons minced fresh cilantro
1 tablespoon red wine vinegar
1 garlic clove, minced
1 teaspoon salt
1/4 teaspoon dried basil
1/8 teaspoon cayenne pepper
Pita breads, cut into wedges

Cut eggplant in half lengthwise. Remove pulp, leaving a 1/2-in. shell. Brush inside of shell with lemon juice; set aside.

Place eggplant pulp in a steamer basket; place in a saucepan over 1 in. of water. Bring to a boil; cover and steam for 5-8 minutes or until tender. Set aside.

In a large skillet, saute the green pepper, celery, onion and carrot in oil for 4-6 minutes or until tender. Stir in the tomatoes, cilantro, vinegar, garlic, salt, basil, cayenne and eggplant pulp. Cook and stir over medium heat for 10-15 minutes or until thickened.

Spoon the dip into the eggplant shells. Serve with pita wedges. **Yield:** 3 cups.

Marinated Grilled Lamb

(Pictured on page 150)

It's fun to fire up the grill on Easter, especially if you live in a cold climate!
A mild marinade from our home economists wonderfully flavors the lamb.

1 boneless leg of lamb (3 to 4 pounds), trimmed
1/4 cup lemon juice
1/4 cup dry white wine *or* chicken broth
3 tablespoons olive oil
8 garlic cloves, minced
3 tablespoons minced fresh rosemary
1 tablespoon minced fresh thyme
1 tablespoon minced fresh oregano
1 teaspoon salt
1/2 teaspoon coarsely ground pepper
1 sprig fresh rosemary
Additional salt and pepper

If leg of lamb is tied, untie it. In a resealable plastic bag, combine the lemon juice, wine or broth, oil, garlic, rosemary, thyme, oregano, salt and pepper; add lamb. Seal bag and turn to coat. Refrigerate for 4 hours.

Prepare grill for indirect medium heat. Remove lamb from marinade; discard marinade. Place rosemary sprig on lamb; roll up and tie with kitchen string, leaving a small section of the sprig exposed. Sprinkle with additional salt and pepper.

Grill lamb, covered, over indirect medium heat for 1-1/2 to 2 hours or until meat reaches desired doneness (for medium-rare, a meat thermometer should read 145°; medium, 160°; well-done, 170°). Remove rosemary sprig. Let meat stand for 10 minutes before slicing. **Yield:** 10 servings.

Olive Tapenade

To tie into the Mediterranean feel of this Easter dinner, our home economists created an easy appetizer.
The salty tapenade pairs well with the toasted baguette slices.

1 tablespoon capers, drained
2 teaspoons olive oil
1 teaspoon minced fresh oregano *or* 1/4 teaspoon dried oregano
1 teaspoon lemon juice
1/2 teaspoon anchovy paste
1/8 teaspoon pepper

20 Greek olives, pitted and finely chopped
15 slices French bread baguette (1/4 inch thick), toasted

In a small bowl, combine the first six ingredients. Add the olives and toss to coat. Serve with the toasted baguette slices. **Yield:** 15 appetizers.

Simple Spring Centerpiece

(Pictured at right)

YOU DON'T need to spend a fortune—or be a professional florist—to create a stunning centerpiece for your formal Easter dinner.

For an eye-catching arrangement, all you need are a few seasonal items and a container that you already have on hand.

In the pretty picture at right, we gathered enough parrot tulips to fill an everyday enamel container. Cut and arrange the stems so that they slightly spill over the sides. Then we tucked in some simple pussy willow stems.

With the right amount of care, your display can last for several days. See the tips in Tending to Tulips, below.

TENDING TO TULIPS

TULIPS can last from three to seven days if you follow these guidelines.

- Purchase tulips with colorful, closed buds and healthy green stems and leaves.
- At home, cut off at least 1/2 inch of the stems on an angle with a sharp nonserrated knife. (Cut off the firm, white base of the stem if not already done.) Place tulips in cold water. Do not refrigerate.
- Tulips prefer cool room temperatures, so keep them away from sources of heat, including sunlight.
- Unlike many other flowers, tulips continue to grow once cut. To keep the shape of your arrangement, trim the stems daily.
- Add fresh water every day.

Side Dishes Celebrate Spring

THINK SPRING and thoughts of budding trees and blooming flowers probably come to mind. But what about the bounty of fresh spring produce?

Tender asparagus stalks...sweet carrots...crisp peas...succulent beets...assorted baby greens. Showcase the spring's best with an Easter menu that incorporates deliciously simple side dishes.

A platter of eye-catching Herb-Buttered Baby Carrots captures the essence of the season by adding color and rustic charm to the table.

Add new life to your Easter fare by introducing guests to two innovative dishes. The slightly sweet, mellow flavor of Leek Potato Pancakes puts a delightful spin on a traditional favorite, while Couscous Salad with Lemon Vinaigrette treats guests to bold, wonderful flavors. (All recipes are shown at right.)

FRESH FLAVORS
(Clockwise from bottom)

Herb-Buttered Baby Carrots (p. 166)

Couscous Salad with
Lemon Vinaigrette (p. 168)

Leek Potato Pancakes (p. 162)

Apple Broccoli Salad

Everyone is sure to eat their broccoli when it's dressed up in this tasty salad.
Each bite has plenty of crunch and just the right amount of sweetness.
—Mary Javor, Hastings, Michigan

4 cups fresh broccoli florets
1 medium red apple, chopped
1 medium green apple, chopped
1 cup halved seedless red grapes
1/2 cup golden raisins
1/2 cup chopped pecans
1/3 cup thinly sliced red onion

POPPY SEED DRESSING:
1 cup canola oil
3/4 cup sugar
1/3 cup cider vinegar
2 tablespoons poppy seeds
1-1/2 tablespoons lemon juice
1 teaspoon salt
1 teaspoon ground mustard

In a large bowl, combine the broccoli, apples, grapes, raisins, pecans and onion. In a jar with a tight-fitting lid, combine the dressing ingredients; shake until sugar is dissolved. Pour over salad and toss to coat. Cover and refrigerate for at least 1 hour before serving. **Yield:** 10 servings.

Leek Potato Pancakes

(Pictured on page 161)

My great-grandmother brought this recipe over from England, where they enjoyed leeks immensely. Flecks of green add color and interest to this unique side dish.
—Suzanne Kesel, Cohocton, New York

1/2 pound russet potatoes, peeled and quartered
2 pounds medium leeks (white portion only), thinly sliced
4 eggs, lightly beaten
1/2 cup dry bread crumbs
1/3 cup grated Parmesan cheese
1 teaspoon salt
1/4 teaspoon pepper
1/4 cup canola oil, *divided*
6 tablespoons sour cream

Place potatoes in a large saucepan and cover with water. Bring to a boil. Reduce heat; cover and cook for 20 minutes, adding leeks during the last 3 minutes. Drain.

Transfer potatoes to a large bowl; mash with eggs, bread crumbs, Parmesan cheese, salt and pepper. Stir in leeks. Cover and refrigerate for 1 hour.

Heat 1 tablespoon oil in a large nonstick skillet over medium heat. Drop batter by 1/4 cupfuls into oil. Fry in batches until golden brown on both sides, using remaining oil as needed. Drain on paper towels. Serve with sour cream. **Yield:** 12 pancakes.

Garlic Fennel Bisque

(Pictured at right)

Featuring a subtle garlic-like flavor, this thick, creamy bisque makes an elegant first course for any special-occasion meal.
—Janet Ondrich, Thamesville, Ontario

>   4 cups water
> 2-1/2 cups half-and-half cream
>   24 garlic cloves, peeled and halved
>   3 medium fennel bulbs, cut into 1/2-inch pieces
>   2 tablespoons chopped fennel fronds
>   1/2 teaspoon salt
>   1/8 teaspoon pepper
>   1/2 cup pine nuts, toasted

In a Dutch oven, bring the water, cream and garlic to a boil. Reduce heat; cover and simmer for 15 minutes or until garlic is very soft. Add fennel and fennel fronds; cover and simmer 15 minutes longer or until fennel is very soft.

Cool slightly. In a blender, process the soup in batches until blended. Return all to the pan. Season with salt and pepper; heat through. Sprinkle each serving with toasted pine nuts. **Yield:** 14 servings.

FENNEL FACTS

FENNEL has a celery-like texture and a sweet anise-like flavor. When buying fennel, look for creamy white bulbs, firm straight stalks and bright green fronds. Avoid withered bulbs or those with brown spots or yellowing. Smaller bulbs are more tender. Store unwashed fennel in the refrigerator crisper drawer for up to 4 days.

Just before using, wash in cold water. Trim off fronds and stalks. Trim base from bulb; cut in half and remove core. Cut, slice or chop the bulb and stalks. Use the fronds as you would use a minced herb or for a garnish.

One fennel bulb (about 10-1/2 ounces) equals about 2 cups sliced.

Chilled Minty Green Beans

You've never tasted green beans like these before. The subtle mint
flavor really perks up this delightfully different salad.
— Patricia Kile, Elizabethtown, Pennsylvania

3 **pounds fresh green beans,**
   trimmed
1/2 **cup red wine vinegar**
1/2 **cup canola oil**
1/3 **cup minced fresh mint**
3 **garlic cloves, minced**
3/4 **teaspoon salt**

Place beans in a Dutch oven and cover with water. Bring to a boil; cover and cook for 5-7 minutes or until crisp-tender. Drain and place in a large bowl.

  In a small bowl, whisk the vinegar, oil, mint, garlic and salt. Pour over beans and toss to coat. Cover and refrigerate until chilled. **Yield:** 13 servings.

Kale with Portobellos

When friends are invited over for dinner, they're quick to request this easy mushroom
dish. The crisp-tender kale and soft portobellos go together wonderfully.
— Karen Rietenbach, Santa Rosa Beach, Florida

1 **pound fresh kale**
3 **large portobello mushrooms,**
  sliced
1 **medium onion, chopped**
2 **garlic cloves, minced**
2 **tablespoons olive oil**
1 **can (15-1/2 ounces) great**
  northern beans, rinsed and
  drained
1/4 **teaspoon sugar**
1/4 **teaspoon salt**

Cut out and discard the thick vein from each kale leaf. Coarsely chop kale. In a Dutch oven, bring 1 in. of water to a boil. Add kale; cover and cook for 10-15 minutes or until tender.

  Meanwhile, in a large skillet, saute the mushrooms, onion and garlic in oil until tender. Drain kale and return to the pan. Stir in the mushroom mixture, beans, sugar and salt; heat through. **Yield:** 8 servings.

Do You Know Your Portobello?

A PORTOBELLO is really just a large cremini mushroom. The diameter can be as big as 6 inches.

  Portobellos have an earthy, meaty flavor with a firm texture. Look for ones that are plump and firm, avoiding those that are limp, dry, shriveled or slippery.

  At home, remove the portobellos from their wrapping; place on a tray and cover with a paper towel. Store in the refrigerator and use within 5 days.

Swiss Angel Hair 'n' Asparagus

(Pictured at right)

An ideal accompaniment for ham or pork, this dish stars tender angel hair pasta coated in a creamy sauce. It's accented by colorful pieces of asparagus.
—Michele Cornish
Blairstown, New Jersey

12 ounces uncooked angel hair pasta
1 pound fresh asparagus, trimmed and cut into 2-inch pieces
1/2 pound sliced fresh mushrooms
1 teaspoon minced chives
3 tablespoons butter
2 tablespoons all-purpose flour
2-1/4 teaspoons salt-free seasoning blend
1/2 teaspoon salt
2-1/4 cups milk
1-1/2 cups (6 ounces) shredded Swiss cheese
Grated Parmesan cheese, optional

Cook pasta according to package directions. Meanwhile, place asparagus in a steamer basket; place in a large saucepan over 1 in. of water. Bring to a boil; cover and steam for 3-5 minutes or until crisp-tender.

In a large saucepan, saute mushrooms and chives in butter until tender. Stir in the flour, seasoning blend and salt; gradually add milk. Bring to a boil; cook and stir for 1-2 minutes or until thickened. Add the Swiss cheese; cook and stir until cheese is melted.

Drain pasta and place in a large bowl. Add asparagus and cheese sauce; toss to coat. Garnish with Parmesan cheese if desired. **Yield:** 10 servings.

New Potatoes in Lemon-Dill Sauce

*The refreshing flavors of lemon and dill really shine through in
the rich, creamy sauce that coats the small red potatoes.*
—Dannealle Misson, Pembina, North Dakota

12 small red potatoes (1 pound)
 2 fresh dill sprigs
 2 tablespoons butter
 1 tablespoon all-purpose flour
1/2 cup half-and-half cream
 2 tablespoons snipped fresh dill
 1 tablespoon lemon juice
1/8 teaspoon salt

Place potatoes and dill sprigs in a large saucepan; cover with water. Bring to a boil. Reduce heat; cover and cook for 15-20 minutes or until tender. Drain, reserving 1/2 cup cooking liquid. Transfer potatoes to a serving bowl; keep warm.

In a small saucepan, melt butter. Stir in flour until smooth; gradually add cream and reserved cooking liquid. Bring to a boil; cook and stir for 2 minutes or until thickened. Add the snipped dill, lemon juice and salt; pour over potatoes and toss to coat. **Yield:** 4 servings.

Herb-Buttered Baby Carrots

(Pictured on page 160)

*A mild herb flavor, tender texture and beautiful color make this side dish a wonderful choice for any spring
celebration. Best of all, the herb butter can be used on other vegetables and poultry, too.*
—Sandra Corey, Caldwell, Idaho

1/2 cup butter, melted
 1 garlic clove, minced
 1 teaspoon dried parsley flakes
1/2 teaspoon dried basil
1/4 teaspoon *each* dried oregano, marjoram and thyme
1/4 teaspoon dried rosemary, crushed
 1 pound fresh baby carrots, trimmed

In a large bowl, combine the butter, garlic and herbs. Add carrots and stir until coated. Transfer to a greased 1-1/2-qt. baking dish.

Cover and bake at 375° for 50-60 minutes or until tender, stirring once. **Yield:** 6 servings.

COLOR YOUR MENU WITH RAINBOW CARROTS

FOR THE PHOTO of Herb-Buttered Baby Carrots on page 160, we used mini rainbow carrots instead of the traditional orange variety. Available at specialty grocery stores and farmer's markets, rainbow carrots are packed with vitamins and anitoxidants.

Sweet 'n' Sour Onions

(Pictured at right)

If you love onions and want to serve something deliciously different at your next gathering, this recipe is for you. The simple and wonderful combination is something I serve on a regular basis.
— Penny Vanderhoff, Ellijay, Georgia

  3 cups water
2-2/3 cups green onions (white
     portion only)
  1/4 cup butter, cubed
  1/4 cup minced fresh parsley
  1/4 cup white wine vinegar
  4 teaspoons honey
  1/2 teaspoon salt
  1/4 teaspoon pepper

In a large saucepan, bring water to a boil. Add onions; cover and boil for 3 minutes. Drain and immediately place onions in ice water. Drain and pat dry.

In a large skillet, saute onions in butter until tender. Stir in the parsley, vinegar, honey, salt and pepper; heat through. **Yield:** 4 servings.

Couscous Salad with Lemon Vinaigrette

(Pictured on page 161)

The lemon vinaigrette is a nice contrast to the sweet basil, tart cherries and spicy arugula that star in my colorful salad. I like to garnish it with a lemon wedge.
—Maria Breiner, Schwenksville, Pennsylvania

2 cups reduced-sodium chicken broth
1 tablespoon plus 1/2 cup olive oil, *divided*
1 package (10 ounces) couscous
2 cups fresh baby arugula *or* spinach
3/4 cup crumbled feta cheese
1/2 cup dried cherries
1/4 cup pine nuts, toasted
12 fresh basil leaves, thinly sliced

1/4 cup lemon juice
1-1/2 teaspoons salt
1 teaspoon pepper

In a small saucepan, bring broth and 1 tablespoon oil to a boil. Stir in couscous. Cover and remove from the heat; let stand for 5 minutes or until water is absorbed. Fluff with a fork. Transfer to a large bowl; cool.

Just before serving, add the arugula, feta cheese, cherries, pine nuts and basil. In a small bowl, whisk the lemon juice, salt, pepper and remaining oil. Pour over salad and toss to coat. **Yield:** 9 servings.

Dilled Leek Soup

My friend was lucky enough to get this recipe from a chef of a very popular Toronto restaurant. The original recipe called for blue cheese, but my friend and I discovered it is just as delicious with Parmesan.
—Agnes Ward, Stratford, Ontario

3 medium leeks (white portion only), chopped
2 large onions, chopped
1/3 cup butter, cubed
1 tablespoon Dijon mustard
4 cups chicken broth
4 cups cubed peeled potatoes
1/2 teaspoon dill weed
1/8 teaspoon white pepper
1/8 teaspoon ground nutmeg
1 cup half-and-half cream

1 tablespoon snipped fresh dill
Grated Parmesan cheese and additional nutmeg, optional

In a Dutch oven, saute leeks and onions in butter until tender. Stir in mustard. Add the broth, potatoes, dill weed, pepper and nutmeg. Bring to a boil. Reduce heat; cover and simmer for 20 minutes or until potatoes are tender.

Reduce heat to low. Stir in cream and fresh dill; heat through. Garnish with Parmesan cheese and additional nutmeg if desired. **Yield:** 12 servings (about 2 quarts).

Roasted Radishes

(Pictured at right)

Our Test Kitchen staff developed this surprisingly sweet, roasted side. Even those who aren't usually fond of radishes enjoy every bite.

2-1/4 **pounds radishes, trimmed and quartered**
3 **tablespoons olive oil**
1 **tablespoon minced fresh oregano** *or* 1 **teaspoon dried oregano**
1/4 **teaspoon salt**
1/8 **teaspoon pepper**

In a large bowl, combine all of the ingredients. Transfer to a greased 15-in. x 10-in. x 1-in. baking pan. Bake, uncovered, at 425° for 30 minutes or until radishes are crisp-tender, stirring once. **Yield:** 5 servings.

VEGETABLES TASTE OF SPRING

BELOW is a list of veggies that are typically in season during spring (depending on where you live). Make a medley of seasonal sides!

Artichokes
Asparagus
Avocadoes
Bok choy
Broccoli
Cabbage
Carrots
Cauliflower
Fennel

Green beans
Greens (kale, spinach, Swiss chard)
Kohlrabi
Leeks
Lettuce (arugula, radicchio, watercress)
New potatoes
Onions (green and sweet)
Peas (snow and snap)
Radishes
Rhubarb
Scallions
Turnips

Venetian Rice

I often serve this creamy rice with roasted turkey in lieu of mashed potatoes.
The addition of bright green peas adds a pretty touch.
—*Nita Cinquina, Surprise, Arizona*

1 medium onion, chopped
3 tablespoons butter
1 cup uncooked long grain rice
1 can (14-1/2 ounces) chicken
   broth
1 cup water
1 teaspoon dried basil
1/2 teaspoon seasoned salt
Dash pepper
2/3 pound fresh *or* frozen peas,
   thawed
2 tablespoons grated Parmesan
   cheese

In a large saucepan, saute onion in butter until tender. Add the rice; saute until golden, about 5 minutes.

Stir in the broth, water, basil, seasoned salt and pepper. Bring to a boil. Reduce heat; cover and simmer for 15-18 minutes or until rice is tender (some liquid will remain).

Stir in the peas. Remove from the heat; cover and let stand for 5 minutes. Stir in the Parmesan cheese. **Yield:** 6 servings.

Raspberry Red Cabbage Slaw

For a colorful and flavorful switch from traditional coleslaw, turn to this change-of-pace idea.
Raspberries lend a delicious sweetness to the spring salad's contrasting tart flavors.
—*Roxanne Chan, Albany, California*

4 cups shredded red cabbage
2 cups shredded radicchio
2 cups watercress
2 cups fresh raspberries
1 jar (16 ounces) pickled beets,
   drained and chopped
1/4 cup chopped red onion
1/4 cup minced fresh parsley
1/3 cup canola oil
1/4 cup rice vinegar

2 tablespoons red wine vinegar
2 tablespoons seedless raspberry jam
1/2 teaspoon ground allspice
1/4 teaspoon salt
1/4 teaspoon crushed red pepper flakes
Sliced almonds, optional

In a large bowl, combine the first seven ingredients. In a small bowl, whisk the oil, vinegars, jam, allspice, salt and pepper flakes until blended. Drizzle the dressing over the salad and toss to coat. Garnish with almonds if desired. **Yield:** 13 servings.

Cran-Orange Swiss Chard

(Pictured at right)

If you have never sampled Swiss chard before, this is a recipe you must try! The colorful side salad could not be simpler to prepare.
—Joan Jackaman, Nobleton, Ontario

  1 medium onion, sliced
  1 tablespoon olive oil
 10 cups chopped Swiss chard
1/4 cup orange juice
  2 tablespoons dried cranberries
Dash salt and pepper
  2 tablespoons coarsely chopped
     walnuts, toasted

In a large skillet, saute onion in oil until tender. Add chard; saute for 3-5 minutes or just until wilted.

Stir in the orange juice, cranberries, salt and pepper. Cook for 1-2 minutes or until the cranberries are softened. Sprinkle with the walnuts. **Yield:** 4 servings.

Buying Swiss Chard

SWISS CHARD is a member of the beet family and considered a good source of copper, calcium, vitamin B2, and Vitamin B6. It has a tangy flavor with a hint of lemon.

When buying Swiss chard, choose plants with bright green, shiny leaves and without marks or blemishes. The stalks should be white and crisp. Store it unwashed in a plastic bag in the fridge, where it will keep for several days.

One bunch (12 ounces) yields approximately 9 cups chopped.

Marvelous Muffins & Scones

WHAT could be more inviting than biting into a warm-from-the-oven muffin or a freshly baked scone topped with butter or your favorite jam?

Wonderfully delicious and easy to make, the popular bakery delights aren't just for breakfast anymore. Bake a batch as an afternoon snack, a simple dessert or even a flavorful side with soup or salad.

Sweet or savory, moist or crumbly, the right combination of ingredients can turn these delectable gems into the perfect bite any time of day.

When the occasion calls for something sunny and sweet, indulge in heavenly Lemon Meringue Muffins, buttery Tangerine Chip Tea Scones or tropical Mango Colada Scones. (All recipes shown at right.)

BAKED GOODIES

(Clockwise from top)

Tangerine Chip Tea Scones (p. 174)

Mango Colada Scones (p. 176)

Lemon Meringue Muffins (p. 176)

Tangerine Chip Tea Scones

(Pictured on page 172)

My family and I are all tea-lovers. Since my son likes the flavors of chocolate
and citrus together, I came up with this scone recipe in his honor.
—Joyce Manier, Beech Grove, Indiana

1 package (8 ounces) cream
  cheese, softened
1/2 cup sour cream
2 tablespoons confectioners'
  sugar
1 teaspoon vanilla extract
DOUGH:
2 cups all-purpose flour
1/4 cup plus 1/2 teaspoon sugar,
  divided
2 teaspoons baking powder
3/4 teaspoon salt
1/2 teaspoon baking soda
1/2 teaspoon ground coriander
5 tablespoons cold butter
1 cup (8 ounces) sour cream
1 egg, *separated*
1/2 cup miniature semisweet
  chocolate chips
2 teaspoons grated tangerine
  peel (about 2 tangerines)
1/2 teaspoon water

In a small bowl, combine the cream cheese, sour cream, confectioners' sugar and vanilla. Cover and refrigerate until ready to serve.

In a large bowl, combine the flour, 1/4 cup sugar, baking powder, salt, baking soda and coriander. Cut in butter until mixture resembles coarse crumbs. Add sour cream and egg yolk just until moistened. Stir in chocolate chips and tangerine peel.

Turn onto a floured surface; knead 10 times. Pat into a 9-1/2-in. circle. Cut into eight wedges; separate the wedges and place on an ungreased baking sheet. Beat the egg white and water; brush over the dough. Sprinkle with the remaining sugar.

Bake at 400° for 15-20 minutes or until golden brown. Serve with cream cheese spread. **Yield:** 8 servings.

HISTORY OF THE SCONE

IT IS BELIEVED that this Scottish quick bread got its name from the Stone of Destiny (or Scone), the place where Scottish kings were once crowned. The original triangular-shaped treat was made with oats and baked on a griddle.

Today, scones are usually flour-based and baked in the oven. While the traditional triangle shape is still popular, they also come in rounds, squares and diamonds. Both savory and sweet versions are usually enjoyed for breakfast or with tea.

Coconut Chocolate Muffins

(Pictured at right)

With a rich, dark chocolate flavor and luscious cream cheese-coconut topping, these irresistible muffins taste more like a decadent dessert than a morning treat.
—Sonia Daily, Midland, Michigan

1/2 cup cream cheese, softened
3 tablespoons sugar
2 tablespoons all-purpose flour
1 egg
1 cup (6 ounces) semisweet chocolate chips, *divided*
1/2 cup flaked coconut
1/3 cup chopped pecans, toasted

BATTER:
1-1/2 cups all-purpose flour
1 cup packed brown sugar
1/4 cup baking cocoa
1 teaspoon baking soda
1/4 teaspoon ground cinnamon
1 cup brewed coffee, room temperature
1/3 cup canola oil
2 tablespoons cider vinegar

In a small bowl, beat the cream cheese, sugar and flour until smooth. Beat in egg. Stir in 2/3 cup chocolate chips; set aside. In another bowl, combine the coconut, pecans and remaining chips; set aside.

In a large bowl, combine the flour, brown sugar, cocoa, baking soda and cinnamon. Combine the coffee, oil and vinegar; stir into dry ingredients just until moistened.

Fill paper-lined muffin cups half full. Drop a rounded tablespoonful of cream cheese mixture into the center of each; sprinkle with 1 tablespoon coconut mixture.

Bake at 350° for 20-25 minutes or until a toothpick comes out clean. Cool for 5 minutes before removing from pans to wire racks. **Yield:** 14 muffins.

Editor's Note: This cupcake batter does not contain eggs.

Lemon Meringue Muffins

(Pictured on page 172)

With their cute presentation and wonderful lemon flavor, these light,
tender muffins take center stage on the breakfast tray.
—*Nancy Kearney, Massillon, Ohio*

6 tablespoons butter, softened
1 cup sugar, *divided*
2 eggs
1/2 cup plain yogurt
2 tablespoons lemon juice
1 tablespoon grated lemon peel
1/4 teaspoon lemon extract
1-1/3 cups all-purpose flour
1/2 teaspoon baking powder
1/2 teaspoon baking soda
2 egg whites

In a large bowl, cream butter and 2/3 cup sugar until light and fluffy. Add eggs, one at a time, beating well after each addition. Stir in the yogurt, lemon juice, peel and extract. Combine the flour, baking powder and baking soda; add to creamed mixture just until moistened. Fill greased or paper-lined muffin cups three-fourths full. Bake at 350° for 18 minutes.

Meanwhile, in a small bowl, beat egg whites on medium speed until soft peaks form. Gradually beat in remaining sugar, 1 tablespoon at a time, on high until stiff glossy peaks form and sugar is dissolved.

Transfer meringue to a heavy-duty resealable plastic bag; cut a small hole in a corner of bag. Pipe onto muffins. Bake 5-8 minutes longer or until meringue is golden brown and a toothpick inserted into muffin comes out clean. Cool for 5 minutes before removing from pan to a wire rack. Serve warm. Refrigerate leftovers. **Yield:** 1 dozen.

Mango Colada Scones

(Pictured on page 173)

One bite of this tropical-inspired scone and you'll know it's something special. The flaky exterior,
soft bits of mango and sweet toasted coconut topping can only be described as paradise.
—*Cheryl Perry, Elizabeth City, North Carolina*

2-1/2 cups biscuit/baking mix
2 tablespoons brown sugar
3 tablespoons cold butter
1/2 cup frozen non-alcoholic pina colada mix, thawed
1 cup chopped peeled mango
3 tablespoons flaked coconut
1/4 cup macadamia nuts, chopped

In a large bowl, combine the biscuit mix and brown sugar. Cut in 2 tablespoons butter until the mixture resembles coarse crumbs. Stir in the pina colada mix just until moistened. Fold in mango.

Turn onto a floured surface; knead 10 times. Pat into a 9-in. x 7-in. rectangle. Cut into 10 rectangles; separate rectangles and place on a greased baking sheet. Melt remaining butter; brush over scones.

Bake at 400° for 12 minutes. Sprinkle with coconut and nuts; bake 2-4 minutes longer or until golden brown. Serve warm. **Yield:** 10 scones.

Chippy Cinnamon Scones

(Pictured at right)

If you love cinnamon rolls but don't want to spend the time making them, these sweet, sticky scones will do the trick. The addition of chocolate chips and bits of toffee make them extra special.
—Camilla Saulsbury
Nacogdoches, Texas

1-2/3 cups all-purpose flour
1/4 cup packed brown sugar
2 teaspoons baking powder
1 teaspoon ground cinnamon
1/8 teaspoon salt
1 cup heavy whipping cream
1/2 cup miniature semisweet
   chocolate chips
1/4 cup chopped pecans, toasted
1/4 cup milk chocolate English
   toffee bits
1 tablespoon butter, melted
GLAZE:
1/4 cup confectioners' sugar
4-1/2 teaspoons spreadable cream
   cheese
2-1/4 teaspoons milk
1/4 teaspoon vanilla extract

In a large bowl, combine the flour, brown sugar, baking powder, cinnamon and salt. Stir in cream just until moistened. Stir in the chocolate chips, pecans and toffee bits.

Turn onto a floured surface; knead 10 times. Pat dough into an 8-in. circle; cut into six wedges. Separate wedges and transfer to a lightly greased baking sheet. Brush with butter.

Bake at 375° for 16-20 minutes or until golden brown. Combine the glaze ingredients; drizzle over scones. Serve warm. **Yield:** 6 scones.

Lemon-Raspberry Jumbo Muffins

Sweet raspberries add delightful color and flavor to my large, lemon-infused muffins.
They're perfect for company brunches or as a Saturday morning indulgence.
—*Laura Siegrist, Jermyn, Pennsylvania*

1/2 cup butter, softened
1-1/4 cups sugar
4 eggs
1 cup buttermilk
1 teaspoon vanilla extract
3 cups all-purpose flour
1 teaspoon baking powder
1/2 teaspoon baking soda
1/2 teaspoon salt
1-1/4 cups fresh *or* frozen
  raspberries
3 teaspoons grated lemon peel
GLAZE:
1 cup confectioners' sugar
3 to 4 tablespoons lemon juice

In a large bowl, cream butter and sugar until light and fluffy. Add eggs, one at a time, beating well after each addition. Stir in buttermilk and vanilla. Combine the flour, baking powder, baking soda and salt; add to creamed mixture just until moistened. Fold in raspberries and lemon peel.

Fill paper-lined jumbo muffin cups half full. Bake at 350° for 23-28 minutes or until a toothpick comes out clean. Cool for 5 minutes before removing from pan to a wire rack. Combine glaze ingredients; drizzle over warm muffins. **Yield:** 1 dozen.

Editor's Note: If using frozen raspberries, do not thaw before adding to batter.

Sausage 'n' Broccoli Corn Muffins

Here in the Southwest, we enjoy foods that are intense with flavors from our region.
This savory muffin is one example, chock-full of hot pork sausage and green chilies.
—*Verlene Hendricks, Roswell, New Mexico*

1 cup yellow cornmeal
1 cup whole wheat flour
1 teaspoon baking soda
1/2 teaspoon salt
1/2 teaspoon garlic powder
1/4 teaspoon cayenne pepper
2 eggs
1 cup buttermilk
1/4 cup canola oil
1-1/2 cups crumbled cooked hot
  pork sausage
2/3 cup fresh broccoli florets, cooked, finely chopped
  and patted dry
1/2 cup chopped green chilies

In a large bowl, combine the cornmeal, flour, baking soda, salt, garlic powder and cayenne. In another bowl, whisk the eggs, buttermilk and oil. Stir into dry ingredients just until moistened. Combine the sausage, broccoli and chilies; fold into batter.

Fill greased or paper-lined muffin cups three-fourths full. Bake at 400° for 18-23 minutes or until a toothpick comes out clean. Cool for 5 minutes before removing from the pan to a wire rack. Serve warm. Refrigerate leftovers. **Yield:** 1 dozen.

Upside-Down Turtle Muffins

(Pictured at right)

These gems feature an ooey-gooey caramel center and a glossy chocolate glaze topped with sweet pecans. They're perfect when you want something sweet.
—Patrice Bruwer, Lowell, Michigan

  1 **cup all-purpose flour**
1/4 **cup chopped pecans**
  1 **teaspoon baking soda**
1/2 **teaspoon salt**
1/2 **cup semisweet chocolate chips**
  3 **tablespoons butter**
1/3 **cup packed brown sugar**
1/3 **cup buttermilk**
  1 **egg, lightly beaten**
  1 **teaspoon vanilla extract**
16 **Riesen's chewy chocolate-covered caramels,** *divided*
24 **pecan halves**

In a small bowl, combine the flour, chopped pecans, baking soda and salt; set aside. In a microwave-safe bowl, melt chocolate chips and butter; stir until smooth. Cool slightly. Stir in the brown sugar, buttermilk, egg and vanilla. Stir into dry ingredients just until moistened.

Fill greased muffin cups three-fourths full. Press one caramel into the center of each muffin cup. Bake at 400° for 12-14 minutes or until a toothpick inserted into the edge comes out clean.

Cool for 1 minute; invert onto a baking sheet. Top muffins with remaining caramels; return to the oven for 1-2 minutes or until caramel is softened. Place three pecan halves on each muffin. Serve warm. **Yield:** 8 muffins.

MAGNIFICENT MUFFINS

TO BAKE the ideal batch of muffins, follow these simple tips:

- Even if you are using pre-sifted flour, you'll get better results if you sift the flour before measuring.
- To make sure all of the muffins in the pan are evenly browned, bake them on the middle rack of the oven.

- Muffin batter should be lumpy. Stir the batter just until the dry ingredients are moistened. If the batter is too smooth, the muffins will be tough and have pointed peaks.
- To produce muffins with a high, rounded crown, be sure to use fresh baking powder and baking soda. Also, only grease the bottom of the muffin cups, avoiding the sides.

Poppy Seed Banana Muffins

If you're a fan of lemon poppy seed muffins or banana bread, then you'll enjoy this recipe that combines poppy seeds with delicious banana flavor. They make a great on-the-go breakfast or snack.
—Gloria Olds, Troy, Montana

1-1/2 cups all-purpose flour
1/2 cup sugar
1-1/2 teaspoons baking powder
1/2 teaspoon salt
1/4 teaspoon baking soda
1 egg
1/2 cup milk
1/4 cup canola oil
2 medium ripe bananas, mashed
2-1/2 teaspoons poppy seeds

In a small bowl, combine the flour, sugar, baking powder, salt and baking soda. In another bowl, combine the egg, milk and oil. Stir into dry ingredients just until moistened. Fold in bananas and poppy seeds.

Fill paper-lined muffin cups three-fourths full. Bake at 400° for 15-20 minutes or until a toothpick comes out clean. Cool for 5 minutes before removing from the pan to a wire rack. Serve warm. **Yield:** 1 dozen.

Streusel-Topped Blueberry Muffins

Here in Michigan, fresh blueberries are plentiful in the summer. My sister-in-law passed along this recipe to me. Every bite is bursting with juicy blueberry flavor.
—Brenda Hoffman, Stanton, Michigan

1 cup sugar
1 tablespoon butter, softened
1 egg
1 cup (8 ounces) sour cream
2 cups all-purpose flour
1/2 teaspoon baking powder
1/2 teaspoon baking soda
1 cup fresh *or* frozen blueberries
TOPPING:
1/2 cup packed brown sugar
1/3 cup all-purpose flour
1/4 cup cold butter

GLAZE:
1/2 cup confectioners' sugar
1-1/2 teaspoons water
1/4 teaspoon vanilla extract

In a large bowl, combine sugar and butter. Add egg and sour cream; mix well. Combine the flour, baking powder and baking soda; add to sugar mixture just until combined. Fold in blueberries.

Fill paper-lined muffin cups two-thirds full. For topping, combine brown sugar and flour in a small bowl; cut in butter until crumbly. Sprinkle over batter.

Bake at 350° for 20 minutes or until a toothpick comes out clean. Cool for 5 minutes before removing from pan to a wire rack. Combine glaze ingredients; drizzle over warm muffins. **Yield:** 1 dozen.

Spicy Ginger Scones

(Pictured at right)

Candied ginger gives these tasty bites that special "zing." Crumbly on the outside, but soft on the inside, the golden treats pack in plenty of tongue-tingling flavor.
—Rebecca Guffey, Apex, North Carolina

2 cups biscuit/baking mix
2 tablespoons sugar
1 teaspoon ground cinnamon
1/4 teaspoon ground ginger
1/4 teaspoon ground nutmeg
2/3 cup half-and-half cream
1/2 cup golden raisins
2 tablespoons candied *or* crystallized ginger, chopped
Additional half-and-half cream and sugar

In a large bowl, combine the biscuit mix, sugar, cinnamon, ginger and nutmeg. Stir in cream just until moistened. Stir in raisins and ginger.

Turn onto a floured surface; knead 10 times. Transfer dough to a greased baking sheet. Pat into a 9-in. circle. Cut into eight wedges, but do not separate. Brush tops lightly with additional cream; sprinkle with additional sugar.

Bake at 425° for 12-15 minutes or until golden brown. Serve warm. **Yield:** 8 scones.

Family Traditions

EACH Easter Sunday, members of our community gather on top of Ravalli Hill for a "Son Rise" service. Afterwards, we serve a continental breakfast, featuring an abundance of foods, including fresh-baked breads and muffins.
—Joy Maynard
St. Ignatius, Montana

SPECIAL *Celebrations*

Occasions throughout the year call for special celebrations.
You'll be on track for good times with an Indy 500 gala.
In the sunny days of summer, celebrate Father's Day
in the great outdoors. Or prepare delightful dishes
with the season's finest fruit. When fall comes calling,
you can't resist the appeal of festive Oktoberfest fare
or the spirited fun of a Halloween gathering.
Celebrating a wedding anniversary? Serve a tasty meal for two!

SPECIAL *Celebrations*

Lovely Anniversary Dinner

WEDDING anniversaries are eventful occasions to remember. So celebrate with your sweetie in a special way.

Forego fancy food at an expensive restaurant by preparing a romantic dinner for two at home.

You and your spouse will fall head over heels for Tenderloin for Two with Cherry-Brandy Sauce. It's an elegant yet easy entree that both novice and experienced cooks can prepare.

With tender potatoes and a creamy cheese sauce, Fontina Potatoes Au Gratin is a perfect partner for the beefy main dish.

Simply Delicious Italian Bread and Rosemary Lemon Butter is a match made in heaven…just like you and your loved one! (All recipes shown at right.)

TABLE FOR TWO
(Pictured above)

Tenderloin for Two with Cherry-Brandy Sauce (p. 186)

Fontina Potatoes Au Gratin (p. 186)

Simply Delicious Italian Bread (p. 188)

Rosemary Lemon Butter (p. 188)

Tenderloin for Two With Cherry-Brandy Sauce

(Pictured on page 185)

An evening alone with my husband is truly a special occasion. So I make this elegant entree for those nights.
—Gina Hardy, La Vernia, Texas

1/4 cup beef broth
1/4 cup port wine *or* additional beef broth
1 shallot, thinly sliced
1 teaspoon tomato paste
1/2 teaspoon grated horseradish
1/4 teaspoon whole peppercorns
1 bay leaf
2 beef tenderloin steaks (6 ounces *each*)
1-1/2 teaspoons olive oil
1 tablespoon butter, *divided*
1/4 cup cherry liqueur
1-1/2 teaspoons cherry preserves

In a small saucepan, combine the first seven ingredients. Bring to a boil. Reduce heat; simmer, uncovered, until liquid is slightly thickened and reduced to about 1/3 cup. Strain and discard the shallot, peppercorns and bay leaf; set liquid aside.

In a large skillet over medium heat, cook steaks in oil and 1-1/2 teaspoons butter for 5-8 minutes on each side or until meat reaches desired doneness (for medium-rare, a meat thermometer should read 145°; medium, 160°; well-done, 170°). Remove steaks and keep warm.

Remove pan from the heat; add the reserved broth mixture, then the liqueur. Return pan to the heat. Bring to a boil; cook for 5 minutes or until liquid is thickened and reduced to about 1/4 cup. Stir in preserves and remaining butter. Return steaks to the pan; heat through. **Yield:** 2 servings.

Fontina Potatoes Au Gratin

(Pictured on page 185)

Our home economists use a white sauce and fontina cheese to coat sliced potatoes in this casserole for two.

2 tablespoons butter
2 teaspoons all-purpose flour
1/2 teaspoon salt
1/8 teaspoon pepper
2/3 cup milk
3 medium potatoes, peeled and cut into 1/4-inch slices
1/4 cup shredded fontina cheese
2 tablespoons minced chives
1 tablespoon grated Parmesan cheese

In a small saucepan, melt butter. Stir in the flour, salt and pepper until smooth. Gradually stir in milk. Bring to a boil; cook and stir for 2 minutes or until thickened.

In a greased 3-cup baking dish, layer half of the potatoes, fontina cheese, white sauce and chives. Top with remaining potatoes, fontina, sauce and chives.

Cover and bake at 400° for 30 minutes. Uncover; sprinkle with Parmesan cheese. Bake 10-15 minutes longer or until potatoes are tender and top is lightly browned. Let stand for 5 minutes before serving. **Yield:** 2 servings.

Snow Crab Legs with Dipping Sauces

(Pictured at right)

Whenever I prepare crab legs for my family, I serve these three dipping sauces on the side. They really enhance the already-fabulous crab flavor.
—Suzy Horvath, Sheridan, Oregon

DILL BUTTER SAUCE:
- 1/4 cup butter, melted
- 1-1/2 teaspoons lemon juice
- 1/4 teaspoon dill weed
- 1/8 teaspoon garlic salt
- Dash white pepper

HORSERADISH CHILI SAUCE:
- 1/4 cup chili sauce
- 1/2 teaspoon rice vinegar
- 1/2 teaspoon prepared horseradish

AVOCADO CREAM SAUCE:
- 1/2 medium ripe avocado, peeled and mashed
- 1/3 cup sour cream
- 1/4 teaspoon ground cumin
- 1 teaspoon lime juice
- 1/8 teaspoon hot pepper sauce

CRAB LEGS:
- 1 pound cooked snow crab legs
- 1 tablespoon olive oil

In three separate small bowls, combine the ingredients for dill butter sauce, horseradish chili sauce and avocado cream sauce; set aside.

Brush both sides of crab legs with oil. Grill, covered, over medium heat for 3-4 minutes on each side or until heated through. Serve with dipping sauces. **Yield:** 2 servings.

A Lesson in Crab Legs

CRAB LEGS are sold cooked and only need to be adequately heated before serving. They can either be sold thawed or frozen.

Thawed crab legs should be prepared within a day of purchase and should not be refrozen.

You can store frozen crab legs in your home freezer for up to 3 months. To use, thaw overnight in the refrigerator and then heat as directed.

Simply Delicious Italian Bread

(Pictured on page 185)

It's always a joy to watch people's faces when I present them with homemade bread.
This recipe makes two loaves—one for you to enjoy and one to share with others.
—Nicole Gillenardo, St. Peters, Missouri

1 **package (1/4 ounce) active dry yeast**
1 **cup warm water (110° to 115°)**
2 **teaspoons sugar**
1 **teaspoon salt**
2-1/2 **to 3 cups all-purpose flour**
1 **teaspoon cornmeal**
1 **teaspoon butter, softened**

In a large bowl, dissolve yeast in warm water. Add the sugar, salt and 1 cup flour. Beat until smooth. Stir in enough remaining flour to form a soft dough.

Turn onto a floured surface; knead until smooth and elastic, about 6-8 minutes. Place in a greased bowl, turning once to grease top. Cover and let rise in a warm place until doubled, about 1 hour.

Punch dough down. Turn onto a lightly floured surface; divide in half. Roll each portion into an 8-in. x 6-in. rectangle. Roll up jelly-roll style, starting with a long side; pinch seams to seal and tuck ends under.

Grease a baking sheet; sprinkle with cornmeal. Place loaves seam side down on prepared pan. With a sharp knife, make four shallow slashes across the top of each loaf. Cover and let rise until doubled, about 30 minutes.

Bake at 400° for 15-20 minutes or until golden brown. Remove to a wire rack; spread with butter. **Yield:** 2 loaves (12 slices each).

Rosemary Lemon Butter

(Pictured on page 185)

In our Test Kitchen, we dressed up ordinary butter with rosemary, lemon and a dash of pepper.
It's a tasty spread on savory bread.

2 **tablespoons butter, softened**
1 **teaspoon grated lemon peel**
1 **teaspoon minced fresh rosemary**
Dash coarsely ground pepper

In a small bowl, combine all ingredients. Cover and refrigerate until serving. **Yield:** 2 tablespoons.

Chocolate Hazelnut Torte

(Pictured at right)

Most cake recipes feed a group. So our home economists came up with this six-serving cake. That's enough for two...with just the right amount of leftovers!

1/3 cup butter, softened
  1 cup packed brown sugar
  1 egg
  1 teaspoon vanilla extract
  1 cup all-purpose flour
1/4 cup baking cocoa
  1 teaspoon baking soda
1/8 teaspoon salt
1/2 cup sour cream
1/2 cup brewed coffee, room
    temperature
FROSTING:
  7 squares (1 ounce *each*)
    semisweet chocolate,
    chopped
  1 cup heavy whipping cream
  2 tablespoons sugar
1/3 cup chocolate hazelnut
    spread
**Chocolate curls and hazelnuts,
    optional**

In a small bowl, cream butter and brown sugar until light and fluffy, about 5 minutes. Beat in egg and vanilla. Combine the flour, cocoa, baking soda and salt; add to creamed mixture alternately with sour cream and coffee. Beat just until combined.

Pour into two greased and floured 6-in. round baking pans. Bake at 350° for 25-30 minutes or until a knife inserted near the center comes out clean. Cool for 10 minutes before removing from pans to wire racks to cool completely.

For frosting, in a small saucepan, melt chocolate with cream and sugar over low heat; stir until smooth. Remove from the heat; whisk in hazelnut spread. Transfer to a small bowl; cover and refrigerate until frosting reaches spreading consistency, stirring occasionally.

Spread frosting between layers and over top and sides of cake. Garnish with chocolate curls and hazelnuts if desired. **Yield:** 6 servings.

Green Beans with Red Pepper

I'm of the belief that simple sides are best. These basic but beautiful beans deliciously prove my theory correct!
— *Betty Ellis, Boaz, Alabama*

1/3 **pound fresh green beans, trimmed**
3 **tablespoons chopped sweet red pepper**
1 **green onion, thinly sliced**
1 **small garlic clove, minced**
1 **tablespoon butter**
Dash salt and pepper

Place beans in a large saucepan and cover with water. Bring to a boil. Cook, uncovered, for 8-10 minutes or until crisp-tender.

Meanwhile, in a small skillet, saute the red pepper, onion and garlic in butter until tender. Remove from the heat; sprinkle with salt and pepper. Drain beans and transfer to a serving dish. Add red pepper mixture and stir gently to coat. **Yield:** 2 servings.

ANNIVERSARY DINNER AGENDA

A Few Weeks Before:
- Prepare two grocery lists—one for nonperishable items to purchase now and one for perishable items to purchase a few days before.
- Bake Simply Delicious Italian Bread. Freeze each loaf in a heavy-duty resealable plastic bag.

Two Days Before:
- Buy remaining grocery items.
- Make Rosemary Lemon Butter; cover and refrigerate.

The Day Before:
- Make the sauce for Fontina Potatoes Au Gratin; cover and chill.
- Clean and trim the beans and chop the red pepper for Green Beans with Red Pepper. Place in separate resealable plastic bags; refrigerate.
- For Tenderloin for Two with Cherry-Brandy Sauce, prepare the sauce, but don't add liqueur. Cover tightly and chill.
- Prepare the Horseradish Chili and Avocado Cream Sauces for Snow Crab Legs with Dipping Sauces. Refrigerate in separate covered containers.
- Bake the Chocolate Hazelnut Torte; cover and chill.

The Day of Your Dinner:
- In the morning, peel and slice the potatoes for Fontina Potatoes Au Gratin. Place in a bowl of cold water and chill.
- Thaw one Simply Delicious Italian Bread at room temperature. (Keep the other loaf frozen for future use.)
- Reheat the sauce for Fontina Potatoes Au Gratin. Assemble the dish; bake.
- Prepare Green Beans with Red Pepper.
- Make the Dill Butter Sauce and grill the crab legs.
- Cook the steaks as directed and finish making the sauce.
- Serve slices of bread with Rosemary Lemon Butter.
- Slice Chocolate Hazelnut Torte.

Unforgettable Anniversary Table

(Pictured above)

SET a romantic, intimate mood at your special anniversary dinner by creating a simply pretty tablescape.

Start with low lighting in the room. Then use plenty of candles to add a little spark…and to kindle some new memories.

Display framed images of the two of you through the years. These treasured photos allow you to reminisce about your years of wedded bliss and serve as a picture-perfect reminder of your lovely life together.

Finally, as a symbol of your flourishing love, scatter flower petals onto the tabletop, being careful to keep them away from the candle flames.

Indy 500 Fun!

LADIES and gentlemen start your appetites! Even if you can't be in the stands at this year's Indy 500, hosting a themed get-together with plenty of race-day fare will place you in the Winner's Circle.

Like the box lunch sold at the race, this hearty meal will refuel you and your guests.

Sink your teeth into a Brickyard Bistro Sandwich, piled high with meat and cheese and seasoned with a zesty olive oil dressing.

Then rev up your taste buds with Checkered-Flag Curry Vegeatable Dip, Speedway Snack Mix and Thirst-Quenching Limeade.

Sweet-Taste-of-Victory Butter-scotch Cookies are the perfect thing to enjoy with a cold glass of milk. (All recipes shown at right.)

RACE-DAY FARE
(Pictured above)

Thirst-Quenching Limeade (p. 196)

Checkered-Flag Curry Vegetable Dip (p. 196)

**Sweet-Taste-of-Victory
Butterscotch Cookies** (p. 198)

Brickyard Bistro Sandwich (p. 194)

Speedway Snack Mix (p. 198)

Pit Stop Potatoes

(Pictured at far right)

*We love fried potatoes and experimented with several recipes until we came up
with this yummy grilled version. Using a disposable foil pan means easy cleanup.*
—*Annette Frahmann, Shelton, Washington*

2 large potatoes, thinly sliced
1/4 cup chopped onion
1/4 cup sliced baby portobello
    mushrooms
1/4 cup chopped green pepper
1/2 teaspoon salt
1/2 teaspoon pepper

1/2 teaspoon Southwest seasoning
2 tablespoons butter, cut into small cubes

In a greased disposable foil pan, layer the potatoes, onion, mushrooms and green pepper. Sprinkle with salt, pepper and Southwest seasoning; dot with butter.

    Cover with foil. Grill over medium-hot heat for 20-25 minutes or until potatoes are tender. **Yield:** 3 servings.

Brickyard Bistro Sandwich

(Pictured on page 193)

*Even the heartiest of appetites will be satisfied with this impressive sandwich created by our home economists.
Piled high with meat and cheese, it's topped with a flavorful olive oil and balsamic dressing.*

1 loaf (1 pound) focaccia bread
2 tablespoons olive oil
1 tablespoon balsamic vinegar
2 teaspoons minced fresh
    oregano
1 teaspoon minced fresh
    rosemary
2 slices red onion, separated
    into rings
2 ounces sliced deli smoked
    turkey
2 ounces thinly sliced hard
    salami
2 ounces sliced deli roast beef
2 ounces sliced provolone
    cheese
1 plum tomato, sliced
2 lettuce leaves

Cut focaccia in half horizontally. In a small bowl, combine the oil, vinegar, oregano and rosemary; brush over cut sides of bread.

    On bread bottom, layer the onion, turkey, salami, roast beef, cheese, tomato and lettuce; replace bread top. Cut into four wedges. **Yield:** 4 servings.

Race Day Burgers

(Pictured at right)

I once ended up with a bumper crop of fresh basil and needed to find a way to use it all. These juicy burgers were just the thing! They have great Italian flavor and an irresistible gooey cheese center.
—Virginia Kochis, Springfield, Virginia

> 4 **sun-dried tomatoes (not packed in oil)**
> 1 **cup boiling water**
> 1 **cup mayonnaise**
> 4 **pieces string cheese**
> 1/2 **cup minced fresh basil**
> 4 **teaspoons Worcestershire sauce**
> 4 **teaspoons Italian seasoning**
> 4 **garlic cloves, minced**
> 1 **teaspoon salt**
> 1 **teaspoon pepper**
> 3 **pounds ground beef**
> 2 **loaves (14 ounces *each*) ciabatta bread, halved lengthwise**
> 4 **slices part-skim mozzarella cheese**

Fresh basil leaves

Place tomatoes and water in a small bowl; let stand for 5 minutes. Drain well; place tomatoes in a food processor. Add mayonnaise; cover and process until blended. Transfer to a bowl; cover and refrigerate until serving.

Cut each piece of string cheese in half lengthwise and widthwise; set aside. In a large bowl, combine the minced basil, Worcestershire sauce, Italian seasoning, garlic, salt and pepper. Crumble beef over mixture and mix well. Shape into 16 thin patties. Place two pieces of string cheese on eight patties; top with remaining patties. Press edges firmly to seal.

Grill patties, covered, over medium heat for 5-7 minutes on each side or until meat is no longer pink. Place four burgers on the bottom of each loaf of bread; top with mozzarella cheese, basil leaves and tomato mayonnaise. Replace bread tops. Cut each loaf into four servings. **Yield:** 8 servings.

Thirst-Quenching Limeade

(Pictured on page 192)

Beat the heat with this refreshing concoction from our home economists.

5-1/2 cups water, *divided*
1-1/4 cups sugar
   3/4 cup lemon juice (about 4
      lemons)
   3/4 cup lime juice (about 4 limes)
    1 teaspoon grated lemon peel
    1 teaspoon grated lime peel
Ice cubes

In a large saucepan, bring 1-1/2 cups water and sugar to a boil. Reduce heat; simmer, uncovered, for 10 minutes. Cool to room temperature.

Transfer to a 2-qt. pitcher. Stir in juices and peels. Cover and refrigerate for at least 1 hour. Stir in remaining water. Serve over ice. **Yield:** 7 servings (1-3/4 quarts).

Checkered-Flag Curry Vegetable Dip

(Pictured on page 193)

Curry powder makes ordinary vegetable dip extra special. I usually double the recipe for get-togethers because it disappears quickly every time.
—*Michelle Mackey, Erie, Pennsylvania*

    1 cup mayonnaise
1/2 cup sour cream
    1 tablespoon dried parsley
      flakes
    1 teaspoon Italian salad
      dressing mix
1/2 teaspoon lemon juice
1/2 teaspoon Worcestershire
      sauce
1/4 teaspoon salt
1/8 teaspoon curry powder
Assorted fresh vegetables

In a small bowl, combine the first eight ingredients. Cover and refrigerate for at least 1 hour. Serve with the vegetables. **Yield:** 1-1/2 cups.

HELP YOUR INDY 500 PARTY TAKE FLIGHT

FEW sporting events are as tradition-rich as the Indy 500. Why not try adapting one of those customs for your own Indy celebration?

Every year thousands of multicolored balloons are released into the air. Re-create the tradition by having each guest release a helium-filled balloon at the start of the car race, or decorate your house with bunches of colorful balloons.

Roasted Pepper Mushroom Salad

(Pictured at right)

This is a colorful, pretty dish to serve and it's always a big hit. One bite and people can't stop eating it.
—Bonnie Hawkins
Burlington, Wisconsin

 1 large sweet red pepper
 1 large green pepper
 2 cups whole fresh mushrooms
 1 small red onion, sliced
 1/2 cup pitted ripe olives
 1/3 cup Italian salad dressing
 1 garlic clove, minced
 1 teaspoon dried basil
 1/2 teaspoon salt
 1/2 teaspoon dried oregano
 1/2 teaspoon pepper
Lettuce leaves

Broil peppers 4 in. from the heat until skins blister, about 10 minutes. With tongs, rotate peppers a quarter turn. Broil and rotate until all sides are blis-tered and blackened. Immediately place peppers in a bowl; cover and let stand for 15-20 minutes.

Peel off and discard charred skin. Remove stems and seeds. Cut peppers into thin slices. In a large bowl, combine the peppers, mushrooms, onion and olives.

In a small bowl, combine the salad dressing, garlic, basil, salt, oregano and pepper. Pour over vegetables and toss to coat. Cover and refrigerate overnight. Serve on lettuce leaves. **Yield:** 6 servings.

Sweet-Taste-of-Victory Butterscotch Cookies

(Pictured at far right and on page 193)

Loaded with chocolate, butterscotch and toffee chips, these cookies are a winner every time.
—Jerry Huff, Oakland, California

1 cup butter, softened
1 cup sugar
1 cup packed brown sugar
3 eggs
3 teaspoons vanilla extract
3-3/4 cups all-purpose flour
2 teaspoons ground cinnamon
1 teaspoon baking soda
1/2 teaspoon salt
Pinch *each* ground ginger, nutmeg and cloves
1-1/2 cups semisweet chocolate chips

1 cup butterscotch chips
1 cup chopped walnuts
1/2 cup English toffee bits *or* almond brickle chips

In a large mixing bowl, cream butter and sugars until light and fluffy. Add eggs, one at a time, beating well after each addition. Beat in vanilla. Combine the flour, cinnamon, baking soda, salt, ginger, nutmeg and cloves; gradually add to creamed mixture. Stir in the chips, walnuts and toffee bits.

Drop cookie dough by rounded tablespoonfuls 2 in. apart onto ungreased baking sheets. Bake at 350° for 12-14 minutes or until lightly browned. Remove to wire racks. **Yield:** about 5 dozen.

Speedway Snack Mix

(Pictured on page 193)

Our Taste of Home Test Kitchen guarantees your cookout will be off to a good start when you pass around a bowl of this crunchy, satisfying snack.

12 cups pretzel sticks
2 cups dry roasted peanuts
3/4 cup butter, melted
3 tablespoons Worcestershire sauce
2 teaspoons chili powder
1/2 teaspoon garlic salt
1/2 teaspoon seasoned salt
1/4 teaspoon cayenne pepper

In a large bowl, combine pretzels and peanuts. Combine the remaining ingredients; pour over pretzel mixture and toss to coat.

Transfer to two greased 15-in. x 10-in. x 1-in. baking pans. Bake at 300° for 30 minutes or until lightly toasted, stirring once. Cool on wire racks. Store in airtight containers. **Yield:** 3-1/2 quarts.

Finish-Line Pie Bars

(Pictured at right)

A custard-like filling makes these dessert bars simply delectable. If you serve the yummy treats at an outdoor picnic, our home economists recommend that you keep them cold in a cooler.

    2 cups all-purpose flour
    1 teaspoon salt, *divided*
  1/2 teaspoon baking powder
  1/2 cup shortening
    2 egg yolks
  1/4 cup cold water
    1 tablespoon lemon juice
    3 cups sugar
  3/4 cup cornstarch
7-1/2 cups half-and-half cream
    1 cup plus 2 tablespoons butter,
      cubed
    3 teaspoons vanilla extract
  1/2 teaspoon ground nutmeg
Additional ground nutmeg

In a large bowl, combine the flour, 1/2 teaspoon salt and baking powder. Cut in shortening until mixture resembles coarse crumbs. In a small bowl, whisk the egg yolks, water and lemon juice; gradually add to flour mixture, tossing with a fork until dough forms a ball. Chill for 30 minutes.

Roll out dough between two large sheets of waxed paper into a 17-in. x 12-in. rectangle. Transfer to an ungreased 15-in. x 10-in. x 1-in. baking pan. Press pastry onto the bottom and up the sides of pan; trim pastry even with top edges. Bake at 325° for 10 minutes.

Meanwhile, in a large saucepan, combine the sugar, cornstarch and remaining salt. Add cream; stir until smooth. Cook and stir over medium heat until mixture comes to a boil. Cook and stir 1-2 minutes longer or until thickened. Remove from the heat; stir in butter, vanilla and nutmeg. Pour into crust. Sprinkle with additional nutmeg.

Bake for 40-45 minutes or until a knife inserted near the center comes out clean and crust is golden brown. Cool on a wire rack. Cover and refrigerate for at least 1 hour before cutting. Refrigerate leftovers. **Yield:** 4 dozen.

The Great Outdoors With Dad

FATHER'S DAY is a time to celebrate Dad—and all of those great guys who act as father figures. Whether it's a stepfather, grandfather, uncle or even a big brother, show him how much he means with a fun-filled camping trip.

Not only does time outdoors provide a terrific opportunity to create special memories, it's also a chance to enjoy your favorite campfire foods.

This year, keep the usual hot dogs and hamburgers at home and let Dad feast on flame-cooked faves such as Campfire Fried Fish, Grilled Romaine Salad and Horseradish-Dill Grilled Corn. (All recipes shown at right.)

Campfire Fried Fish

(Pictured on page 201)

*Flaky and flavorful with a golden cornmeal coating, this fried fish from
our home economists is a keeper! It's wonderful whether you use walleye,
bluegill or perch. Experiment with other seasonings if you like.*

2 eggs
3/4 cup all-purpose flour
1/2 cup cornmeal
1 teaspoon salt
1 teaspoon paprika
3 pounds walleye, bluegill
  or perch fillets
Vegetable oil

In a shallow bowl, whisk eggs. In a large resealable plastic bag, combine the flour, cornmeal, salt and paprika. Dip fillets in eggs, then roll in flour mixture.

Add 1/4 in. of oil to a large cast-iron skillet; place skillet on grill rack over medium-hot heat. Fry fillets in oil in batches for 3-4 minutes on each side or until fish flakes easily with a fork. **Yield:** 6 servings.

Grilled Romaine Salad

(Pictured on page 201)

*Our Test Kitchen gives romaine hearts, fresh cucumbers and ripe tomatoes a unique but delicious
treatment in this grilled salad. Drizzled with a robust oil-vinegar dressing, it packs plenty of zing.
If eating away from home, the dressing can be made in advance. Shake before using.*

1/3 cup plus 3 tablespoons olive
  oil, *divided*
2 tablespoons white wine
  vinegar
1 tablespoon dill weed
1/2 teaspoon garlic powder
1/8 teaspoon crushed red pepper
  flakes
1/8 teaspoon salt
6 green onions
4 plum tomatoes, halved
1 large cucumber, peeled and
  halved lengthwise
2 romaine hearts

In a jar with a tight-fitting lid, combine 1/3 cup oil, vinegar and seasonings; shake well. Set aside.

Brush the onions, tomatoes, cucumber and romaine with remaining oil. Grill the onions, tomatoes and cucumber, uncovered, over medium heat for 4-5 minutes on each side or until onions are crisp-tender. Grill romaine for 30 seconds on each side or until heated through.

Chop the vegetables; place in a large bowl. Shake dressing and pour over salad; toss to coat. Serve immediately. **Yield:** 12 servings.

Molasses Steak Sandwiches

(Pictured at right)

A brown sugar-molasses marinade created in our Test Kitchen makes these hearty steak sandwiches irresistible. Topped with mellow Swiss cheese and grilled mushrooms, they're a satisfying change-of-pace meal.

1/4 cup molasses
2 tablespoons brown sugar
1 tablespoon olive oil
1 tablespoon Dijon mustard
4 beef tenderloin steaks (4 ounces *each*)
2 large portobello mushrooms, stems removed
4 kaiser rolls, split
4 slices Swiss cheese

In a large resealable plastic bag, combine the molasses, brown sugar, oil and mustard; add steaks. Seal bag and turn to coat; refrigerate for up to 2 hours.

Drain and discard marinade. Grill steaks, covered, over medium heat for 4-6 minutes on each side or until meat reaches desired doneness (for medium-rare, a meat thermometer should read 145°; medium, 160°; well-done, 170°).

Grill mushrooms for 3-4 minutes or until lightly browned, turning every minute. Place buns, cut sides down, on grill for 2-3 minutes or until golden brown. Cut mushrooms into 1/4-in. slices.

Place steaks, cheese and mushrooms on bun bottoms; replace tops. Serve immediately. **Yield:** 4 servings.

Horseradish-Dill Grilled Corn

(Pictured on page 201)

Horseradish is the secret ingredient for this crowd-pleaser.
Our home economists guarantee you'll never prepare corn on the cob any other way!

5 medium ears sweet corn
  in husks
1/3 cup butter, softened
1 tablespoon prepared
  horseradish
1/2 teaspoon salt
1/4 teaspoon garlic powder
1/4 teaspoon white pepper
1/4 teaspoon snipped fresh dill
10 fresh dill sprigs

Soak the corn in cold water for 1 hour. Meanwhile, in a small bowl, combine the butter, horseradish, salt, garlic powder, pepper and snipped dill; set aside.

Carefully peel back husks from corn to within 1 in. of bottom; remove silk. Spread butter mixture over corn; place two sprigs of dill on opposite sides of each ear. Rewrap husks and secure with kitchen string.

Coat grill rack with cooking spray before starting the grill. Grill corn, covered, over medium heat for 25-30 minutes or until tender, turning occasionally. Cut string and peel back husks. Remove and discard dill sprigs before serving. **Yield:** 5 servings.

Grilled Cajun Green Beans

This quick and fabulous recipe gives you one more reason to fire up the grill.
Cajun seasoning adds a delicious kick to garden-fresh green beans.
—Shannon Lewis, Andover, Minnesota

1 pound fresh green beans,
  trimmed
1/2 teaspoon Cajun seasoning
1 tablespoon butter

Place green beans on a double thickness of heavy-duty foil (about 18 in. square). Sprinkle with Cajun seasoning and dot with butter. Fold foil around beans and seal tightly.

Grill, covered, over medium heat for 10 minutes. Turn the packet over; grill 8-12 minutes longer or until the beans are tender. Carefully open the foil to the allow steam to escape. **Yield:** 4 servings.

SAVE TIME TRIMMING BEANS

TO EASILY trim green beans, gather the beans into a bunch and line up the stem ends. Cut off the ends with a sharp knife. Repeat on the other side.

Granola Trail Mix

(Pictured at right, bottom)

This homemade granola stores well, so it's an ideal take-along treat for trips. My family can't stop munching on it.
—Shelley Riddlespurger, Amarillo, Texas

1 package (18 ounces) granola without raisins
1 package (15 ounces) raisins
1 package (14 ounces) milk chocolate M&M's
1 can (12 ounces) honey roasted peanuts

In a large bowl, combine all of the ingredients. Store in an airtight container. **Yield:** about 3 quarts.

Cinnamon-Glazed Peanuts

(Pictured above, top)

You won't be able to stop snacking on these buttery, sweet peanuts from our Test Kitchen. Because they're prepared on a grill, the nuts are an easy treat to make while camping.

1 can (12 ounces) salted peanuts
1/2 cup packed brown sugar
3/4 teaspoon ground cinnamon
2 teaspoons honey
3 tablespoons butter
1/2 teaspoon vanilla extract

Place peanuts in a greased 11-in. x 7-in. x 2-in. disposable foil pan. Sprinkle with brown sugar and cinnamon. Drizzle with honey and dot with butter.

Grill, uncovered, over medium heat for 10 minutes, stirring occasionally, or until sugar is bubbly and peanuts are golden brown. Remove from the grill; stir in vanilla. Transfer to waxed paper to cool completely. Store in an airtight container. **Yield:** 2-1/2 cups.

Vanilla Ice Cream in a Bag

(Pictured at far right)

This summertime delight is fun for kids of all ages. Enjoy fresh, homemade ice cream anywhere!
—Erin Hoffman, Canby, Minnesota

1 cup milk
2 tablespoons sugar
2 tablespoons evaporated milk
1 teaspoon vanilla extract
4 cups coarsely crushed ice
3/4 cup salt

In a small resealable plastic bag, combine the milk, sugar, evaporated milk and vanilla. Press out air and seal. In a large resealable plastic bag, combine the ice and salt; add the sealed small bag.

Seal the large bag; place in another large resealable plastic bag and seal. Shake and knead for 5-7 minutes or until cream mixture is thickened. Serve immediately or freeze. **Yield:** 1 cup.

MAKING ICE CREAM IN A BAG

1. Place the sealed plastic bag with the milk mixture into a larger plastic bag that contains the ice and salt. Place in another large resealable plastic bag; seal.

2. Shake and knead the bag for 5-7 minutes until the cream mixture thickens.

Campfire Cobbler

(Pictured at right)

Put away the marshmallows and try this cobbler from our Test Kitchen instead! The delectable dessert can be prepared right over your campfire using a Dutch oven. Add variety by substituting other pie fillings.

1-1/4 cups biscuit/baking mix
    1 envelope instant maple and
      brown sugar oatmeal
  1/4 cup cold butter, cubed
  1/3 cup milk
    2 cans (21 ounces *each*)
      blueberry pie filling
  3/4 cup unsweetened apple juice
Vanilla Ice Cream in a Bag
  (recipe on opposite page), optional

Prepare grill or campfire for low heat, using 12-16 charcoal briquettes or large wood chips.

In a large resealable plastic bag, combine biscuit mix and oatmeal. Add butter; squeeze bag until mixture resembles coarse crumbs. Gradually add milk; knead to form a soft dough. Spread into a greased ovenproof Dutch oven. Combine pie filling and apple juice; pour over dough.

Cover Dutch oven. When briquettes or wood chips are covered with white ash, place Dutch oven directly on top of 6-8 of them. Using long-handled tongs, place 6-8 briquettes on pan cover. Cook for 15 minutes or until filling is bubbly.

To check for doneness, use the tongs to carefully lift cover. If necessary, cook 5 minutes longer. Serve with ice cream if desired. **Yield:** 6 servings.

Sugar Cookie S'mores

Our home economists give the classic s'more a yummy makeover by using sugar cookies and Milky Way candy bars. They're the perfect addition to any cookout or camping trip.

8 fun-size Milky Way candy
  bars
8 sugar cookies (3 inches)
4 large marshmallows

Place two candy bars on each of four cookies; place on grill rack. Grill, uncovered, over medium-hot heat for 1 to 1-1/2 minutes or until bottoms of cookies are browned.

Meanwhile, using a long-handled fork, toast marshmallows 6 in. from the heat until golden brown, turning occasionally. Remove marshmallows from fork and place over candy bars; top with remaining cookies. Serve immediately. **Yield:** 4 servings.

Fresh Summer Fruit

SAY "summer" and people's minds likely turn to lazy, carefree days...family picnics in the park...bright blue and sunny skies...and roadside stands featuring the season's finest fruit!

From cherries, berries and melon to peaches, plums and pineapple, this chapter offers ripe-for-the-picking recipes that will let you delight in all of your favorite fruits.

Enhance the natural flavors of grilled chicken and chops by serving zesty Gingered Peach Chutney on the side.

You can also showcase summer's finest at the end of a meal by offering guests Majestic Cherry Pie, fresh-from-the-oven Cherry Turnovers or a bowl of vanilla ice cream topped with Fresh Fruit Sauce. (All recipes shown at right.)

Fresh 'n' Fruity
(Clockwise from top right)

Cherry Turnovers (p. 212)

Majestic Cherry Pie (p. 210)

Fresh Fruit Sauce (p. 213)

Gingered Peach Chutney (p. 210)

Majestic Cherry Pie

(Pictured on page 209)

*Here's a cherry pie fit for a king! Sweet, lightly colored Rainier cherries
blend beautifully with tart, deep red Bing cherries to create this impressive pie.*
—*Louise Piper, Rolfe, Iowa*

1 cup plus 1 tablespoon sugar, *divided*
2 tablespoons all-purpose flour
2 tablespoons quick-cooking tapioca
1/8 teaspoon salt
3-1/2 cups pitted fresh Rainier cherries
1 cup halved pitted fresh Bing cherries
1 tablespoon lemon juice
4-1/2 teaspoons butter
Pastry for double-crust pie (9 inches)
2 teaspoons milk

In a large bowl, combine 1 cup sugar, flour, tapioca and salt. Add cherries and lemon juice; toss to coat. Let stand for 15 minutes.

Line a 9-in. pie plate with bottom pastry; trim even with edge of plate. Add filling; dot with butter. Roll out remaining pastry to fit top of pie; place over filling. Trim, seal and flute edges. Cut slits in pastry. Brush with milk and sprinkle with remaining sugar.

Cover edges loosely with foil. Bake at 400° for 45-50 minutes or until crust is golden brown and filling is bubbly. Cool on a wire rack. **Yield:** 6-8 servings.

Gingered Peach Chutney

(Pictured on page 208)

*This peach chutney is spectacular served over grilled chicken breasts or pork chops. The fresh flavor
is accented by ginger, garlic and other seasonings, with a slight kick from a touch of chili powder.*
—*Marlene Wiczek, Little Falls, Minnesota*

4 cups chopped peeled fresh peaches
1-1/2 cups cider vinegar
1 cup plus 2 tablespoons packed brown sugar
1 small onion, finely chopped
1/2 cup raisins
1/3 cup chopped candied *or* crystallized ginger
1 tablespoon mustard seed
1 tablespoon chili powder
1 teaspoon salt
1 small garlic clove, minced

In a Dutch oven, combine all ingredients. Bring to a boil over medium heat. Reduce heat; simmer, uncovered, for 45-50 minutes or until thickened and reduced to about 3-1/2 cups, stirring occasionally.

Serve warm or at room temperature. Refrigerate leftovers. **Yield:** 3-1/2 cups.

Americana Smoothies

(Pictured at right)

Creamy, fruity and refreshing, these patriotic smoothies are a welcome treat on warm summer days.
—Donna-Marie Ryan
Topsfield, Massachusetts

1 carton (6 ounces) strawberry
   yogurt
1/2 cup fresh strawberries, hulled
1/2 cup fresh blueberries
2 tablespoons honey
2 cups cubed seedless
   watermelon, frozen
Small watermelon wedges, optional

In a blender, combine the yogurt, berries and honey. Cover and process for 30-45 seconds or until blended, stirring if necessary. Add watermelon; cover and process until smooth. Pour into chilled glasses; garnish with melon wedges if desired. Serve immediately. **Yield:** 4 servings.

Family Traditions

OUR area has several pick-your-own berry farms that yield a very tasty crop. When my children were younger, we would spend beautiful summer afternoons selecting the best-looking strawberries so I could make their favorite freezer jam.
—*Sharon Parsons, Killingworth, Connecticut*

Cherry Turnovers

(Pictured on page 209)

These cherry pie pockets are a welcome treat, especially when they're served warm from the oven.
—*Lori Daniels, Beverly, West Virginia*

2-2/3 cups all-purpose flour
1 teaspoon salt
3/4 cup shortening
6 tablespoons cold water
FILLING:
2 cups fresh *or* frozen pitted tart cherries, thawed
1/2 cup sugar
2 tablespoons plus 1-1/2 teaspoons cornstarch
1/4 teaspoon ground cinnamon
GLAZE:
1 cup confectioners' sugar
1 to 2 tablespoons milk
1/2 teaspoon vanilla extract

In a large bowl, combine flour and salt; cut in shortening until crumbly. Gradually add water, tossing with a fork until dough forms a ball. Wrap in plastic wrap; refrigerate for 30 minutes.

Meanwhile, in a large saucepan, combine cherries and sugar. Mash slightly; let stand for 15-20 minutes. Stir in cornstarch until blended. Bring to a boil over medium heat; cook and stir for 2 minutes or until thickened. Remove from the heat; stir in cinnamon. Cool.

Divide dough into eight portions. On a lightly floured surface, roll out each portion into a 5-in. circle. Place about 3 tablespoons cherry mixture on one side of each circle; fold dough over filling. Press edges with a fork to seal. Prick tops with a fork.

Place on a greased baking sheet. Bake at 375° for 30-35 minutes or until golden brown. Combine glaze ingredients; drizzle over turnovers. Serve warm. **Yield:** 8 servings.

Plum Crisp

With its slightly sweet oat topping, this dessert is a mouth-watering way to feature a late-summer fruit.
—*Lillian Julow, Gainesville, Florida*

3-1/2 cups chopped fresh plums (about 2 pounds)
6 tablespoons brown sugar, *divided*
5 teaspoons all-purpose flour, *divided*
1/8 teaspoon pepper
Pinch ground nutmeg
Pinch ground cloves
2/3 cup old-fashioned oats
2 tablespoons butter, melted
1-1/2 teaspoons finely grated orange peel

In a large bowl, combine plums and 3 tablespoons brown sugar. Combine 2 teaspoons flour, pepper, nutmeg and cloves; sprinkle over plums and toss to coat. Transfer to a greased shallow 1-qt. baking dish.

In a small bowl, combine oats with remaining brown sugar and flour. Stir in butter and orange peel until crumbly. Sprinkle over plum mixture.

Bake at 375° for 20-25 minutes or until topping is golden brown and plums are tender. Serve warm. **Yield:** 6 servings.

Plum Dumplings

(Pictured at right)

Special meals call for elegant desserts like this. Sweet plums are halved then tucked inside a pretty pastry pocket.
—Martha Voss, Dickinson, North Dakota

1-1/2 cups all-purpose flour
1/4 cup sugar
1 teaspoon baking powder
1/8 teaspoon salt
6 tablespoons milk
1 egg, lightly beaten
3 medium black plums, halved and pitted
1 cup water
3 tablespoons butter
Melted butter and cinnamon-sugar

In a large bowl, combine the flour, sugar, baking powder and salt. Stir in milk and egg just until blended. Divide into six portions.

On a lightly floured surface, pat each portion of dough into a 5-in. circle. Place a plum half on each circle. Gently bring up corners of dough to center; pinch edges to seal.

In a Dutch oven, bring water and butter to a boil. Carefully add dumplings. Reduce heat; cover and simmer for 20-25 minutes or until a toothpick inserted into a dumpling comes out clean. Serve warm with pan juices, melted butter and cinnamon-sugar. **Yield:** 6 servings.

Fresh Fruit Sauce

(Pictured on page 208)

Summer is the perfect time to enjoy ice cream, especially when it's topped with this delectable fruit sauce.
—Katie Koziolek, Hartland, Minnesota

1 tablespoon cornstarch
1 cup orange juice
1/3 cup honey
1 cup sliced fresh peaches
1 cup sliced fresh plums
Vanilla ice cream

In a small saucepan, combine cornstarch and orange juice until smooth; stir in honey. Bring to a boil over medium heat; cook and stir for 1 minute or until thickened. Remove from the heat. Stir in peaches and plums. Serve with ice cream. **Yield:** 2-1/4 cups.

Cherry Chocolate Fruit Tart

These pretty tarts burst with fresh fruit flavors—pineapple, kiwi,
blueberries and two kinds of cherries. It's a unique combination that proves to be irresistible.
—Cherry Wiest, Yakima, Washington

3/4 cup butter, softened
1/2 cup confectioners' sugar
1-1/2 cups all-purpose flour
1-1/2 cups vanilla *or* white chips
1 package (8 ounces) cream cheese, softened
1/4 cup heavy whipping cream
1 can (20 ounces) unsweetened pineapple chunks
3 tablespoons sugar
2 teaspoons cornstarch
1/2 teaspoon lemon juice
1 pint fresh Rainier cherries, pitted and halved
1 pint fresh dark sweet cherries, pitted and halved
1 to 2 medium kiwifruit, peeled and sliced
1/3 cup fresh blueberries

In a small mixing bowl, cream butter and confectioners' sugar. Gradually add flour until the mixture forms a ball. Press into an ungreased 9-in. fluted tart pan with a removable bottom. Bake at 350° for 25-30 minutes or until golden brown. Cool on a wire rack.

In a small microwave-safe bowl, melt vanilla chips at 70% power. In a small mixing bowl, beat cream cheese until smooth; beat in melted chips and cream. Spread over crust. Cover and refrigerate for 30 minutes or until set.

Drain pineapple, reserving 1/2 cup juice; set pineapple aside. In a small saucepan, combine the sugar, cornstarch, lemon juice and reserved pineapple juice until smooth. Bring to a boil; cook and stir for 2 minutes or until thickened. Cool slightly.

Arrange the cherries, kiwi, blueberries and pineapple over filling. Brush with pineapple juice mixture. Cover and refrigerate for at least 1 hour before serving. **Yield:** 8 servings.

Kielbasa Fruit Kabobs

If you want to serve something that's deliciously different at your next cookout, look no further.
Apricots, plums and sausage create these unique and zesty kabobs.
—Mary Relyea, Canastota, New York

3 tablespoons orange marmalade
1 teaspoon Chinese five-spice powder
1 pound smoked kielbasa *or* Polish sausage, cut into 1-inch pieces
3 medium apricots, pitted and quartered
2 medium plums, pitted and quartered

In a small bowl, combine marmalade and five-spice powder; set aside.

Alternately thread the kielbasa, apricots and plums onto four metal or soaked wooden skewers. Grill, covered, over medium heat or broil 4-6 in. from the heat for 6-8 minutes or until heated through, turning and basting occasionally with marmalade mixture. **Yield:** 4 servings.

Mojito Marinated Fruit

(Pictured at right)

A mojito is a popular Cuban cocktail featuring rum, lime juice, sugar and fresh mint. In this recipe, our home economists created a mojito-type syrup in which to marinate assorted fruit.

2/3 cup sugar
1/3 cup water
1/2 cup light rum
2 tablespoons lime juice
1 teaspoon grated lime peel
2 cups *each* cantaloupe, honeydew and seedless watermelon balls
2 cups cubed fresh pineapple
3 mint sprigs
Additional mint sprigs, optional

In a small saucepan, combine sugar and water. Cook and stir over medium heat until sugar is dissolved. Remove from the heat. Stir in the rum, lime juice and peel. Cool.

In a large bowl, combine the melon, pineapple and mint. Add marinade; toss to coat. Cover and refrigerate overnight. Discard mint. Spoon fruit with syrup into serving cups. Garnish with additional mint if desired. **Yield:** 10 servings.

Sweet 'n' Savory Peach Chicken

(Pictured at far right, bottom)

Juicy chicken breasts topped with a mouth-watering peach sauce create this tangy entree.
You might also try making this dish using nectarines in place of the peaches.
—*Regena Hofer, Meadows, Manitoba*

3 tablespoons all-purpose flour
1 teaspoon salt
1/2 teaspoon pepper
1 broiler/fryer chicken
   (3-1/2 to 4 pounds), cut up
2 to 3 tablespoons vegetable oil
1 cup orange juice
2 tablespoons cider vinegar
2 tablespoons honey
1 tablespoon minced fresh
   parsley
3 medium peaches, peeled and
   sliced

In a large resealable plastic bag, combine the flour, salt and pepper. Add chicken, a few pieces at a time, and shake to coat.

In a large skillet, fry chicken in oil until browned on all sides. Transfer to a greased 13-in. x 9-in. x 2-in. baking dish.

In a small bowl, combine the orange juice, vinegar, honey and parsley; pour over chicken. Cover and bake at 350° for 40 minutes.

Uncover; add peaches. Bake 5-10 minutes longer or until chicken juices run clear and peaches are heated through. **Yield:** 4 servings.

Berries and Cream Wonton Cups

These delightful bites look so elegant when served on a pretty platter, but are really quite easy to prepare.
For an extra special touch, garnish the berry cups with a sprinkling of confectioners' sugar and fresh mint.
—*Heidi Hoskinson, Conifer, Colorado*

24 wonton wrappers
1 tablespoon butter, melted
2 tablespoons sugar
1-1/2 cups fresh raspberries, *divided*
1 cup whipped topping
1 carton (6 ounces) raspberry
   yogurt
1/2 cup fresh blueberries
Confectioners' sugar and fresh
   mint, optional

Brush wonton wrappers with butter and sprinkle with sugar. Press sugar side up into ungreased miniature muffin cups. Bake at 350° for 8-10 minutes or until lightly browned. Cool completely.

Place 1/2 cup raspberries in a small bowl; mash slightly. Add whipped topping and yogurt; stir to combine. Spoon into wonton cups. Top with blueberries and remaining raspberries. Garnish with confectioners' sugar and mint if desired. **Yield:** 2 dozen.

Melon Salad With Poppy Seed Vinaigrette

(Pictured at right, top)

With a hint of sweetness, the poppy seed vinaigrette dressing complements colorful melon and sliced cucumber in this summertime salad. When arranged on a bed of tender baby spinach, this salad has a pretty presentation, too.
—*Priscilla Gilbert*
Indian Harbour Beach, Florida

1 cup *each* cubed cantaloupe, honeydew and seedless watermelon
1/2 cup chopped cucumber
2 tablespoons coarsely chopped fresh mint
2 tablespoons sugar
2 tablespoons white wine vinegar
1/2 teaspoon salt
1/4 teaspoon ground mustard
1/4 cup vegetable oil
1 tablespoon plain yogurt
1 teaspoon poppy seeds
4 cups fresh baby spinach

In a large bowl, combine the melon, cucumber and mint; cover and refrigerate until serving.

For vinaigrette, in a small saucepan, combine the sugar, vinegar, salt and mustard. Cook and stir over medium heat until sugar is dissolved. Cool. Transfer to a blender. While processing, gradually add oil in a steady stream. Stir in yogurt and poppy seeds.

Pour half of the vinaigrette over melon mixture; toss to coat. Arrange spinach on a serving platter; top with melon. Drizzle with remaining vinaigrette. **Yield:** 4 servings.

SWEETER MELONS

IF YOU cut up a cantaloupe or watermelon and it's not as sweet as you'd like, sprinkle a little artificial sweetener over it and let it sit an hour or so.

Peach Cobbler with Praline Biscuits

Praline biscuits add a scrumptious twist to traditional peach cobbler. With old-fashioned flavor in every bite, this comforting dessert is one your family will request often when peaches are ripe.
—Jacqueline Rusnak, Emporium, Pennsylvania

1-1/2 cups sugar
  3 tablespoons cornstarch
  1 teaspoon ground cinnamon
  1 cup water
  8 cups sliced peeled fresh
    peaches
BISCUITS:
  1 cup chopped pecans
  1/4 cup packed dark brown sugar
  3 tablespoons butter, melted
  2 cups self-rising flour
  2 teaspoons sugar
  1/8 teaspoon salt
  1/2 cup shortening
  3/4 cup buttermilk

In a large saucepan, combine the sugar, cornstarch, cinnamon and water until smooth. Stir in peaches. Bring to a boil; cook and stir for 1-2 minutes or until thickened. Remove from the heat. Pour into a greased 13-in. x 9-in. x 2-in. baking dish; set aside.

In a small bowl, combine the pecans, brown sugar and butter; set aside. In a large bowl, combine the flour, sugar and salt. Cut in shortening until mixture resembles coarse crumbs. Stir in buttermilk just until moistened.

Turn dough onto a well-floured surface; knead 3-4 times. Roll into a 12-in. x 8-in. rectangle. Sprinkle with reserved pecan mixture to within 1/2 in. of edges. Roll up jelly-roll style, starting with a long side; pinch seam to seal. Cut into 1/2-in. slices; place cut side down over peach mixture.

Bake at 400° for 30-35 minutes or until biscuits are golden brown. Serve warm. **Yield:** 12 servings.

Editor's Note: As a substitute for each cup of self-rising flour, place 1-1/2 teaspoons baking powder and 1/2 teaspoon salt in a measuring cup. Add all-purpose flour to measure 1 cup.

Summertime Orzo Salad

This chilled salad is an ideal warm-weather refresher. Chopped apricots and peaches are tossed with crunchy almonds and a zesty dressing to bring the very best of summer to the table.
—Cheryl DeVecchis, Glassboro, New Jersey

1-1/3 cups uncooked orzo pasta
  1 teaspoon vegetable oil
  2 apricots, peeled and chopped
  1 medium peach, peeled and
    chopped
  4 green onions, thinly sliced
  1/3 cup sliced almonds, toasted
  1 tablespoon grated fresh
    gingerroot
  1 teaspoon minced fresh cilantro
  1/4 teaspoon ground coriander
  1/4 teaspoon salt
  1/4 teaspoon pepper
  3 tablespoons lemon juice

Cook orzo according to package directions; drain and rinse with cold water. Transfer to a large bowl. Stir in oil; set aside.

In a small bowl, combine the apricots, peach, onions, almonds, ginger, cilantro, coriander, salt and pepper. Sprinkle with lemon juice; toss to coat. Add to orzo and stir to coat. Refrigerate until serving. **Yield:** 5 servings.

Stuffed Cherries Dipped in Chocolate

(Pictured at right)

If you like chocolate-covered cherries, you're in for a real treat with these decadent little gems. Dark sweet cherries are filled with a luscious cream cheese mixture before being dipped in chocolate. They're almost too pretty to eat!
—Judy Bond, Duncan, British Columbia

1-1/2 **pounds fresh dark sweet cherries with stems**
   1 **package (8 ounces) cream cheese, softened**
   2 **tablespoons ground hazelnuts**
   2 **tablespoons maple syrup**
   2 **cups vanilla *or* white chips**
 12 **teaspoons shortening, *divided***
1-1/2 **cups milk chocolate chips**
1-1/2 **cups semisweet chocolate chips**

Pit cherries through the sides, leaving stems intact. In a small mixing bowl, beat cream cheese until smooth. Stir in hazelnuts and syrup. Pipe into cherries.

In a small microwave-safe bowl, melt vanilla chips and 5 teaspoons shortening at 70% power; stir until smooth. In another bowl, melt milk chocolate chips with 3-1/2 teaspoons shortening; stir until smooth. Repeat with semisweet chips and remaining shortening.

Holding stems, dip a third of the stuffed cherries into melted white chocolate; allow excess to drip off. Place on waxed paper; let stand until set. Repeat with remaining cherries and milk and semisweet chocolate. Dip the white-coated cherries a second time to completely cover; let stand until set.

Reheat remaining melted chocolate if necessary. Drizzle white chocolate over cherries dipped in milk or semisweet chocolate. Drizzle milk or semisweet chocolate over white chocolate-dipped cherries. Store in an airtight container in the refrigerator. **Yield:** 5 dozen.

SPECIAL Celebrations

Neighborhood Block Party

IN THIS busy age where we run to work, school and extra-curricular activities, you may be home hardly long enough to see your family much less your neighbors.

One great way to connect with your neighbors is by planning a potluck block party. Instead of firing up the grill for ordinary hamburgers, make gourmet-style Spinach Feta Burgers. Just five ingredients are all you need for Three-Bean Baked Beans, while Chopped Garden Salad is easily assembled ahead of time.

Kids of all ages won't be able to keep their hands off of richly decadent Deluxe Marshmallow Brownies and scrumptious Chocolate Chip Molasses Cookies. (All recipes are shown at right.)

NEIGHBORHOOD POTLUCK
(Pictured above, left to right)

Chopped Garden Salad (p. 226)

Chocolate Chip Molasses Cookies (p. 224)

Three-Bean Baked Beans (p. 224)

Spinach Feta Burgers (p. 222)

Italian Sausage Sandwiches (p. 225)

Deluxe Marshmallow Brownies (p. 222)

Deluxe Marshmallow Brownies

(Pictured on page 221)

You'll have to open wide to take a bite of these rich, decadent morsels! The big batch is perfect for potlucks.
—*Martha Stine, Johnstown, Pennsylvania*

1 cup butter, cubed
4 squares (1 ounce *each*)
  unsweetened chocolate,
  coarsely chopped
2 cups sugar
4 eggs
2 teaspoons vanilla extract
1-1/2 cups all-purpose flour
1-1/2 teaspoons baking powder
1 cup chopped walnuts *or* pecans
TOPPING:
1/2 cup butter, cubed
4 squares (1 ounce *each*)
  unsweetened chocolate,
  coarsely chopped
1 cup sugar
1 can (5 ounces) evaporated milk
3-3/4 cups confectioners' sugar
3 teaspoons vanilla extract
4 cups miniature marshmallows

In a microwave-safe bowl, melt butter and chocolate; stir until smooth. Cool. In a large mixing bowl, combine the sugar, eggs, vanilla and melted chocolate. Combine flour and baking powder; add to chocolate mixture and beat just until blended. Fold in nuts.

Spread into a greased 15-in. x 10-in. x 1-in. baking pan. Bake at 325° for 25-30 minutes or until a toothpick inserted near the center comes out clean.

Meanwhile, in a large heavy saucepan, melt butter and chocolate. Stir in sugar and milk. Cook over low heat for 20 minutes, stirring frequently. Gradually whisk in confectioners' sugar until smooth. Remove from the heat; stir in vanilla.

Place marshmallows over warm brownies; pour warm topping over marshmallows. Cool on a wire rack for at least 2 hours before cutting. **Yield:** about 3 dozen (35 servings).

Spinach Feta Burgers

(Pictured on page 221)

Mixed with feta, spinach, tomato, onion and a blend of seasonings, these hearty patties satisfy the biggest appetites.
—*Suzanne Kern, Louisville, Kentucky*

1 cup torn fresh spinach
1/2 cup crumbled feta cheese
1/2 cup chopped seeded plum
  tomatoes
2 green onions, chopped
1-1/2 teaspoons dill weed
1 teaspoon salt
1 teaspoon pepper
2 pounds ground beef
8 hamburger buns, split

In a large bowl, combine the first seven ingredients. Crumble the beef over mixture and mix well. Shape into eight 4-in. patties.

Grill, covered, over medium heat for 4-5 minutes on each side or until no longer pink. Serve on buns. **Yield:** 8 servings.

Scrumptious Scrambled Salad

(Pictured at right)

This pretty salad is chock-full of fresh ingredients. You can make it ahead, so it's great for parties.
— *Becky Muldrow, Highlands, Texas*

  2 large bunches romaine, torn
12 green onions, thinly sliced
1-1/2 cups sliced water chestnuts, coarsely chopped
  1 package (16 ounces) frozen peas, thawed
2-1/4 cups mayonnaise
1/2 cup plus 1 tablespoon evaporated milk
1/4 cup plus 1-1/2 teaspoons cider vinegar
3/4 teaspoon garlic powder
  2 cups (8 ounces) shredded cheddar cheese
  3 medium tomatoes, chopped

  1 pound sliced bacon, cooked, crumbled and drained
  3 hard-cooked eggs, sliced

In a very large salad bowl, layer the romaine, onions, water chestnuts and peas. Combine the mayonnaise, milk, vinegar and garlic powder; spread over peas. Sprinkle with cheese. Cover and refrigerate for 8 hours or overnight.

Just before serving, add the tomatoes, bacon and eggs; toss gently. **Yield:** 24 servings.

Speedy Salsa

Enjoy homemade salsa in a snap with this fresh-tasting recipe. Just combine the ingredients, chill and serve!
— *Dana Sapp, Scottsville, Kentucky*

  4 cans (14-1/2 ounces *each*) diced tomatoes, drained
  2 medium onions, chopped
1/2 cup minced fresh cilantro
  2 jalapeno peppers, seeded and minced
  2 tablespoons sugar
  1 teaspoon salt
Tortilla chips

In a large bowl, combine the tomatoes, onions, cilantro, jalapenos, sugar and salt. Cover and refrigerate until serving. Serve with tortilla chips. **Yield:** 7 cups.

Editor's Note: When cutting hot peppers, disposable gloves are recommended. Avoid touching your face.

Chocolate Chip Molasses Cookies

(Pictured on page 220)

Molasses adds an irresistible richness to these yummy chocolate chip cookies.
The cookie monsters in your house are bound to gobble them up quickly.
—Mellowdee Jae Brooks, Moscow, Idaho

1 cup shortening	In a large mixing bowl, beat the shortening, sugar and molasses. Add eggs, one at a time, beating well after each addition. Combine the flour, baking soda and salt; gradually add to creamed mixture. Stir in chocolate chips.
1-1/2 cups sugar	
1/2 cup molasses	
2 eggs	
3 cups all-purpose flour	Roll into 1-in. balls. Place 2 in. apart on ungreased baking sheets. Bake at 375° for 8-10 minutes or until edges are firm. Remove to wire racks. **Yield:** 7-1/2 dozen.
1-1/2 teaspoons baking soda	
1 teaspoon salt	
2 cups (12 ounces) semisweet chocolate chips	

Three-Bean Baked Beans

(Pictured on page 221)

Green chilies and chipotle peppers deliver the perfect amount of zip to these baked beans.
For large crowds, you can easily double the recipe for this scrumptious side.
—Darlene Brenden, Salem, Oregon

1 can (16 ounces) maple-cured bacon baked beans	In a large bowl, combine all the ingredients. Transfer to a greased 11-in. x 7-in. x 2-in. baking dish. Cover and bake at 350° for 1 hour. Uncover; bake 15-20 minutes longer or until bubbly. **Yield:** 8 servings.
1 can (15-1/2 ounces) hot chili beans	
1 can (15 ounces) black beans, rinsed and drained	
1 can (10 ounces) diced tomatoes and green chilies, undrained	
1-1/2 teaspoons minced chipotle peppers in adobo sauce	

Italian Sausage Sandwiches

(Pictured at right and on page 221)

These hearty sandwiches created by our Test Kitchen are packed with robust flavor. The grilled sausages smothered in a well-seasoned sauce are sure to become a staple at all your cookouts.

2 jars (26 ounces *each*) meatless
   spaghetti sauce
2 medium green peppers,
   cut into strips
2 medium onions, thinly sliced
1/2 teaspoon garlic powder
1/2 teaspoon fennel seed, crushed
2 packages (20 ounces *each*)
   Italian turkey sausage links
10 sandwich buns, split

In a 3-qt. slow cooker, combine the spaghetti sauce, green peppers, onions, garlic powder and fennel seed. Cover and cook on low for 4 hours or until vegetables are tender.

   Grill sausages according to package directions. Serve on buns with sauce. **Yield:** 10 servings.

Homemade Potato Chips

(Pictured above)

You won't settle for store-bought chips again after munching on these crunchy snacks from our home economists. Seasoned with garlic powder, celery salt and pepper, you'll keep going back to the bowl for more!

7 unpeeled medium potatoes
   (about 2 pounds)
2 quarts ice water
5 teaspoons salt
2 teaspoons garlic powder
1-1/2 teaspoons celery salt
1-1/2 teaspoons pepper
Oil for deep-fat frying

Using a vegetable peeler or metal cheese slicer, cut potatoes into very thin slices. Place in a large bowl; add ice water and salt. Soak for 30 minutes.

   Drain potatoes; place on paper towels and pat dry. In a small bowl, combine the garlic powder, celery salt and pepper; set aside.

   In an electric skillet, heat 1-1/2 in. of oil to 375°. Fry potatoes in batches for 3-4 minutes or until golden brown, stirring frequently. Remove with a slotted spoon; drain on paper towels. Immediately sprinkle with seasoning mixture. Store in an airtight container. **Yield:** 8-1/2 cups.

Chopped Garden Salad

(Pictured on page 220)

This simple salad travels well, making it an ideal dish to pass. The homemade dressing comes together easily and offers a delicious punch of flavor.
—*Anna Sutherland, Camp, Arkansas*

6 medium tomatoes
2 medium green peppers
2 large cucumbers
2 medium red onions
1-1/4 cups water
3/4 cup cider vinegar
4-1/2 teaspoons sugar
1-1/2 teaspoons mustard seed
1-1/2 teaspoons celery salt
1/2 teaspoon salt
1/8 teaspoon pepper

Dice the tomatoes, green peppers, cucumbers and onions; place in a 3-qt. salad bowl.

In a small saucepan, combine the remaining ingredients. Bring to a boil. Reduce heat; simmer, uncovered, for 1 minute, stirring occasionally. Cool slightly. Pour over vegetables and toss to coat. Cover and refrigerate overnight. Serve with a slotted spoon. **Yield:** 16 servings.

Pesto Pasta Medley

With just a handful of ingredients, this pasta salad is one quick-to-fix dish you can depend on.
—*Beth Lepore, Winchester, Massachusetts*

3 packages (7 ounces *each*) dried cheese tortellini
1 package (12 ounces) tricolor spiral pasta
1 can (14 ounces) water-packed artichoke hearts, rinsed, drained and quartered
2 jars (3-1/2 ounces *each*) prepared pesto
1 jar (6 ounces) oil-packed sun-dried tomatoes, drained and chopped
1/2 teaspoon salt
Grated Parmesan cheese, optional

Cook tortellini and spiral pasta according to package directions; drain and place in a large serving bowl. Add the artichokes, pesto, tomatoes and salt. Sprinkle with Parmesan cheese if desired. Serve warm or at room temperature. Refrigerate leftovers. **Yield:** 16 servings.

Cannellini Bean Hummus

(Pictured at right)

My version of hummus features a delightful nuttiness from tahini, a peanut butter-like paste made from ground sesame seeds.
—Marina Castle, Burbank, California

  2 garlic cloves, peeled
  1 can (15 ounces) cannellini *or* white kidney beans, rinsed and drained
1/4 cup tahini
  3 tablespoons lemon juice
1-1/2 teaspoons ground cumin
1/4 teaspoon salt
1/4 teaspoon crushed red pepper flakes
  2 tablespoons minced fresh parsley
Pita breads, cut into wedges

Place garlic in a food processor; cover and process until minced. Add the beans, tahini, lemon juice, cumin, salt and pepper flakes; cover and process until smooth.

Transfer to a small bowl; stir in parsley. Refrigerate until serving. Serve with pita wedges. **Yield:** 1-1/4 cups.

BLOCK PARTY PLAN

START getting to know your neighbors even before the party begins by forming a block party committee.

Not only will working together make the party easier to organize, you'll make some new friends in the process. Have one person act as the main contact person, then assign other groups to handle the following:

• Permits and other legal requirements.

• Food and refreshments. Potlucks are an easy way to make sure there's a variety of tasty fare at your block party. To keep from having a buffet full of chips or desserts, cir-

culate a sign-up sheet with assigned categories such as salads, veggies and desserts. For the main course, charge a per-person fee and purchase grill meat or have each family supply their own.

• Activities. Bicycle decorating contests, scavenger hunts, relay races…the sky's the limit when it comes to planning the fun and games for your neighborhood block party. To make sure both the young and young at heart have a good time, include a variety of activities that appeal to a wide age range.

• Set up and clean up.

SPECIAL *Celebrations*

Oktoberfest Fare

OKTOBERFEST is a sixteen-day festival held annually in Munich, Germany during late September and early October. Known as the Largest People's Fair in the World, this event attracts nearly six million visitors every year.

Besides beer, a main attraction at the festival is the cuisine! For true comfort food, nothing compares to hearty German fare.

If a trip to Bavaria isn't in your plans come autumn, host your own Oktoberfest celebration.

Welcome guests with mugs of Hot Spiced Cherry Cider, then offer assorted authentic dishes such as Wiener Schnitzel, German-Style Cabbage and Beans, Old-Country Sauerbraten, Potato Dumplings and Pumpernickel Bread. (All recipes shown at right.)

WILLKOMMEN!

(Clockwise from top right)

Pumpernickel Bread (p. 232)

German-Style Cabbage and Beans (p. 236)

Hot Spiced Cherry Cider (p. 230)

Wiener Schnitzel (p. 230)

Old-Country Sauerbraten (p. 234)

Potato Dumplings (p. 232)

Hot Spiced Cherry Cider

(Pictured on page 229)

Ideal on a brisk, fall day, this cherry cider is great to have simmering in your slow cooker.
—*Marlene Wiczek, Little Falls, Minnesota*

1 gallon apple cider *or* juice
2 cinnamon sticks (3 inches)
2 packages (3 ounces *each*) cherry gelatin

Place cider in a 6-qt. slow cooker; add cinnamon sticks. Cover and cook on high for 3 hours. Stir in gelatin; cook 1 hour longer. Discard cinnamon sticks before serving. **Yield:** 4 quarts.

Wiener Schnitzel

(Pictured on page 229)

For added convenience, chill the veal cutlets for 30 minutes after coating. While the cutlets chill, you'll have extra time to prepare the rest of the meal.
—*Emma West, Leoma, Tennessee*

4 veal cutlets (4 ounces *each*)
3/4 teaspoon salt
3/4 teaspoon pepper
1/2 cup all-purpose flour
2 eggs, lightly beaten
3/4 cup dry bread crumbs
1/4 cup butter
4 lemon slices

Sprinkle veal with salt and pepper. Place the flour, eggs and bread crumbs in separate shallow bowls. Coat veal with flour, then dip in eggs and coat with crumbs.

In a large skillet over medium heat, cook veal in butter for 2-3 minutes on each side or until juices run clear. Serve with lemon. **Yield:** 4 servings.

WURST AT ITS BEST

OKTOBERFEST requires one essential element—wurst, or sausage. German sausage comes in two basic categories, fresh sausages (such as Bratwurst, Knockwurst and Weisswurst) and slicing or spreading sausages (such as Liverwurst and Blutwurst, also called blood sausage).

More than a thousand varieties of wurst exist, with some being widely available and others being local specialties. Almost all wurst is made of pork (but sometimes beef or veal) and is seasoned with spices and peppercorns.

However, it's the addition of other ingredients, such as regional spices, cheeses, apples and vegetables that make the various types of wurst distinctive.

Beer 'n' Gouda Pretzels

(Pictured at right)

Our Test Kitchen created these soft, chewy pretzels that are just as much fun to make as they are to eat! Shredded Gouda cheese gives them a unique, distinct flavor that everybody loves.

4-3/4 to 5-1/4 cups all-purpose
     flour
    2 tablespoons sugar
    1 envelope (1/4 ounce)
     quick-rise yeast
1-1/2 teaspoons salt
    1 teaspoon caraway seeds
    1 cup milk
  1/2 cup beer *or* nonalcoholic beer
    2 tablespoons canola oil
    2 eggs, lightly beaten
    1 cup (4 ounces) shredded
     Gouda cheese
Coarse salt

In a large mixing bowl, combine 2 cups flour, sugar, yeast, salt and caraway seeds. In a small saucepan, heat the milk, beer and oil to 120°-130°; add to dry ingredients. Beat just until moistened. Stir in enough remaining flour to form a soft dough.

Turn onto a floured surface; knead until smooth and elastic, about 4-6 minutes. Cover and let rest for 10 minutes. Divide dough into 14 equal portions; roll each into a 20-in. rope. Cover and let rest 10 minutes longer.

Twist into pretzel shapes. Place on greased baking sheets; brush with eggs. Bake at 350° for 15 minutes.

Brush again with eggs; sprinkle with Gouda and coarse salt. Bake 12-15 minutes longer or until golden brown. Remove to wire racks. Serve warm. **Yield:** 14 pretzels.

Harry's Hot Mustard

(Pictured above)

Perfect for dipping pretzels or accompanying cooked sausage, this hot mustard delivers a serious kick. If you like spicy foods, this is one recipe you'll use time and again.
— Harry Goeschko, Waukesha, Wisconsin

3-1/2 cup ground mustard
1-1/2 teaspoons sugar
  1/2 teaspoon salt
    3 tablespoons water
    2 tablespoons white vinegar
Fully cooked bratwurst *or*
    smoked sausage

In a small bowl, combine the mustard, sugar and salt. Stir in water and vinegar until smooth. Transfer to a jar with a tight-fitting lid. Store in the refrigerator. Serve with sausage. **Yield:** 1/2 cup.

Pumpernickel Bread

(Pictured on page 229)

This dense, moist bread created by our Test Kitchen is a delightful classic.
Round out any meal by serving thick slices of the hearty loaf.

1 cup water
1 cup buttermilk
3 tablespoons olive oil
4-1/2 teaspoons molasses
1 teaspoon salt
3-1/2 cups rye flour
2/3 cup all-purpose flour
3 teaspoons active dry yeast

Heat water and buttermilk to 70°-80°. In bread machine pan, place all ingredients in order suggested by manufacturer. Select dough setting (check dough after 5 minutes of mixing; add 1 to 2 tablespoons of water or flour if needed).

When cycle is completed, turn dough onto a lightly floured surface. Shape into an 8-in. round loaf. Place on a greased baking sheet. Cover and let rise in a warm place until doubled, about 30 minutes.

Bake at 350° for 40-45 minutes or until the bread sounds hollow when tapped. Remove to a wire rack to cool. **Yield:** 1 loaf (2-1/4 pounds).

Potato Dumplings

(Pictured on page 228)

Potato dumplings (called Kartoffel Kloesse in Germany) are a delightful addition
to any German feast. The browned butter sauce is delectable.
—Arline Hofland, Deer Lodge, Montana

3 to 10 medium potatoes
   (about 3 pounds), peeled
   and quartered
1 cup all-purpose flour
3 eggs, beaten
2/3 cup dry bread crumbs
1 teaspoon salt
1/2 teaspoon ground nutmeg
12 cups water
BROWNED BUTTER SAUCE:
1 cup butter, cubed
2 tablespoons chopped onion
1/2 cup dry bread crumbs

Place potatoes in a Dutch oven and cover with water. Bring to a boil. Reduce heat; cover and simmer for 15-20 minutes or until tender. Drain.

In a large bowl, mash the potatoes. Stir in the flour, eggs, bread crumbs, salt and nutmeg. Shape into 2-in. balls.

In a Dutch oven, bring water to a boil. Carefully add dumplings. Reduce heat; simmer, uncovered, for 8-10 minutes or until a toothpick inserted into a dumpling comes out clean.

Meanwhile, in a large heavy saucepan, cook butter and onion over medium heat for 5-7 minutes or until butter is golden brown. Stir in bread crumbs. Serve with dumplings. **Yield:** 7 servings.

German Meatballs And Gravy

(Pictured at right)

*Paired with hot mashed potatoes,
this authentic entree serves
a hearty helping of Old World flavor.*
—Marshelle Greenmyer-Wagner
Englevale, North Dakota

1 egg
3-1/2 cups milk, *divided*
1/2 teaspoon Worcestershire
 sauce
1 cup finely shredded
 uncooked peeled potatoes
2 tablespoons finely chopped
 onion
2 teaspoons salt
1/2 teaspoon ground nutmeg
1/4 teaspoon ground ginger
1/4 teaspoon ground allspice
1/8 teaspoon pepper
2 pounds ground beef
1/4 cup butter, cubed
1/4 cup all-purpose flour
Hot mashed potatoes

In a large bowl, combine the egg, 1/2 cup milk, Worcestershire sauce, shredded potatoes, onion, salt, nutmeg, ginger, allspice and pepper. Crumble beef over mixture and mix well. Shape into 48 balls.

In a large skillet over medium heat, cook meatballs in butter in batches until no longer pink; remove and keep warm.

Stir flour into drippings until blended; gradually add the remaining milk. Bring to a boil; cook and stir for 2 minutes or until thickened. Return meatballs to the pan; heat through. Serve with mashed potatoes. **Yield:** 8 servings.

Old-Country Sauerbraten

(Pictured on page 228)

Enjoy a taste of the Old Country with this scrumptious German dish.
A traditional gravy adds wonderful flavor to the tender slices of beef served over hot spaetzle.
—Inge Perreault, Oxford, New Jersey

2 bay leaves
4 whole cloves
2 cups water
2 cups white vinegar
2 medium onions, sliced
2 garlic cloves, minced
2 teaspoons salt
1/2 teaspoon pepper
1 boneless beef top sirloin roast
   (3 to 4 pounds)
3 tablespoons butter
1/4 cup sugar
2 tablespoons molasses
1 to 2 tablespoons cornstarch
2 tablespoons cold water
5 to 6 gingersnap cookies,
   crushed
Hot cooked spaetzle

Place bay leaves and cloves on a double thickness of cheese-cloth; bring up corners of cloth and tie with kitchen string to form a bag. In a large saucepan, combine the water, vinegar, onions, garlic, salt and pepper. Add spice bag. Bring to a boil. Remove from the heat; cool completely.

Place the roast in a 2-gal. resealable plastic bag. Add marinade. Seal bag and turn to coat; refrigerate for 3 days, turning once each day.

Remove meat from marinade; reserve marinade. In a Dutch oven, brown roast in butter on all sides. Sprinkle with sugar. Add reserved marinade. Bring to a rolling boil for 1 minute. Stir in molasses. Reduce heat; cover and simmer for 1-1/4 to 1-1/2 hours or until meat is tender.

Remove roast to a cutting board. Cut into thin slices; set aside. Skim fat from cooking juices. Discard spice bag. In a small bowl, combine cornstarch and cold water until smooth; gradually stir into juices. Add gingersnaps. Bring to a boil; cook and stir for 2 minutes or until thickened. Return meat to gravy; heat through. Serve over spaetzle. **Yield:** 10 servings.

MAKING HOMEMADE SPAETZLE

HERE'S a traditional spaetzle recipe to accompany Old-Country Sauerbraten:

In a bowl, combine 2 cups all-purpose flour, 1 teaspoon salt, 2 eggs, lightly beaten and 1 cup milk. Let the mixture stand for 5 minutes. In a large saucepan, bring 2 quarts water or beef broth to a rapid boil. Place the spaetzle batter in a colander or spaetzle press. While holding the colander over the boiling liquid, press the batter through holes. Cook and stir for 5 minutes or until the spaetzle are tender; drain.

Black Forest Cheesecake

(Pictured at right)

This decadent dessert puts a delicious spin on the classic Black Forest cake. Top each serving with canned cherry pie filling, a dollop of whipped cream and chocolate curls for an elegant presentation.
—Carey Lynn Enns, Aylmer, Ontario

   2 packages (8 ounces *each*)
      cream cheese, softened
 3/4 cup sugar
   2 eggs, lightly beaten
   1 teaspoon vanilla extract
 1/2 teaspoon almond extract
Dash salt
BATTER:
 1-1/2 cups sugar
 1/2 cup canola oil
   1 egg
 1-1/2 teaspoons vanilla extract
 2-1/4 cups all-purpose flour
 1/3 cup baking cocoa
   1 teaspoon baking soda
 1/2 teaspoon baking powder
 1/4 teaspoon salt
 1-1/2 cups buttermilk *or* sour
      cream
TOPPING:
   1 can (21 ounces) cherry
      pie filling
Whipped topping and
   chocolate curls, optional

In a large mixing bowl, beat cream cheese and sugar until smooth. Add eggs; beat on low speed just until combined. Stir in extracts and salt; set aside.

In another large mixing bowl, beat the sugar, oil, egg and vanilla until well blended. Combine the flour, cocoa, baking soda, baking powder and salt; gradually add to sugar mixture alternately with buttermilk.

Spoon half of the batter into a greased and floured 10-in. fluted tube pan; spread with half of the cream cheese mixture. Repeat layers. Bake at 375° for 45-50 minutes or until a knife inserted near the center comes out clean. Cool for 10 minutes before removing from pan to a wire rack to cool completely.

Slice cake; serve with pie filling. Garnish with whipped topping and chocolate curls if desired. Refrigerate leftovers. **Yield:** 12 servings.

German-Style Cabbage and Beans

(Pictured on page 229)

I've taken this crisp, flavorful side dish to many potlucks where it's always a winner.
Against the green beans, the red cabbage adds a very festive, light pink color.
—Winifred Winch, Wetmore, Michigan

1 pound fresh green beans, cut into 1-1/2-inch pieces
3 bacon strips, cut into 1-inch pieces
1/2 cup cider vinegar
1/4 cup sugar
3 tablespoons chopped onion
1/2 teaspoon salt
1/4 teaspoon pepper
3 cups shredded red cabbage

Place 1 in. of water in a large saucepan; add beans. Bring to a boil. Reduce heat; cover and simmer for 8-10 minutes or until crisp-tender. Drain and set aside.

In a large skillet, cook bacon over medium heat until crisp. Remove to paper towels; drain, reserving 2 tablespoons drippings. Add the vinegar, sugar, onion, salt and pepper to the drippings. Bring to a boil.

Add cabbage. Reduce heat; cover and simmer for 5 minutes. Add beans; cook 3-5 minutes longer or until heated through. Stir in bacon. **Yield:** 6 servings.

Smoked Pork Chop Casserole

My family and I enjoy the taste of smoked pork chops with apples and potatoes
so I serve this often. If you prefer, you can also use non-smoked pork chops in this recipe.
—Patricia Sue Kopecky, Lake Arrowhead, California

8 medium potatoes, peeled and cut into 1/4-inch slices
1 large tart apple, peeled and cut into 1/4-inch slices
1 tablespoon chopped onion
1 cup (4 ounces) shredded Swiss cheese
6 smoked pork chops (6 ounces *each*)
SAUCE:
2 tablespoons butter
2 tablespoons all-purpose flour
1 cup milk
4 teaspoons Dijon mustard
Salt and pepper to taste

Place potatoes in a Dutch oven and cover with water. Bring to a boil. Reduce heat; cover and simmer for 8-10 minutes or until tender. Drain. Stir in apple and onion.

Transfer to a greased 13-in. x 9-in. x 2-in. baking dish. Sprinkle with cheese; top with pork chops. Cover and bake at 350° for 30 minutes.

In a small saucepan, melt butter over medium heat. Stir in flour until smooth; gradually add milk. Bring to a boil; cook and stir for 1-2 minutes or until thickened. Stir in the mustard, salt and pepper.

Pour over pork chops. Bake, uncovered, for 30 minutes or until heated through. **Yield:** 6 servings.

Pronto Potato Pancakes

(Pictured at right)

One of my favorite foods at our local Oktoberfest is potato pancakes with applesauce. Using a food processor makes preparing these potato pancakes at home easy and quick.
— *Darlene Brenden, Salem, Oregon*

2 eggs
1 small onion, halved
2 medium potatoes, peeled and cut into 1-inch cubes
2 to 4 tablespoons all-purpose flour
1/2 teaspoon salt
1/8 teaspoon cayenne pepper
4 to 6 tablespoons canola oil
Applesauce, optional

Place eggs and onion in a blender; cover and process until blended. Add potatoes; cover and process until finely chopped. Transfer to a small bowl. Stir in the flour, salt and cayenne.

Heat 2 tablespoons oil in a large nonstick skillet over medium heat.

Drop batter by 1/4 cupfuls into oil. Fry in batches until golden brown on both sides, using remaining oil as needed. Drain on paper towels. Serve with applesauce if desired. **Yield:** 8 pancakes.

SPECIAL Celebrations

Halloween Graveyard Gathering

SCARE UP frightful fun for friends and family on Halloween by hosting a ghost in the graveyard gathering.

To get into the spirit of the spooky celebration, prepare the creepy cuisine featured here.

Welcome guests to your haunt with a hair-raising beverage like Bloodthirsty Punch.

Capture the attention of carnivores and pass a platter piled high with finger-lickin'-good Juicy Bat Wings and Stack of Bones.

To send shivers down the backs of family and friends, serve spine-tingling Spiderweb Trap and Oozy Green Eyeballs! (All recipes shown at right.)

EERIE EATING
(Left to right)

Juicy Bat Wings (p. 242)

Spiderweb Trap (p. 242)

Oozy Green Eyeballs (p. 240)

Stack of Bones (p. 244)

Bloodthirsty Punch (p. 241)

Stained-Glass Spooks

(Pictured at far right)

Our Test Kitchen staff concocted these eye-catching candies. Dangle them with fishing line above your spooktacular table for a devilish decoration.

1-1/2 cups sugar
3/4 cup water
2/3 cup light corn syrup
1/2 teaspoon cream of tartar
1/2 teaspoon orange oil
Paste food coloring in colors
of your choice
Fishing line

Butter 10-12 assorted metal Halloween cookie cutters. Place on a parchment paper-lined baking sheet; set aside.

In a small heavy saucepan, combine the sugar, water, corn syrup and cream of tartar. Cook and stir over medium heat until sugar is dissolved. Bring to a boil. Cook, without stirring, until a candy thermometer reads 300° (hard-crack stage).

Remove from the heat; stir in orange oil. Pour into large ramekins or custard cups; tint with food coloring as desired.

Working quickly, pour sugar mixture into prepared cutters to a depth of 3/16 in. Cool for 1 minute. Using a wooden skewer, poke a hole in the top of each candy. (If sugar mixture hardens before pouring into cutters, microwave in a large ramekin or custard cup for 10 seconds on high.)

Remove cutters just before candy is set. String fishing line through holes; knot each line, forming a loop. Hang as desired. **Yield:** 10-12 candy ornaments.

Editor's Note: This recipe was tested with LorAnn orange oil. It can be found at candy and cake decorating supply shops or at www.lorannoils.com. We recommend that you test your candy thermometer before each use by bringing water to a boil; the thermometer should read 212°. Adjust your recipe temperature up or down based on your test.

Oozy Green Eyeballs

(Pictured on page 239)

Because it calls for frozen prepared meatballs, this unique appetizer takes mere minutes to prepare.
—*Carole Resnick, Cleveland, Ohio*

36 frozen cooked Italian meatballs
(1/2 ounce *each*), thawed
1 cup beef broth
1/4 cup mango chutney
4 teaspoons jalapeno pepper jelly
1 teaspoon red wine vinegar
1 tablespoon cornstarch
2 tablespoons mango nectar
1 tablespoon cold water
Dash pepper

Bake meatballs according to package directions. Meanwhile, in a small saucepan, combine the broth, chutney, jelly and vinegar. Cook and stir over medium heat for 3-4 minutes or until blended.

Combine the cornstarch, mango nectar and water; stir into broth mixture. Bring to a boil; cook and stir for 1-2 minutes or until thickened.

Drain meatballs; transfer to a serving dish. Drizzle with sauce; toss gently to coat. **Yield:** 3 dozen.

Bloodthirsty Punch

(Pictured at right and on page 239)

Years ago, a friend gifted me with a recipe box packed with her favorites... this refreshing punch was one of them. It's excellent for any occasion.
— Dianne Berst, Snohomish, Washington

2 quarts black cherry soda, chilled, *divided*
1 quart orange soda, chilled
1 quart lemon-lime soda, chilled

Pour 1 qt. black cherry soda into ice cube trays; freeze for at least 4 hours.

Just before serving, combine the orange soda, lemon-lime soda and remaining black cherry soda in a punch bowl or large pitcher. Add black cherry ice cubes. **Yield:** 3 quarts (about 2 dozen ice cubes).

RED-RIMMED GLASSES

FOR a terror-filled twist when serving Bloodthirsty Punch, coat the rims of your glasses with colored sugar. Here's how:

Place 1/4 in. of water in a small bowl; place red colored sugar in another small bowl. Dip the rims of cocktail glasses in water, then in colored sugar. You can prepare the glasses the morning of your party. Let stand at room temperature.

Spiderweb Trap

(Pictured on page 239)

Our home economists use a spaghetti squash "web" to capture gnocchi "bugs" in this savory side dish.

1 medium spaghetti squash
2 packages (16 ounces *each*) potato gnocchi
3 cups loosely packed basil leaves
3 tablespoons pine nuts, toasted
3 tablespoons grated Parmesan cheese
1 garlic clove, peeled
1/2 teaspoon salt
6 tablespoons olive oil

Cut squash in half lengthwise; discard seeds. Place squash, cut side down, on a microwave-safe plate. Microwave, uncovered, on high for 15-20 minutes or until tender. Meanwhile, cook gnocchi according to package directions.

For pesto, place the basil, pine nuts, Parmesan cheese, garlic and salt in a food processor; cover and process until chopped. While processing, gradually add oil in a steady stream; process until blended.

When squash is cool enough to handle, use a fork to separate strands. Drain gnocchi; place in a large bowl. Add spaghetti squash and pesto; toss to coat. **Yield:** 10 servings.

Editor's Note: This recipe was tested in a 1,100-watt microwave. Look for potato gnocchi in the pasta, ethnic or frozen section of your grocery store.

Juicy Bat Wings

(Pictured on page 239)

These wings are guaranteed to have your guests licking their fingers clean! If desired, you can replace the seasonings listed in the recipe with 1/4 cup purchased blackened seasoning.
—*Corey Russo, Orono, Minnesota*

Oil for deep-fat frying
2-1/2 to 3 pounds chicken wings
1/2 cup cider vinegar
1/2 cup honey
1 tablespoon dried thyme
2 teaspoons sugar
1 teaspoon each salt, onion powder, garlic powder, paprika and pepper
1/2 teaspoon ground cumin
1/2 teaspoon dried oregano
1/2 teaspoon cayenne pepper
1/4 teaspoon ground nutmeg

In an electric skillet or deep-fat fryer, heat oil to 375°. Fry chicken wings, a few at a time, for 3-4 minutes on each side or until juices run clear. Drain on paper towels; keep warm.

Meanwhile, in a small saucepan, combine the remaining ingredients. Bring to a boil; cook until liquid is syrupy and reduced by about half, keeping face away from mixture as odor is very strong. Place chicken wings in a large bowl; drizzle with syrup and toss to coat. **Yield:** about 1 dozen.

Ghosts in the Graveyard Cake

(Pictured at right)

This spooky cake from our Test Kitchen is easy to make and fun to decorate. To save time, bake and freeze the brownies weeks in advance, then thaw at room temperature overnight before decorating.

1 package fudge brownie mix
(13-inch x 9-inch pan size)
1 package fudge brownie mix
(8-inch square pan size)
3 pretzel rods
1 cup (6 ounces) semisweet
chocolate chips, melted
6 ounces white candy coating,
melted
3 lollipop sticks
6 chocolate jimmies
1 can (16 ounces) chocolate
frosting
2/3 cup confectioners' sugar
1 tablespoon baking cocoa
Black paste food coloring
Vanilla frosting
1 cup chocolate wafer crumbs
1/4 cup flaked coconut, toasted

Line a 13-in. x 9-in. x 2-in. baking pan and an 8-in. square baking dish with foil and grease the foil. Prepare brownie batter and bake according to package directions, using prepared pans. Cool on wire racks.

Break pretzel rods into various sizes; dip into melted chocolate. Arrange into a tree shape on a waxed paper-lined baking sheet.

Place melted white candy coating in a heavy-duty resealable plastic bag; cut a small hole in a corner of bag. Outline three small ghosts on waxed paper. Fill in ghost outlines, adding a lollipop stick to each for support. Place jimmies on ghosts for eyes. Let dry completely.

Using foil, lift brownies out of pans. Discard foil; place 8-in. square brownie on a large serving plate for graveyard. Spread chocolate frosting over top and sides.

Cut remaining brownie into 3-in. x 1-1/2-in. tombstone shapes. Combine confectioners' sugar and cocoa; sprinkle over tombstones. With black food coloring, tint vanilla frosting gray; decorate tombstones.

Using toothpicks, insert three tombstones into graveyard. Insert tree into graveyard (support as needed with brownie scraps). Insert ghosts into graveyard; sprinkle with wafer crumbs for dirt and coconut for grass. Place remaining tombstones on a serving platter. **Yield:** 1 graveyard cake (9 servings) and 20 tombstones.

R.I.P. (Rest In Pizza)

This pizza is light but full of flavor thanks to plenty of fresh vegetables.
—Julie Stoner, Peoria, Illinois

1 package (1/4 ounce) active
   dry yeast
1-2/3 cups warm water (110° to 115°)
2 tablespoons sugar
2 tablespoons olive oil
1 teaspoon salt
1 teaspoon lemon juice
2 cups all-purpose flour
2 to 2-1/2 cups whole wheat
   flour

HEART-Y BLOOD SAUCE:
1 can (8 ounces) tomato sauce
1 can (6 ounces) tomato paste
3/4 cup water
2 tablespoons olive oil
4 garlic cloves, minced
1 tablespoon finely shredded
   carrot
1 tablespoon brown sugar
1 tablespoon honey
1 teaspoon dried basil
1/4 teaspoon dried thyme
1/2 teaspoon dried oregano
1/4 teaspoon salt
1/8 teaspoon pepper

TOPPINGS:
1 large green pepper, finely chopped
1 small sweet red pepper, finely chopped
1/4 cup finely chopped red onion
1 cup finely chopped fresh pineapple
1 cup finely chopped fully cooked ham
1/2 cup grated Romano cheese
1/4 cup shredded Italian cheese blend

In a large bowl, dissolve yeast in warm water. Add the sugar, oil, salt, lemon juice and all-purpose flour. Beat until smooth. Stir in enough whole wheat flour to form a soft dough.

Turn onto a lightly floured surface; knead until smooth and elastic, about 6-8 minutes. Cover and rest for 10 minutes.

Meanwhile, in a small saucepan, combine the sauce ingredients. Bring to a boil. Reduce heat; simmer, uncovered, for 8-10 minutes or until slightly thickened, stirring occasionally.

Roll dough into a 15-in. circle. Transfer to an ungreased 14-in. pizza pan, building up edges slightly. Do not let rise. Bake at 425° for 12-15 minutes or until lightly browned.

Spread sauce over crust. Sprinkle with toppings. Bake 8-10 minutes more or until cheese melts and edges are golden. **Yield:** 12 slices.

Stack of Bones

(Pictured on page 239)

My husband devours these delicious ribs! They're prepared in a slow cooker so they turn out tender every time.
—Linda South, Pineville, North Carolina

1 cup chili sauce
2 green onions, chopped
2 tablespoons brown sugar
2 tablespoons balsamic vinegar
1 tablespoon Dijon mustard
1 tablespoon Worcestershire
   sauce
1 tablespoon soy sauce

1 teaspoon ground ginger
1/4 teaspoon crushed red pepper flakes
4 pounds pork baby back ribs

In a large bowl, combine the first 10 ingredients. Cut ribs into individual pieces; dip each into sauce. Transfer to a 5-qt. slow cooker; top with remaining sauce. Cover and cook on low for 4-5 hours or until meat is tender. **Yield:** 4 servings.

Terrifying Tombstone

(Pictured above)

MAKING centerpieces for your graveyard gathering doesn't have to be a monumental undertaking. You can create the haunting headstone above with relative ease.

First cover a table with black burlap. Cut a purchased Styrofoam tombstone at an angle about two-thirds up from the bottom so the height is appropriate for your table. Use floral pins to attach the tombstone to a slightly larger piece of green Styrofoam. Place it on the table.

Add some devilish decorations such as stuffed rats, Spanish moss, dusty miller plants, dried Queen Anne's lace, twigs and leaves. Using a glue gun, add glue strings to the centerpiece as desired to resemble cobwebs. You can even add to the spooky effect of the table topper by setting a skull candle next to the centerpiece.

If hosting a big party, make a Terrifying Tombstone for each dinner table and send them home as party favors.

REFERENCE INDEX

Use this index as a guide to the many helpful hints, food facts, decorating ideas and step-by-step instructions throughout the book.

GENERAL RECIPE INDEX

This handy index lists every recipe by food category, major ingredient and/or cooking method.

ALPHABETICAL INDEX

Refer to this index for a complete alphabetical listing of all recipes in this book.

Here's *Your* Chance To Be Published!

Send us your special-occasion recipes and you could have them featured in a future edition of this classic cookbook.

YEAR AFTER YEAR, the recipe for success at every holiday party or special-occasion celebration is an attractive assortment of flavorful food.

So we're always on the lookout for mouthwatering appetizers, entrees, side dishes, breads, desserts and more…all geared toward the special gatherings you attend or host throughout the year.

Here's how you can enter your family-favorite holiday fare for possible publication in a future *Holiday & Celebrations Cookbook:*

Print or type each recipe on one sheet of 8-1/2" x 11" paper. Please include your name, address and daytime phone number on each page. Be specific with directions, measurements and the sizes of cans, packages and pans.

Please include a few words about yourself, when you serve your dish, reactions it has received from family and friends and the origin of the recipe.

Send to "Celebrations Cookbook," 5400 S. 60th Street, Greendale WI 53129 or E-mail to *recipes@reimanpub.com.* Write "Celebrations Cookbook" on the subject line of all E-mail entries and include your full name, postal address and phone number on each entry.

Contributors whose recipes are printed will receive a complimentary copy of the book…so the more recipes you send, the better your chances of "being published!"